Prospective Eu

The European Initiative

Series Editor: PROFESSOR DAVID G. MAYES
National Institute of Economic and Social Research, London, and
Co-ordinator of the Economic and Social Research Council (ESRC)
research project *The European Initiative*.

The late 1980s and early 1990s have produced major events and
changes in Europe which are set to produce fundamental shifts in the
economic, political and social changes throughout the continent. The
European Community's Single Market Programme due for completion
at the end of 1992 and the sweeping political reforms and revolution in
eastern Europe have been the catalysts. This new series of books has
been established to publish the best research and scholarship on
European issues and to make an important contribution to the
advancement of knowledge on European issues.

Professor Mayes is Co-ordinator of a major research initiative on
European issues by the Economic and Social Research Council. The
Series, in addition to publishing the leading contributions made by that
initiative, will also publish other titles drawn from all disciplines in the
Social Sciences, including Economics, Political Science and Sociology.

Titles in the Series:

The European Challenge: Industry's Response to the 1992 Programme
edited by David G. Mayes

The External Implications of European Integration
edited by David G. Mayes

The New Europe: Changing Economic Relations between East and West
by Susan Senior Nello

To Adrian
Thanks for your help

Prospective Europeans

New Members for the European Union

edited by

John Redmond
University of Birmingham

John Redmond

HARVESTER
WHEATSHEAF

New York   London   Toronto   Sydney   Tokyo   Singapore

First published 1994 by
Harvester Wheatsheaf
Campus 400, Maylands Avenue
Hemel Hempstead
Hertfordshire, HP2 7EZ
A division of
Simon & Schuster International Group

Printed and bound in Great Britain by
BPC Wheatons Ltd, Exeter

British Library Cataloguing in Publication Data

A catalogue record for this book is available from
the British Library

ISBN 0-7450-1594-8

1 2 3 4 5   98 97 96 95 94

To the memory of Alice Pinder Redmond

Contents

Contents

Tables

Contributors

William Hale is Senior Lecturer with special reference to Turkey at the School of Oriental and African Studies (SOAS), University of London.

Karl Koch is Senior Lecturer in German Studies and Head of the German Section, Department of Linguistics and International Studies at the University of Surrey.

Gunnar Helgi Kristinsson is Reader in Government at the University of Iceland.

Lee Miles is Lecturer in European Studies at the Humberside Business School, University of Humberside.

John Pinder is Chairman of the Federal Trust and Visiting Professor at the College of Europe in Bruges.

John Redmond is Senior Lecturer in European Political Economy at the University of Birmingham.

René Schwok is Associate Professor in Political Science at the University of Geneva and Lecturer at the Graduate Institute of International Studies, Geneva.

Tony Verheijen is Lecturer in Public Administration at the University of Limerick.

Preface

The principal purpose of the book is to provide a country-specific examination of the forthcoming enlargement of the European Union (EU). Whilst various authors have considered subsets of the applicant countries and all of them are discussed in the monographs and book chapters which consider enlargement in general, there seems to be no complete book which focuses systematically on the countries which currently aspire to EU membership. This is possibly because it is probably beyond the scope of a single author. What this book does, therefore, is to draw on a wide range of expertise, including authors from the applicant countries, in an attempt to fill this gap. Some general issues are also addressed in the introduction and conclusion. Clearly, the enlarging of the EU is very much an ongoing subject in the 1990s and any book can only provide a snapshot in time. However, the major issues remain much the same and efforts to resolve the difficult ones will continue even after the 'prospective Europeans' have acceded to the EU.

The brief of each contributor, with some concessions to style and approach, was to explore the historical background of the EU's relations with the country or countries which they were examining, its (or their) current situation with regard to EU membership and to look to the future. Contributors were commissioned to give the first draft of their paper at the British International Studies Association (BISA) Annual Conference at Swansea in December 1992 in a panel on EU enlargement and some also gave revised versions as papers on a similar panel at the third American European Community Studies Association (ECSA) conference in Washington in May 1993. Final versions were then submitted for inclusion in the book based, in part, on the comments of participants at those conferences which are acknowledged with thanks. In addition, I would like to thank Adrian Treacher for his assistance in preparing the manuscript for publication.

Abbreviations

APEC	Asia Pacific Economic Cooperation
AS	Austrian Schilling
BERD	French acronym for EBRD
BSP	Bulgarian Socialist Party
CAP	Common Agricultural Policy
CFP	Common Fisheries Policy
CFSP	Common Foreign and Security Policy
CIS	Confederation of Independent States
CMEA	Council for Mutual Economic Assistance
COMECON	*see* CMEA
CSCE	Conference on Security and Cooperation in Europe
DCR	Democratic Convention of Romania
DM	Deutschmark
DNSF	(Romanian) Democratic National Salvation Front
EBRD	European Bank for Reconstruction and Development
EC	European Community
ecu	European Currency Unit
EEA	European Economic Area
EFTA	European Free Trade Association
EIB	European Investment Bank
EMS	European Monetary System
EMU	Economic and Monetary Union
EPC	European Political Cooperation
ERM	Exchange Rate Mechanism
EU	European Union
FM	Finnish Markkaa
FTA	Free Trade Agreement
G7	Group of Seven
GATT	General Agreement on Tariffs and Trade

GDP	Gross Domestic Product
GMP	Global Mediterranean Policy
GNP	Gross National Product
GSP	Generalised System of Preferences
IMF	International Monetary Fund
LO	(Swedish) Labour Federation
MFN	Most Favoured Nation
MRF	(Bulgarian) Movement for Rights and Freedoms
MTK	Confederation of (Finnish) Agricultural Producers
NAFTA	North American Free Trade Agreement
NATO	North Atlantic Treaty Organisation
NSF	(Romanian) National Salvation Front
OECD	Organisation for Economic Cooperation and Development
ÖVP	Austrian People's Party
PHARE	Poland and Hungary Assistance for Economic Restructuring
PKK	Kurdistan Workers' Party
SAF	Swedish Employers Federation
SEA	Single European Act
SEE	(Turkish) State Economic Enterprise
SEM	Single European Market
SK	Swedish Kronor
SPÖ	Socialist Party of Austria
TCA	Trade and Cooperation Agreement
TRNC	Turkish Republic of Northern Cyprus
UDF	(Bulgarian) Union of Democratic Forces
Visegrad	Poland, Hungary, Czech and Slovak Republics
WEU	Western European Union

Part 1

Introduction

Part I

Introduction

1   Introduction

A remarkable transformation has taken place in Europe in the last decade. Ten years ago the then European Community had not yet emerged from the Euroscelerosis of the early 1980s and was still enmeshed in the seemingly interminable internal conflicts over its budget and the reform of its common agricultural policy. The post-war division of Europe into east and west seemed set to continue indefinitely and, within the west, the economic division between an intergovernmental EFTA and an EU with supranational tendencies seemed unlikely to change much either. Finally, the Mediterranean enlargement that the EU was contemplating was the accession of Spain and Portugal. The accession of Greece and the military intervention in Turkey at the beginning of the 1980s, together with the situation in Cyprus meant that the prospects of Turkey and Cyprus joining the EC were on nobody's agenda. Meanwhile, Malta had moved into a second decade of rule by an essentially anti-EU Labour Government.

Yet, by the early 1990s, the enlargement of the EU has arguably become the central issue in Europe. In early 1994 no less than 13 countries were actively pursuing EU membership[1] with many more in the wings in the medium-term (mainly located in the former Soviet bloc); only Iceland and Switzerland[2] seem to have turned their backs on the EU, at least for the time being. Why has this happened? There are obviously a number of factors, but three are particularly important.

The first of these is internal to the EU; there has been a resurgence in the spirit of European integration which began with the Cockfield White Paper on the creation of a single EU market and culminated in the Maastricht Treaty. The reasons for this rejuvenation are complex and perhaps not entirely clear, but the impact on non-EU Europe was plain. There were two principal effects:

(1)   The EU's position as the major player in Europe was firmly established. In the early 1980s there were times, particularly when

3

the acrimony which surrounded the internal dispute over the budget was at its height, that it seemed as likely that the EU would regress as progress and that Europe's future might lie not in the development of the EU but elsewhere. This is no longer an issue. Whatever Europe becomes in the coming years, the EU will be the central component for the foreseeable future.

(2)   Those European countries which were not members of the EU had to re-examine their relationships with the revitalised Union. The main problem that they perceived was basically an economic one: how to ensure continued market access to the EU. This is the issue that preoccupies most countries, whether they are European or not, in their dealings with the EU. What is feared can be summarised in two words: Fortress Europe. However, whilst non-European countries were limited in the action that they could take, non-EU European countries had the additional option of applying to join the EU. Gradually, they have exhausted the alternatives and concluded that full membership is the only means by which this dilemma of maintaining their access to EU markets can be permanently resolved. The deepening of the EC into the EU by the Maastricht Treaty has accentuated these fears of exclusion which now spread beyond the economic sphere into politics and security.

To summarise, the net result of the internally generated rejuvenation of the EU has been to establish it as the only viable 'club' in Europe and to increase the costs of non-membership to a level that most countries that are eligible to join find unacceptable.

The second development occurred in Europe but outside the EU. There were momentous changes in central and eastern Europe which have transformed the economic, political and strategic balance of the continent. After over 40 years, the old post-war certainties have vanished and a range of new possibilities and alternative scenarios have opened up. Most important of all, Europe is once more a whole, or at least potentially so. Rather amazingly, the hitherto unimaginable prospect of EU membership is now attracting many former Soviet bloc countries, some of which did not even exist as separate nations until very recently. However, there have also been important effects in western Europe, most obviously the relaxation of the security constraint for the EFTA countries, particularly Finland.

The third factor is global rather than European. The failure to resolve the Uruguay Round amicably and on schedule meant that the future of the GATT was shrouded in uncertainty as the negotiations meandered along their tortuous route. The relevant direct inference is that the negotiations illustrated the importance of the EU (and the impotence of other Europeans) by degenerating into a power struggle between the US and the EU, clearly the two main participants, whilst the rest of the world (including non-EU European countries) had to look on ineffectively or, at best, seek to exert influence at the fringes. Clearly, non-EU membership does not only exclude countries from influencing internal EU decisions (such as the rules of the single market), but also external decisions taken at global level. In short, any loss of sovereignty implied by joining the EU has clearly to be offset by the ever-increasing loss of sovereignty implied by not joining.

A less direct but more insidious consequence of the prolonged Uruguay Round negotiations has been that their near-collapse has encouraged the development of regional trade blocs. Specifically, NAFTA has been created in North America with the possibility of extension to Latin America and even the entire Asia-Pacific region through APEC. Whether the threat of a world economy dominated by a small number of trade blocs is a realistic scenario is perhaps debatable. Nevertheless, the speculation has been sufficient to intensify the feeling of isolation amongst non-EU European states and to make the lure of their only available port (the EU) in the (potentially) imminent storm even stronger. At the very least, EU membership seems to be an attractive insurance policy.

These three factors, particularly the first two, lie at the heart of the dash to join the EU currently in progress on its fringes. They have either been critical in changing the minds of Governments (the EFTA applicants) or have been essential for the very idea of EU membership to become a possibility (the former Soviet bloc countries in eastern and central Europe). Of course, there are also additional factors in individual cases and these are comprehensively examined in the main chapters of the book.

Eligibility and Procedures

At this point, it is useful to consider briefly the actual mechanics of the application procedure for EU membership and the conditions which the EU requires prospective members to fulfil. Turning first to the former, the first step is a formal application which has to be made, in writing, to the Council. The Council may then decide to reject the application (as it did with the Moroccan application in 1987) or request an Opinion (*avis*) from the Commission. This can tend to the positive (the EFTAns) or the negative (Greece and the current Mediterranean applicants, in the sense of proposing an alternative to accession). The Council then usually endorses the Opinion which implies the next stage (negotiations) if it is positive or the end of the process if negative, although rejection has usually been qualified to the effect that the application may be considered again at some later date and, in the meantime, some alternative status is offered.[3] The decision to proceed has to be unanimous and the approval of the European Parliament has also been required since the Single European Act. Negotiations take place between the Government of the applicant state and the Council (represented by the Presidency) assisted by the Commission. The EU negotiates with individual applicants rather than groups although parallel negotiations take place when several countries apply simultaneously, as is the case with the recent negotiations with Austria, Sweden, Finland and Norway.

The EU currently requires new members to meet the following eight criteria:

(1)   Be European;
(2)   Be a democracy;
(3)   Respect human rights (the European Parliament applies this condition with great stringency);
(4)   Accept the *acquis communautaire*, that is, all the existing law of the European Union;
(5)   Accept the *acquis politique*, that is the common foreign and defence policy, both as it already exists and as it will be extended by the implementation of the Maastricht Treaty;
(6)   Subscribe to the *finalités politiques*, that is, the long-term objective of European Union;
(7)   Have a 'functioning and competitive market economy';[4] it is not clear to what extent prospective members have specifically to fulfil the conditions (relating to inflation, interest rates, budget deficits and national debt) required to join fully in economic and monetary union;
(8)   Have 'an adequate legal and administrative system in the public and private sector';[5] that is, new members must be able to implement EU policies.

The first of these is the only condition imposed formally by the Treaty of Rome. In fact, there is a little ambiguity because what the Treaty actually says is that 'any European nation can apply' (Article 237), which is not quite the same as saying only European states can apply. Indeed, this ambiguity has been amplified by the Commission which explicitly chose not to define 'European' in the context of enlargement in a submission to the Lisbon summit in mid-1992.[6] Criteria (2), (3) and (4) simply evolved and were formalised at the Maastricht and Lisbon summits in 1991-92, which also added (5), (6), (7) and (8). Whilst the former group are clearly general, the latter seems to have been developed with the current round of applications in mind. Specifically, (5) would appear to be directed at the EFTA neutrals and (7) and (8) at the central and eastern Europeans.

Alternatives to EU Membership

In one sense, the three developments outlined above - the surge in European integration, the end of the Cold War and the uncertainties of the Uruguay Round - do not necessarily generate a rationale for large numbers of non-EU members applying to join the EU. They imply a re-examination and perhaps intensification of relations with the EU, but this could stop short of full membership. Indeed, alternatives to membership are very much what the EU has sought to offer (and still is offering most) aspiring members. It is possible for non-members to pursue a whole range of relationships with the EU from a simple non-preferential trade agreement to full membership. The options for the current applicants preferred by the EU have been the European Economic Area (EEA) for the members of EFTA and association for the central, eastern and Mediterranean Europeans. The problem with these alternatives is essentially that they are considered inadequate and inferior to full membership by the countries to which they are being offered.

Association with the EU has effectively been reserved either for former colonies, through Articles 131-136 of the Treaty of Rome ('Part Four association'), or for European states that are eligible for EU accession (Article 238). For the latter group, it is an ill-defined concept and the Treaty itself is rather imprecise. Article 238 refers to 'creating ... reciprocal rights and obligations, joint actions and special procedures' but this could mean anything from a mere trade agreement to a relationship verging on full membership. Consequently, association has effectively been defined by practice and would seem to consist of the following six elements:

(1) Either (a) a free trade area or (b) a customs union.
(2) A financial protocol (EU financial aid).
(3) Harmonisation or alignment of economic and related policies.
(4) Association institutions at Council and Parliament level.
(5) Political dialogue.
(6) Cultural dialogue.

On the face of it, this looks as though it could be reasonably considered as a useful preparatory phase for a further agreement leading to accession;

elements (1), (3) and, since Maastricht, (5) would push a country a long way towards membership and, indeed, a successfully implemented association agreement could be construed as the first phase of a transition to full membership.

However, there are a number of problems with this optimistic scenario. In the first place, association by definition falls short of full membership, which means that associates play no role in the EU decision-making process. Furthermore, as only partial members, they are subject to all manner of EU safeguard clauses which can be (and have been) invoked to undermine the free access offered, in principle, to their exports. They also have to accept exclusions; for example, the Association Agreements with the Visegrad countries, Bulgaria and Romania will create free trade in industrial but not agricultural goods. Secondly, Association Agreements have proved difficult to negotiate and implement in practice. In fact, no non-member has come close to achieving a customs union with the EU. This is an essential element of EU membership and is often regarded as a suitable objective for aspiring members but, in a sense, it is difficult to see why it is desired other than as part of EU accession. After all, a customs union potentially amounts to the worst of all worlds: competition from EU producers which now have free market access and loss of sovereignty over the setting of customs tariffs (and also tariff revenue, given that EU tariff levels are frequently lower than those of associates), with no offsetting participation in the EU's decision-making, no agricultural subsidies and no access to the EU's structural funds.

Moreover, the history of EU association is not encouraging. It is true that one former associate (Greece) did proceed to full membership, but this was in spite of rather than because of association; indeed, it was the feeling that the Association Agreement was unsatisfactory and constituted an inappropriate framework for relations with the EU that prompted the Greeks to apply for full membership. Furthermore, the other five countries that have acceded to the EU did so without the dubious assistance of an Association Agreement. For example, Spain and Portugal had simple trade agreements and it is difficult not to conclude that if the EU finds an applicant member truly acceptable, then it will prefer to move to accession negotiations directly; association is for countries about which the EU has doubts. This view is supported by an examination of precisely what Association Agreements have said about future accession. Only in the first two Agreements - with Greece and Turkey - was the intention of full membership on completion of the Agreement included. This largely reflected the EU's desire to win friends in its very early years when even its future was not certain, let alone its eventual pre-eminence in Europe. Subsequent Association Agreements (with Cyprus and Malta) did not refer to membership at all and the EU would have much preferred to carry on in the same vein in its 'Europe Agreements' with the central and eastern Europeans; it was only after sustained pressure from the latter that the EU grudgingly accepted a brief reference in the preamble of the Agreements to the possibility of membership as the ultimate (long-term) objective.

Case histories of the implementation of the Association Agreements of Greece, Turkey, Cyprus and Malta make it clear why the current prospective members do not regard association as a preferred option. Greek association was effectively wrecked by the military takeover in 1967 and eventually amounted to little more than a trade and aid agreement of the kind that is common amongst the EU's dealings with the rest of the world. The Turkish Association Agreement was similarly terminated by the military coup in 1980, although it had already become a dead letter. Neither side had felt able to fulfil their obligations. The EU blocked Turkish exports of sensitive products and the Turks pursued an inward-looking economic policy, based on import substitution, which was wholly incompatible with association. Moreover, neither side seemed to know what association was for; the Turks saw it as further evidence of their European identity, but seemed unwilling or unable to undertake, or simply failed to comprehend, the degree of economic adaptation required; the EU appeared to be primarily concerned with securing the continuation of Turkish involvement in NATO and willing to do no more than was strictly necessary to achieve this objective. In fact, there is much in Turkey's experience to support the argument that association is principally a device to stall those aspiring members about which the EU has doubts.

Cypriot association was also torpedoed by military intervention but, despite its short life prior to the Turkish invasion in 1974, there were already signs of dissatisfaction on the Cypriot side about the extent of EU trade concessions. Indeed, there were clear anomalies; for example, at one point in the early 1970s, the tariff concession of 70 per cent being given to Cyprus (and Malta) was actually less than that being given to many other (non-associated) countries under the EU's GSP (100 per cent). This raises the question very directly of what are the advantages of association. In fact, there is a sense in which the Association Agreement with Cyprus is more of a 'former colony-Lomé-Articles 131-136' type relationship than an Article 238 association. In short, it has nothing to do with EU membership, but is considered the final stage by the EU; it is a means of helping a EU member state's former colony, which is why there is no reference to accession in the agreement. This is also the case with Malta. The EU-Malta Association Agreement was, in fact, effectively stillborn. The pro-EU Nationalist Government which negotiated it was replaced before it came into effect by an anti-EU Labour Government (for 16 years). Nevertheless, the EU's ungenerous treatment of Maltese agricultural exports and use of safeguards to protect its textiles producers contributed to the failure of association.

It is true that in all the above four cases association would not have been successful whatever the EU's attitude, because of developments in the four associates. Nevertheless, it is arguably the case that in the absence of such developments, the EU's attitude might well have frustrated the Agreements anyway. It never has been clear what association was supposed to be and the EU seems to have let it develop into little more than an extended form of Trade and Cooperation Agreement. It has not been a fast track to accession, rather it has been the end of the road. Moreover, the EU seems unable to deliver even the limited commitments of association. The benefits of association are effectively undermined by safeguard clauses, the exclusion of agriculture and other sectors, and the effective erosion of benefits as similar concessions are given to non-associates under the EU's GSP. It would, therefore, be surprising if the current prospective members of the EU saw association as anything other than a short-term palliative and a form of evasive action by the Union.

The same is arguably true of the second alternative being offered by the EU - membership of the EEA. This has been portrayed as a potential next stage for the current associates in central and eastern Europe and the Mediterranean on the way to membership of the EU. In fact this is an unlikely scenario. An agreement between the political and economic equals of the EU and EFTA cannot provide a framework for the EU's dealings with Turkey and the politically and economically backward members of the former Soviet bloc. Moreover, the dissatisfaction with the EEA that has driven four members of EFTA to apply for full EU membership is likely to be felt just as keenly by the Mediterranean and central and eastern European applicants. Indeed, the EEA was created, paradoxically, as a means of preventing enlargement of the EU, rather than promoting it. For the EFTAns, it was a means of ensuring access to the EU's internal market without having to submit to the full rigours of membership. As far as the EU was concerned, the EEA allowed it to continue with the process of deepening - the Maastricht agenda - without the distraction of having to accommodate new members.

The EEA has thus become an unsatisfactory half-way house that has actually proved as difficult to negotiate as accession would have been. It allows EFTA participation in the EU's single market by an extension of the four freedoms of movement (goods, services, people and capital) and involvement in the so-called 'flanking' policies,[7] the creation of formal EEA institutions and a financial mechanism by which the (richer) EFTAns compensate the poorer EU members for access to their markets. However, in many ways, it falls far short of the EFTAns' original aspirations :

- The EFTA countries take no part in determining the rules of the EEA, but simply have to accept extensions of EU rules which are ultimately determined by the members of the EU; the EFTAns play an advisory role, but it amounts to participation in 'decision-shaping' rather than in 'decision-making'.
- EFTAn desires to preserve their higher standards in the fields of the environment, consumer protection, health and safety by mutual recognition of standards and legislation were not met; the EEA's legal framework is the EU's *acquis communautaire*.
- The EFTAns made virtually no progress with their extensive demands for derogations from the *acquis*; most were simply not allowed, some were accepted, but only for short transition periods and just two were fully conceded.[8]
- EFTA requests for specific safeguard clauses were rejected by the EU, which was only prepared to give a general safeguard clause.
- The EFTAn preference for joint EEA surveillance and judicial bodies (the 'one pillar' approach) was ignored in favour of an EFTA Surveillance Authority and an EFTA Court of Justice to parallel equivalent EU bodies (the 'two pillar' approach).
- A number of specific problem issues were not resolved entirely to the satisfaction of the EFTA countries (agriculture and EFTA financial contributions to poorer EU states) and two issues had to be resolved by parallel bilateral agreements with the EFTA members concerned (fisheries and the transit of EU traffic through Austria and Switzerland).

The net result of these concessions was that members of EFTA potentially gave away as much sovereignty by not joining the EU (and becoming members of the EEA) as they would do by joining. The unsatisfactory nature of the EEA soon became apparent, as EFTA countries voted with their feet by applying for full EU membership, in the case of Austria some time before the details of the EEA were finalised. The exceptions were Switzerland, which moved the other way because its population decided that it wanted neither EEA nor EU membership for particular reasons which are outlined in Schwok's chapter below, and the two smallest members of EFTA - Iceland and Liechtenstein - which are apparently content with the EEA, at least for the time being.

The future of the EEA is therefore uncertain and, like association, it is clearly not favoured by those countries wishing to join the EU, and with good reason. Unless it is revised to accommodate more members, the EEA is now set to become a rather curious lop-sided relationship between an EU of sixteen on one side and Iceland and Liechtenstein on the other. It is clearly not an alternative to EU membership. Indeed, there is no feasible long-term alternative to EU membership. Those countries wishing to become EU members are best advised to do so as soon as possible in order to get a seat at the decision-making table before the EU moves on at speeds and in directions which may make future membership impossible. If they cannot get immediate entry, then the half-way houses of association and the EEA offer no firmer guarantee of future membership than a simple Trade or Trade and Cooperation Agreement. Most fundamentally, half-way houses inevitably represent a second-class citizenship, because they do not offer a place at the decision-making table. Whilst some of the current prospective members may have to accept an inferior level of relationship with the EU, at least for the time being, they cannot be expected to accept the EEA or association as acceptable alternatives to full membership of the EU. These countries will not stop knocking at the door.

The Applicants: An Overview

Finally, turning to the current actual and potential applicants, these fall into three broad groups which are summarised in Table 1.1 (which provides some basic data on them). The first group consists of the members of EFTA. This is the most likely source of new EU members in the immediate future and indeed four of them (Austria, Sweden, Finland and Norway) actually negotiated EU accession terms in 1993-4. They share a number of characteristics:

(1)   These are rich, developed democracies which are very similar to existing EU member states and, unlike past and other likely future new EU members, would actually be net contributors to the EU budget.

(2)   They are of a similar size and one which is comparable to a number of existing EU members, thereby avoiding the problems associated with very large and very small aspiring Union members.

(3)   They have a unique and very close trading relationship with the EU; not only is the EU their most important trading partner (which is true of most European and, indeed, some non-European states), but they collectively are the EU's major trading partner, accounting for approximately as much EU trade as the United States and Japan combined.

Table 1.1: Basic Statistics of the Countries Applying for EU Membership

Country	Population in millions (1992)	Employment in agriculture % of total (1991)	Exports to EU % of total (1992)	GDP per capita US dollars (1990)
EC12	327.1	7.1	n/a	16190
EFTA				
Austria	7.88	7.4	63.9	19240
Finland	5.04	8.4	43.9	26070
Iceland	0.26	10.5	56.5	20598
Norway	4.29	5.5	65.2	23120
Sweden	8.68	3.1	53.3	23680
Switzerland	6.90	5.5	56.6	32790
The Mediterranean				
Cyprus	0.72	13.7	47.0	8040
Malta	0.36	2.6	69.6	6630
Turkey	58.78	47.7	46.5	1630
Central and eastern Europe				
Bulgaria	8.96	15.7	4.6	2210
Czechoslovakia	15.73	9.2	18.2	3140
Hungary	10.32	19.3	25.6	2780
Poland	38.36	26.7	23.9	1700
Romania	22.75	29.8	17.6	1640

Sources: Economist, *A Survey of the European Community,* 11 July 1992; United Nations, *Monthly Bulletin of Statistics* (various issues); International Labour Organisation, *Yearbook of Labour Statistics, 1993*; and International Monetary Fund, *Direction of World Trade* (various issues).

(4)   More generally, many of the EFTA countries are already well
       integrated economically into the EU, arguably more so than some
       of the EU's peripheral members, such as Greece.
(5)   They have a specific and unique problem amongst aspiring EU
       members, in that they actually subsidise their agricultural sectors
       more than does the EU.
(6)   The decision to pursue EU membership represents a complete
       change of mind. Until very recently, they all rejected this course of
       action either implicitly by choosing to join EFTA or explicitly by
       voting not to join the EU in a referendum (in the case of Norway).
(7)   The shift to favouring EU accession has been led by Governments,
       with the general populations being much more ambivalent. Now the
       terms of membership have been negotiated for the four current
       applicants from EFTA, they all either have had or intend to hold
       referenda and in each case (to varying degrees) there is a possibility
       that EU accession will be rejected.

Of course, there are significant differences amongst the EFTA applicants,
for example, some are members of NATO and some are neutral, Norway
(and Iceland) are interested in fish, Austria (and Switzerland) in transport
problems and so on. Nevertheless, unlike the two other groups of applicant
countries, it is the similarities rather than the differences within the EFTA
group that are most striking and the general implication of these common
threads is very clear: these countries have comparatively little difficulty in
negotiating EU accession, but may well have grave problems in persuading
their populations to let them join.

The second group of aspiring EU members consists of the
Mediterranean associates. These have a long-standing relationship with the
EU, with association going back more than two or three decades and they
applied before most of the EFTAns (with the exception of Austria which
applied before Cyprus and Malta, although after Turkey). Nevertheless,
despite sharing a common experience of troubled Association Agreements,
it is the differences rather than the similarities within this group which are
most striking. Turkey is a very large country and faces difficulties in
relation to virtually every aspect of accession, except the issue of security.
Cyprus is unique with its bitter political divide which also involves a full
EU member on one side and an associate (and aspiring full) member on the
other. Malta is economically unprepared for EU membership and, as the
most likely micro-state to join the EU in the immediate future, raises

institutional problems within the Union which must be addressed before it could be allowed to accede. Like the EFTAns, these countries have all received formal Commission opinions in response to their applications but, unlike the EFTAns, these opinions have not been sufficiently positive to merit the initiation of accession negotiations. The EU is not prepared to accept these countries as full members in the immediate future and prefers a policy of delay with no firm date for accession.

The third and final group of potential EU members comprises the former members of the Soviet Union and Soviet bloc. In principle, the full list is open-ended but in reality only the Visegrad Four (Poland, Hungary, the Czech and Slovak Republics) and Bulgaria and Romania are considered to be serious contenders, even in the medium to long term. In these cases, the EU has the problem of reconciling the political necessity of responding positively to these countries' aspirations for accession with the economic reality of them being very far from being economically prepared for the rigours of membership. The EU has sought to respond constructively but carefully and it is clear that the prospect of beginning accession negotiations lies some considerable distance in the future. So far, the only step taken (and only then very reluctantly by the EU) has been to refer to accession as the ultimate (but not automatic) objective in the preamble to the Association Agreements that have been negotiated with these six countries. It is, of course, this group which has most difficulty in meeting the EU's conditions for membership. Nevertheless, Poland and Hungary have seen fit to apply formally for EU membership in 1994 and the EU will now be forced to address the question of the accession of these countries directly.

The rest of this book looks at the members of each of these three groups in turn. Part I deals with EFTA, the frontrunners for EU accession. Koch examines the Austrian position and argues that Austria's links with the EU, and especially with Germany, make EU membership essential. Schwok unravels the explanations for Switzerland's rejection of the EEA and considers the implications and future options for the Swiss. Miles analyses the evolution of the relations between the EU and the Nordic neutrals in EFTA, Sweden and Finland, in the context of six factors which have guided the relationships. Finally, Kristinsson describes the EU's troubled relations with the Nordic NATO members of EFTA, Norway and Iceland, focusing on the roles of peripherality and isolation. In Part II, the Mediterranean applicants for EU membership are considered. This is the group that has been effectively rejected, at least for the time being. Hale looks at the history and issues of the long-running saga of EU-Turkish relations and concludes that the EU cannot put off the Turks indefinitely. Redmond focuses on the 'Mediterranean orphans' of Cyprus and Malta. He examines the history of their association with the EU and the content and implications of the superficially positive Commission Opinions issued in mid-1993.

Part III turns to the former members of the Soviet bloc in central and eastern Europe. It is the most speculative section, because this group has the furthest to go in the accession process.[9] Verheijen reviews the Trade and Cooperation and Association Agreements of these countries and contrasts the situation in Bulgaria and Romania. He argues that there is a need to differentiate between these two countries as they are not a 'natural' group in terms of readiness for a closer relationship with the EU. Bulgaria belongs more properly to the Visegrad group and Romania is a more difficult case and is clearly 'the odd man out'. Pinder looks at EU relations with the Visegrad countries and then sets out to examine the conditions for their successful accession to the EU at some stage in the future. He not only highlights what is needed in central Europe (social market economies and pluralist democracies), but also considers the changes that might be required in the EU itself in order to be able to accommodate these countries.

Finally, following Pinder's chapter, the conclusion turns briefly to the most fundamental aspect of the enlargement issue omitted from this introduction: the effect on the EU itself and its future development. Previous enlargements have been undertaken on an incremental, country-by-country, basis. The scale and nature of the forthcoming enlargement of the EU make such an approach impractical; the institutions and policies of the Union will require more than mere tinkering. These issues will be examined in the conclusion to the book.

Notes

1. These are the countries which constitute most of the subject matter of this book: Austria, Sweden, Finland, Norway, Turkey, Cyprus, Malta, Poland, Hungary, the Czech Republic, the Slovak Republic, Bulgaria and Romania.
2. In fact this may only be temporary. The Swiss government still maintains that EU membership is its ultimate objective.
3. The one exception to this has been the Opinion on Greece, which was essentially negative but was overruled by the Council which decided to embark on negotiations which eventually led to Greek accession in 1981.
4. *Agence Europe* (1992) 'European Commission Report on the Criteria and Conditions for Accession of New Members to the Community', Europe Documents, no. 1790, 3 July, paragraph 9.
5. Ibid.
6. Ibid, paragraph 7. The Commission considered that it was 'neither possible nor opportune' to do so.

7. The fields of joint action are research and technological development, information services, the environment, education, training and youth, social policy, consumer protection, small and medium-sized enterprises, tourism, the audio-visual sector and civil protection. See Council and Commission of the ECs (1992) *Agreement on the European Economic Area*, Luxembourg: Office for Official Publications of the ECs, Article 78.
8. The first was a general derogation allowing all EFTA members to continue banning television advertising of alcohol; the second concerned only Norway and Iceland and permitted them to continue their legislation relating to direct investment in their fisheries industries.
9. This is not necessarily the same as being the furthest from actually becoming EU members, as one or more of the Mediterranean applicants may eventually discover to their disappointment.

Part 2

The European Free Trade Association (EFTA)

2 Switzerland: The European Union's Self-appointed Pariah

René Schwok

Switzerland originally refused to join the EU because its aims were seen as incompatible with the principles laid down in the Swiss constitution such as neutrality, direct democracy and federalism. Moreover, the Swiss Government did not want to jeopardise Swiss agriculture by entering the CAP. In the 1950s, the Swiss authorities also focused on the disadvantages of the high EU common customs tariffs, which would make Switzerland less competitive. Therefore, Switzerland preferred to join EFTA in 1960 which gave it the possibility to keep its own lower tariff towards non-European countries.[1]

When the UK, Denmark and Ireland joined the EU in 1973, Switzerland, as well as the other EFTA countries, signed free trade agreements with the Union on the removal of tariffs and quotas on industrial goods, followed by more than a hundred bilateral agreements.[2] In the mid-1980s, when the EU became more serious about the prospect of a genuine common market, Switzerland joined the other EFTA countries in promoting a 'dynamic European Economic Space' because, for mainly economic motives, Berne did not want to stay outside the EU-1992 internal market.[3]

Until January 1989, the Swiss Confederation promoted a bilateral and local approach. In other words, Berne did not want to speak with one voice with the other EFTA countries and deal with all aspects of the EU's internal market (e.g. free movement of labour).[4] But Jacques Delors and the Commission imposed on the EFTA countries the 'one pillar' approach of an homogeneous EEA[5] based only on EU rules (the *acquis communautaire*). Therefore, Switzerland had to accept dealing multilaterally with the EU and to give up all claims of permanent exceptions on free movement of labour, acquisition of land by foreigners, etc. Moreover, Berne did not get a good system of arbitration in the case of disputes in which both sides are equally represented. Finally, Switzerland was not satisfied to be forced to accept *de facto* future EU directives which are relevant to keep a homogeneous EEA.

Therefore, Berne decided to apply for full EU membership (June 1992). In order to justify its new position, the Swiss Government firstly stressed the aforementioned liabilities of the EEA treaty and then pointed out three new elements:

(1)   The end of the Cold War makes it necessary to re-evaluate the conservative Swiss interpretation of its neutrality in order to make it compatible with EU membership;[6]
(2)   The Maastricht Treaty means that the EU will develop further and that it will be even more difficult to join later;
(3)   Switzerland should not let the other main EFTA countries join the EU and get a better deal than the one that Switzerland would obtain later.[7]

Nevertheless, on 6 December 1992, the Swiss voters decided they could not even join the European Economic Area. Switzerland is now the only western European country remaining outside the European Union system; it is a self-appointed pariah. Therefore, one should answer at least three questions:

(1)   What are the underlying motives of the Swiss rejection of EEA membership and EU integration?
(2)   What are the consequences of this solitary course?
(3)   What are the different options left to Switzerland?

Motives for the EEA's Rejection[8]

The Ethno-cleavages

Why did 50.3 per cent of the Swiss taking part in the referendum including 18 of the 26 cantons and half-cantons turn against the EEA ? Why, despite the strong endorsement of it by the two chambers of the parliament, almost all major political parties and the Confederation of Industrialists and the trade unions, did the Swiss-Germans reject this treaty by 56 per cent and the Swiss-Italians by 61.5 per cent?[9] Why, also, were all the

French-speaking cantons in favour of the EEA, by nearly 72 per cent - more than in most referenda about the EU? Why in bilingual cantons such as Berne, Fribourg and Wallis did the Swiss-Germans reject the treaty while the neighbouring French-speaking Swiss support it?[10]

First, it is important to point out that, at least since 1986, all opinion polls showed this overall sympathy of the French-speaking Swiss (Romands) for the EU idea.[11] This means that the ethno-cleavage is independent of the details of the EEA agreement (signed in Oporto in May 1992). So, the differences between the two main Swiss communities have to do with rationalities which are mainly independent of the real nature of the EEA.[12]

Many German-speaking Swiss[13] dislike the EU for a number of reasons. First, they wish to preserve their political power. By joining the EU, some of them fear losing their control of the country. For most of them, notions such as independence, sovereignty, neutrality, direct democracy and federalism seem to keep some meaning. In contrast, the French-speaking Swiss are a minority in Switzerland (around 22 per cent). They tend to doubt that they are independent, as they are not in control of their fate. They have a more relative view of the virtues of sovereignty and direct democracy, although they cherish their cantonal autonomy. Suffering from the relative indifference of the Swiss-Germans, they hope, sometimes mythically, to get more autonomy by playing Brussels against Berne. By supporting by nearly 75 per cent the EEA agreement, the French-speaking Swiss express as much irrationality as do the Swiss-Germans who reject it. Irrationality means here that both communities expressed political behaviours largely independent of the real nature of the EEA.

Second, German-speaking Swiss try to differentiate themselves from Germany, to avoid becoming another '*Land*' and losing their own identity. They fear integration in an EU dominated politically by Germany. However, the French-speaking Swiss have no fear of their Gallic neighbour.

Third, there is a dialectical link between the rise of the two main ethno-nationalisms. The more the Swiss-Germans try to differentiate from the outside word, and especially from the Germans, the more they speak a non-written dialect at the levels of the mass media, the university and even administration. At the same time, the German-speaking Swiss practice the French language less and less as the Anglo-Saxon and German worlds are getting more attractive from a cultural point of view than the French. This makes communication difficult with the French-speaking Swiss, as most of them ignore this non-written dialect. Therefore, most of the Romands cannot communicate with the Swiss-Germans, as they do not understand them.

The Question of Identity

Identity[14] is at the heart of the refusal of the majority of Swiss to integrate with the EEA. The EU is often characterised as hegemonic, centralised and bureaucratic, the opposite of the so-called 'Swiss values' of neutrality, federalism and democracy.[15] Moreover, integration in the EU implies acceptance of the free establishment of all western Europeans. Therefore, many Swiss fear a 'foreign invasion'. Also participation in the EU's Common Agricultural Policy (CAP) - not included in the EEA - could lead to a collapse of Swiss agriculture, especially in Alpine areas. Everyone knows that territory is linked to all nationalisms. Switzerland's nationalism is closely related to the mountains and its landscape. Two Swiss symbols should be pointed out: first, the main Swiss historical site is the Grutli meadow, not a tower, castle, cathedral or triumphal arch; second, during the Second World War, the army planned to defend only the mountainous part of the country, and not the densely populated urban areas, against a German invasion (the concept of *national réduit*).

To sum up, the Swiss have developed a myth that they can reconcile freedom and nature. Many Swiss-Germans still believe that they can maintain their freedom from the outside world, their independence, their smallness,[16] their local autonomy, their ideological purity and their close links with the earth. To be sure, in Swiss-German cities, the myth is weaker, as more people can empirically observe that reality is not dictated by notions such as federalism, direct democracy and neutrality. Awareness of the internationalisation of politics and the economy is much more widespread. And more people realise that stress and over-population do not totally fit the Swiss myths.

In the French-speaking part of Switzerland, the European myth is now stronger than the Swiss myth.[17] The Romands also cherish notions such as direct democracy, federalism and neutrality. And they can be xenophobic and hostile towards foreigners. In other words, the French-speakers like Switzerland and still share most of its myths. They do not have the feeling that they have been forced to join this country or that they lost their prerogatives as some French-speaking Canadians and Belgians believe. But the Romands suffer as a minority in Switzerland. Therefore, the EEA, as an incarnation of the European myth, is seen as a way to get out of the 'ghetto'. For most Romands, 'Europe' means openness, communication with other cultures and the respect of minorities. Paradoxically, French-speaking supporters of the EU have cultivated two myths: the Swiss myth of freedom, autonomy and federalism with the

'European' myth of freedom, autonomy and federalism. In a sense, the French-speaking 'Yes' vote is a conservative revolution.

Erosion of Swiss Identity in the EU

Direct Democracy

For the anti-EEA camp, European integration will lead to the damage of some Swiss specificities. Thus, through the EEA, direct democracy will be limited as, *de facto*, there will be no possibility to adopt new legislation which does not fit EU directives. Direct democracy covers two peculiar features of the Swiss political system: the 'referendum' and the 'initiative'. Any bill approved by the Federal Assembly must be open to a referendum. The bill comes into force only if no petition is made against it within 90 days. If a petition is submitted bearing the signature of no fewer than 50,000 citizens, a referendum is held and the final decision as to whether it shall become law rests with the people. Citizens have another means by which they can actively take part in the affairs of the country, namely by the 'initiative'. By this means, the people, given the support of 100,000 signatures, can demand that the Federal Constitution be amended or partially revised. Should the Federal Constitution be amended, not only is the consent of the majority of the people required in every case, but a majority is settled by first determining the majority of votes, and the proportion of votes for and against the motion in each separate canton. If there is a majority of votes as well as majority of cantons in favour of the motion, the Constitution is then changed.

In the case of Switzerland's application to a supranational organisation like the EU or even for EEA membership, the Constitution demands a vote which requires the double majority of the cantons and the population. Therefore, both the Federal Council and the Parliament always try to anticipate possible opposition and are led to consult the vested organisations and political parties at a very early stage of the decision-making process in order to get the largest possible approval. Here one finds two well-known features of the Swiss political system: consensualism and consociationalism.

But the EEA agreement forces the Swiss citizens to give up some of their prerogatives. Worse, it leads to an automatic diminution of those rights in the future. As a matter of fact, Article 102, point 5 of the Treaty on the European Economic Area[18] implies that if the Swiss population refused any new EU directive relevant to the EEA, the Union could almost automatically suspend the part of the Treaty which is linked to the Swiss opposition. For example, if the Union decides in a few years to ban banking secrecy and the Swiss citizens reject this new directive, then it could suspend its agreements on banking with Switzerland. And there will be no EEA Court of Justice, or even a balanced Court of Arbitration, to assess the legitimacy of the EU's decision, as such courts have been refused by the EU Court of Justice.[19]

In those conditions, it is doubtful that Switzerland, or any EFTA country linked to the EU through the EEA agreement, could avoid adopting the future EU laws although those countries are not members of the Union. Practically, therefore, the use of the instruments of direct democracy will be limited and this would be especially true in the case of Switzerland's membership of the EU.[20]

Many German-speaking Swiss do not want to erode the system of direct democracy, as they see it as a deep expression of their sovereignty. In Switzerland, the population is often called 'the sovereign'. Moreover, in sparsely populated cantons (most of them located in the Swiss-German part), direct democracy is often linked with the concept of *Landsgemeinde*,[21] a deep mythical component of the Swiss-German identity.

The French-speaking Swiss, a minority, also want to keep the instruments of direct democracy. But they are more aware of the limits left to the population to make significant use of it. It is still cherished, but not idolised.

Federalism

Federalism[22] is another important element of the Swiss identity. The Swiss define themselves by their cantonal origin. Switzerland continues to have 26 ministers for education, health, justice, police, finance, economy and agriculture, etc. Integration in the EEA would force cantons partly to harmonise their norms in areas such as education, health and public procurement. For anti-integrationists, membership of the EEA would lead to a transfer of competencies from the cantons to the central state. Participation in the EEA would modify the structure of the federal state. It could diminish the power of the canton in the Swiss system. Anti-integrationists fear that the standardisation of the legislation in the EU system would trigger modifications of cantonal laws. The main problems are recognition of non-Swiss diplomas and new admission procedures in schools and universities.

Anti-integrationists also have questions regarding the control of cars, food, water, air, noise and social insurance. Anti-EU elements also question the free access of EFTA and EU citizens to public positions in the cantons. It will therefore be more difficult to derogate to the federal laws influenced by the EU directives. Moreover, those against the EEA assume that membership will lead automatically to EU membership. Therefore, they criticise a future adoption of the VAT system at EU rates (around 15 per cent for the 'normal' rate against 6.2 per cent in Switzerland) which will lead to a reduction in the cantons' taxation revenue. As a result, with the introduction of the VAT strengthening the federal imposition at the expense of the cantons' imposition, the cantons could lose a part of their fiscal autonomy and be more dependent on the central Government, even if there is financial redistribution. Thus, for Swiss-German anti-EU lobbyists, in a free-border Europe, Switzerland would lose its *raison d'être* and be dissolved in the EU cocktail.[23] According to some Swiss-Germans, the French-speaking Swiss would join France, the Italian-speakers Italy, and the German-speakers would alone remain in Switzerland.[24]

For many German-speaking Swiss, especially in small cantons, federalism is a means to keep the identity of communities jeopardised by the modernisation process coming from the central state. Moreover, the concept of double majority in some popular votes is seen by the small cantons (almost all in the German part) as a protection of their specificities. In the French-speaking part, federalism is also seen as being of value. There is however a hope that by joining the EU the cantons will be less dependent upon the German-speaking majority and that there will be more possibilities to deal with the French region near the Franco-Swiss border.

Neutrality

For those opposing the EEA, Swiss neutrality is not directly challenged by EEA membership. But as they assume that an EEA participation will lead automatically to EU membership, they fear that Switzerland's neutrality will be challenged by the EEA eventually (and hence is challenged indirectly). One should remember that neutrality is not only a strategic, legal and economic element, it is also, in Switzerland, an instrument of political integration in a multi-religious and multi-lingual federal state. Neutrality is often viewed as one of the 'deepest expressions of the essence of Switzerland'.[25] The EU jeopardises the credibility of neutrality. If most frontiers are erased between the EU and the EFTA states, how will it be possible to maintain a credible policy of neutrality? For example, if the EU decides upon economic sanctions against a country, Switzerland is *de facto* forced to follow the EU policy and to take the side of the Union against its enemy.[26] Already without EEA membership, Switzerland is so integrated into the EU system that it has carried out the Union's sanctions against Serbia and Montenegro.

With EU membership, not only is the credibility of Switzerland's neutrality at stake but so is its law of neutrality in peacetime. In fact, a new member of the EU has to adopt all the modifications of the Treaty of Rome decided in the Maastricht Treaty. It must accept that 'the Western European Union, which is an integral part of the development of the European Union, elaborates and implements decisions and actions of the Union which have defence implications'.[27] Moreover, this Western European Union (WEU) has taken the commitment 'to strengthen the European pillar of the Atlantic Alliance'[28] and to 'act in conformity with the positions adopted in the Atlantic Alliance'.[29] One can interpret the policy of neutrality in many ways, but not the law of neutrality. Legally, a neutral state cannot belong to a military alliance in peacetime.[30]

Some people also fear that an integration of the Swiss army into an alliance dominated by the WEU would have consequences on its domestic function. Many officers are leading politicians and businessmen. There is still a lot of cooptation between the political and economic elites which is linked to rank in the army. Moreover, the army is one of the few frameworks where Swiss males meet each other. The integration of the Swiss army into a European defence framework jeopardises one of the most important elements of Swiss identity.

One should keep in mind that the majority of Swiss have a deeply emotional attitude towards neutrality. It is an unconscious instrument of differentiation from foreigners. It is therefore not uncommon that the EU is compared to other attempts to jeopardise Swiss sovereignty. Even in the 1990s, the EU is sometimes compared to Stalin's Soviet Union, Hapsburg Austria, Napoleon's France and Hitler's Germany.[31] In a sense, neutrality is for the Swiss-Germans what monarchy is for the British: a fundamental element of their identity. Most Swiss-Germans are still convinced that history teaches them that neutrality is the best way to save their independence, internal equilibrium and prosperity.

Immigration

Politics towards foreigners constitutes another important reason for Swiss desires to remain apart from the EU. The EEA demands free establishment of persons, free circulation of capital and services, the opening of public procurement and mutual recognition of diplomas and university cooperation, all principles which unsettle traditional Swiss policy towards foreigners. In the 1970s, a series of xenophobic popular initiatives paralysed the Federal Council on Immigration and, to this day, its margin of manoeuvre is limited. In the 1990s, the Swiss fear that their land will be sold off to foreign investors. A drastic law (lex Furgler/Friedrich) strongly limits any sale of real estate to non-Swiss. The takeover of Swiss firms by foreigners is also very difficult and pressures by Swiss bankers to open Swiss companies to foreign capital are still resisted. Many Swiss fear losing their jobs and having to be confronted by an invasion of persons who would neglect Switzerland's identity. In the German part, immigrants from Spain, Italy and Portugal are less integrated than in the French part, for cultural reasons. Moreover, young *Romands* are very attracted by the French, Italian and British cultures.

Agriculture

Agriculture is also closely linked to Swiss identity. In the 1950s, one of the main motives for not joining the then Community was the notion of guaranteeing an agriculture sector capable of supplying the country in time of war. By joining the EU (but not by entering the EEA), Switzerland would have to adopt the CAP. This would lead to an important loss of income for Swiss farmers and would stimulate the rural exodus.[32] If Switzerland adopted the CAP, parts of Swiss agriculture would not be competitive and thousands of farmers would lose their jobs. Areas would be abandoned, especially in the mountains, and the cradle of Switzerland's geography and history neglected. It is therefore obvious that the CAP is seen not only as a material, but also as a symbolic, threat to Switzerland's identity.

Moderation of the EU Dangers

Direct Democracy

Concerning the instruments of direct democracy, it is important to bring some nuances to bear.[33] First, it will still be possible to use the instruments of referendum and popular initiative for all aspects which are not related to the EU. Moreover, even those that concern the *acquis communautaire* could be submitted to the popular vote if there is a question of incorporating EU laws into the Swiss legal order. Finally, most popular rights in the cantons and communes will not be jeopardised. More importantly, a diminution of the possibilities for using the instruments of direct democracy might contribute to reducing the paralysis in the Swiss political system.[34] It is sometimes very difficult to take decisions as threats of referenda are a kind of permanent blackmail.[35] In 1992, around 15 referenda were organised at the federal level, with many more at the cantonal and communal levels. It is impossible for any citizen (even for a professor of political science) to have a sufficient level of knowledge to assess each problem. Thanks to EU integration, some restrictions on the possibilities of referenda might make direct democracy more attractive to the population. Swiss citizens would vote less often, but with better knowledge on issues which are closer to their day-to-day life. They could therefore rediscover the original meaning of direct democracy and vote in larger numbers.[36]

Federalism

One should also avoid exaggerations on federalism. First, studies made by the cantons themselves recognise that adaptations will be very limited and that they will not touch their sovereignty.[37] Second, anti-EU lobbies underestimate the functioning of the Union, the over-representation of the small states in the Commission, in the Council of Ministers and in the Parliament. They also neglect the importance of the new approach in the Single Market White Paper which is based on the principles of a minimal compatibility and the mutual recognition of norms. They also seem to ignore the principle of subsidiarity, which allows the EU to legislate only where it is necessary and gives the Governments the right to complain to the EU Court of Justice in cases of abuse of centralisation.[38] Moreover, those anti-EU lobbies do not want to recognise the fact that the SEA and the Maastricht Treaty authorise the member states to refuse norms which would be inferior to their concepts of safety, health and environment.

Finally, Switzerland's integration into the EU could help it reform the function of the cantons. There are some excesses which should disappear. For instance, some diplomas are not recognised in all cantons. Lawyers from Lausanne have difficulty working in Geneva (60 km away, same language). Most cantons' public-sector contracts are not open to bidders from other cantons. One can already observe that, thanks to the EU challenge, some anomalies and anachronisms have been erased. And there are signs of *rapprochement* between different cantons in order to create more collaboration in education, health, taxation etc. This could lead to more cooperation between the cantons and to the creation of bigger regions which could compete with other European regions.

Neutrality

As for armed neutrality, it is also an exaggeration to predict a dissolution of the Swiss army in a European system of collective security. First, no EU, WEU, NATO, CSCE or Franco-German project wants to dismantle national armies.[39] Moreover, the Maastricht Agreement foresees *de facto* a multi-speed integration:[40] a core of member states will take part in the WEU, but other members of the EU could have a status of observers if they wish so.[41] Moreover, the EU Edinburgh Summit (December 1992) authorised Denmark to opt out *a priori* from the political union, namely from the European Political and Security Cooperation. Switzerland could therefore be a member of the Union without entering a military, or even security, union. With other new EU members who are also neutral (Austria, Sweden, Finland), it would be easier for Switzerland to defend such an option.

It is true that Switzerland could not remain neutral if the EU was attacked by an aggressive country. But Switzerland could, nevertheless, maintain its neutrality in the case of conflicts between its neighbours (i.e. between France and Germany) or between Third World countries.[42] It would not be the same neutrality as today, but it could be more than the neutrality of Sweden and Austria. In this situation, Switzerland could appear as more neutral than the other European countries and continue to use this concept for domestic purposes of integration and identification.

Immigration

Dangers of the free establishment of EU and EFTA citizens should also be put in perspective. First, there will not be a foreign invasion when the EEA agreement comes into force. No expert on immigration expects such a phenomenon for the following reasons:[43]

(1)   There have been no important migrations in the EU, although the principle of free establishment already exists.
(2)   The European worker prefers to stay at home unemployed (with indemnities) rather than being confronted with all the psychological, sociological, cultural and linguistic problems linked to emigration.
(3)   It is mostly the needs and requirements of the country of destination which create migrations.

At the same time, thanks to the principle of free establishment, Swiss citizens will stop their rush for EU nationalities as they will not be discriminated against in western Europe. Such an evolution might lead to a limitation on the number of people with two nationalities. More importantly, it will be easier to integrate EU and EFTA citizens in Switzerland who already live there, i.e. around 70 per cent of the foreign population in this country.[44] The overall atmosphere towards citizens from western Europe could improve in Switzerland if naturalisation procedures were accelerated. Moreover, according to the Maastricht Treaty, if Switzerland joined the EU, those foreigners could vote in local elections and even be elected.[45] All these factors could contribute to the development of a less discriminatory identity.

Agriculture

Finally, as for agriculture, one should also be realistic and keep some sense of history. Before 1914, Switzerland was not protectionist. It imported its wheat from Ukraine and its meat from Argentina. Only with the First World War, the crises of the 1930s and the Second World War did Switzerland develop an agricultural war economy. The EEA Treaty could be an interesting opportunity for reforming and liberalising Swiss agriculture. As a matter of fact, the EEA should lead to cheaper prices (by 30 to 35 per cent) for imported goods such as farm machines, animal feed, chemical fertilisers and insecticides.[46] There are also more and more derogations in the EU. For example, it is possible to get exemptions for agriculture in mountainous regions (above 500 m), and to give direct payments to farmers, as is already very common in Germany, especially in Bavaria.[47] Switzerland can safeguard its agriculture only if it specialises in products that its competitors cannot make and finds niches in the world market. Today, Swiss cheese represents only 1.5 per cent of total EU consumption. Switzerland should therefore develop its specialities. There is still room for Swiss products. Thus, paradoxically, the integration of Swiss agriculture into EU agriculture could strengthen Switzerland's identity.

Implications of the EEA's Rejection

By refusing the EEA, Switzerland chooses a way characterised by three elements: political marginalisation, political satellisation and economic marginalisation.

Political Marginalisation

Political marginalisation[48] implies that Switzerland is out of the main elements of EFTA, as it does not participate in the EEA. It remains in the Secretariat but not in the supranational organisation with its common decision-making process, its Court of Justice and its 'Commission' (European Surveillance Authority, ESA). Switzerland is therefore a second-rank member of EFTA, without any real competence for the important questions of relations with the EU in non-tariff areas. Moreover, under the EEA agreement, the EFTA countries are to contribute 2 billion ecus between 1993 and 1995 to a fund to help the poorer EU countries. This is their entry ticket into the EU internal market. Switzerland was to pay nearly 30 per cent of this. Now the other EFTA countries will have to pay the Swiss share or prompt a crisis with Spain and its EU allies. Symbolically, Switzerland has been forced to give up to Sweden the presidency of EFTA for the first semester of 1993 (similar to the EU's presidency system). The supreme humiliation is that Liechtenstein will join the EEA and will be more integrated in EFTA and the EU than Switzerland. *Vis-à-vis* the EU, the situation is even worse, as Switzerland cannot negotiate through EFTA, cannot conclude substantial bilateral agreements and is no longer viewed as a credible candidate for EU membership.

Political Satellisation

This means that Switzerland is copying the EU directives as well as the EFTA laws without participating in their formulation. The Swiss parliament, Swiss bureaucracy and big industry want to adopt most of the European directives on an autonomous basis. Even at the cantonal level, most governments and bureaucracies are doing everything to impose EU rules. It is a political satellisation, as Switzerland cannot resist the normative attraction of the Union (and the EEA), although it is neither formally, nor practically, in this system.

Economic Marginalisation

By choosing a solitary course, Switzerland already suffers a terrible economic cost, as it remains outside the EU internal market and the future economic union. Even without retaliatory measures and intentional discrimination from the EU and the EFTA countries, Switzerland does not profit from all the advantages of an EEA member state. Compared to an EEA competitor benefiting from the single market, a company based in Switzerland would be submitted to the following disadvantages: the survival of traditional obstacles on rules of origin, the maintainance of border checkpoints, costs of approval, the application of different national regulations, inaccessibility of public markets, penalties for the Swiss consumer, incomplete participation in technological cooperation, the lack of economies of scale and almost no effects of competition.[49] Thus, as Switzerland refuses to play the game of European economic competition, its competitiveness diminishes. This leads to the diversion of investments and trade. According to studies made by the main Swiss banks and some economists, by not joining the EEA, investments will grow by only 0.5 per cent instead of 3.5 per cent. As a consequence, GNP will rise by less than 1 per cent compared to 2.3 per cent if Switzerland entered the EU's internal market.[50] Unemployment will be doubled as compared to the integrative scenario.[51]

Are there other alternatives for Switzerland? Anti-EEA lobbyists suggest concluding bilateral and sector agreements with the EU only in those areas in which Switzerland can benefit.[52] But the Commission has clearly rejected such an option. The EU does not want, and cannot sign, agreements with Switzerland only where that country has an interest. Therefore the Union demands, for instance, the free movement of labour in exchange for the free movement of transport.[53] It is, indeed, materially impossible for the EU to negotiate *à la carte* with each EFTA country.

Some Swiss sectors propose a hyper-liberal course.[54] According to this lobby, Switzerland should become more liberal than the EU and develop a world vocation. This objective usually fits the clichés many foreigners have about Switzerland. They often imagine this country as just a place for offshore banking. But this is simply not the reality. Switzerland has many industries, especially small and medium-sized, plus an agricultural sector, and cannot sacrifice them in the name of hyper-liberalisation. Moreover, even Swiss bankers want Switzerland to join the EEA[55] and the EU.[56] There will certainly be a referendum on the outcome of the Uruguay Round in Switzerland, with a possible rejection. Therefore, only a protectionist *Alleingang* is a realistic option, although this would be negative. It will lead to an impoverishment of Switzerland.

Which Options?

For the EU and EFTA countries, EU-1992 is already an old story. None of those states imagined that it could challenge their national identity. The

Twelve, and most EFTA countries, think beyond 1992. But for Switzerland, the problems raised by EU-1992 are far from being solved. Switzerland has the choice between at least seven different theoretical options.

A Hyper-liberal Course

Switzerland starts on a hyper-liberal course and becomes the Hong Kong of Europe. Advantages: it will be more open to business than the EU countries and attract investments from all over the whole world. Moreover, the GATT Uruguay Round agreement will allow Switzerland to avoid some EU discriminations. Difficulties: it is not certain that Switzerland will ratify the Uruguay Round agreement, as there is strong opposition to it and the agreement is not substantial enough to avoid most EU discrimination on standards, certifications, tests, public procurement, free movement of people, services and transport. Finally, there is no majority in Switzerland for a hyper-liberal policy. Trade unions, small and medium-sized enterprises and farmers have enough power to stop such a policy.

A Few Bilateral Agreements

Berne negotiates only a few bilateral agreements, for instance on technological cooperation and the exchange of students. Advantages: Brussels could more easily accept this narrow approach and Swiss domestic opposition would not be strong. Difficulties: those agreements would not be enough to offset Switzerland's political and economic marginalisation.

Many Bilateral Agreements

Switzerland signs a host of bilateral and local agreements. Advantages: it would avoid important discrimination in such fields as standards, certifications and tests. Difficulties: such a solution could be insufficient, and, above all, would clearly be rejected by Brussels.

An EEA Light

Berne negotiates membership in an EEA light. For instance, Switzerland would obtain an individual opt-out instead of the collective opt-out as foreseen in the EEA treaty. Advantages: Switzerland could then reject future EU directives without having to be confronted by its EFTA partners. Difficulties: there is absolutely no indication that the EU would be ready to grant Switzerland such preferential treatment. Moreover, the other EFTA countries would certainly object to Switzerland getting a better deal than they got.

EEA Membership

A new referendum on EEA membership has been called. This is the idea of the so-called 'Committee born on 7 December 1992' (founded the day after the EEA was rejected). They have successfully campaigned for a second referendum on the EEA by collecting the required 100,000 signatures. Advantages: by 1994 or 1995, the Swiss will have a clearer picture of the political and economic marginalisation of their country. Moreover, there is still a large consensus of the elite, and of the French-speaking part, in support of the EEA. Difficulties: the Swiss do not like to vote many times on an issue they have already rejected. Moreover, EEA could be dead by 1996 if most EFTA countries join the EU.

EU Membership with Opt-Outs

In this case, Switzerland would obtain the same hyper-privileged status as Denmark. For instance, Switzerland could opt out of the CAP as well as the defence aspects of the CFSP. Advantages: Switzerland would be a full member of the EU and therefore could participate in the decision-making process (unlike with EEA membership). And, with opt-outs, some Swiss sectors (i.e. farming) could more easily accept EU membership. Difficulties: the EU is not even ready to grant the 'Danish' status to Sweden, Norway and Finland. *A fortiori*, Brussels will be even more reluctant to give more than the Danish status, for instance on agriculture. And even with several exemptions, it is not certain that the Swiss population would accept EU membership.

Full Membership in the European Union

Berne starts negotiations in order to join the 'Maastricht EU', i.e. full membership in the European Union, without exemptions and special treatment. Advantages: Switzerland remains fully in the European fold; a rich, democratic, federalist country contributing to the construction of Europe. Difficulties: all opinion polls show that the Swiss reject EU membership even more than EEA membership.

Concluding comments

Finally, one should remember that any Swiss membership, either of the EEA or the EU (options 4 to 7), necessitates a double majority of the population and of the cantons. In the December 1992 referendum, 14 cantons and half-cantons (out of 26) rejected EEA membership by a majority of more than 60 per cent. This means, therefore, that an important shift of public opinion is needed in some cantons. This will only happen when the Swiss become fully aware of the political and economic marginalisation of their country.

Notes

1. Du Bois, P. (1989) *La Suisse et le défi européen, 1945-1992*, Lausanne: Favre.
2. Schwok, R. (1991) *Switzerland and the European Common Market*, New York: Praeger.
3. Schwok, R. (1989) 'Switzerland and the Price of the Single European Market' in Möttöla, K. and Patomäki, H. (eds) *Facing the Change in Europe. EFTA Countries' Integration Strategies*, Helsinki: The Finnish Institute of International Affairs, pp. 13-21.
4. Du Bois, P. (1992) *La Suisse et l'Espace économique européen*, Lausanne: L'Age d'homme, pp. 23-46.
5. Broadly speaking, the European Economic Area is an extension of the EU-1992 internal market to the European Free Trade Association (EFTA) countries without formal membership in the EU. Through the EEA, there will be a free movement of goods, services, capital and persons among eighteen western European states. In English, on the European Economic Area, see the following articles by René Schwok: (1992) 'EFTA in the 90s: Revival or Collapse?' in Redmond, J. (ed.) *The External Relations of the European Community: The International Response to 1992*, London: Macmillan, pp. 55-76; (1991) 'EC-EFTA Relations' in Hurwitz, L. and Leuesne, C. (eds) *The State of the European Community: Policies, Institutions & Debates in the Transition Years*, Boulder/Essex: Lynne Rienner/Longman, pp. 329-342; and (1991) 'The EC/EFTA Economic Area: A Compass for Central Europe?' in *Program on Central and Eastern Europe Working Paper*, Harvard University, Series no.14, p. 25.
6. Conseil fédéral (1992) *Rapport sur la question d'une adhésion de la Suisse à la Communauté européenne*, Berne, 18 May, p. 13.
7. Ibid, p. 7.
8. For a more detailed analysis, see Schwok, R. (1994) 'Les clivages entres Romands, Alémaniques et Tessinois sur la question européenne, essai d'interprétation' in *Revue d'Allemagne*, Spring.
9. All the German-speaking cantons except Basle had important majorities against the agreement.
10. *Le Nouveau Quotidien* (1992) '6 décembre 1992, deux Suisses face à l'Europe', 7 December 1992.
11. For a comparison with earlier opinion polls, see Ruffieux, R. and Thurler-Muller, A. (1989) 'L'opinion publique face à l'intégration européenne: que disent et ne disent pas les sondages?' in *La Suisse et son avenir européen*, Lausanne: Payot, pp. 237-52.
12. The Swiss-Italians rejected the EEA treaty for different levels of motives. First, they have made their prosperity on cheap labour, on tourism and on tax evasion of Italian money. Joining the EEA leads to the elimination of the statutes of cross-border workers and of seasonal workers. It also abolishes the Lex Friedrich which forbids foreigners to get Swiss land. 'Tessinois' fear, therefore, that Germans and Italians

buy their fields, and too cheap. They want to keep a tourism of quality. Finally, joining the EEA would mean more administrative cooperation between the European tax bureaucracies. Second, many Swiss-Italians are afraid of the 'anarchy' and the corruption of southern Italy and of the economic, political and cultural power of Northern Italy. By contrast, the *Romands* perceive France as a place of organisation and stability, and they are not confronted by a direct competition at their borders.

13. Of course, expressions such as 'French-speaking' and 'German-speaking' are ideal-types in the Weberian sense and aim only at conceptualising the debate. But, for sure, one can be French-speaking and fight EU integration and German-speaking and be an EU supporter (like most of the Swiss-German political and economic elite).

14. See Schwok, R. (1992) 'EC-1992 and the Swiss National Identity' in *History of European Ideas*, vol. 15, no. 1-3, pp. 241-7.

15. See the monthly bulletins of the main anti-EU lobby: *Aktion für eine unabhängige und neutrale Schweiz*, in particular, 12 May 1990, November 1990 and June 1991. See also, Bütler, H. (1991) 'Der europäische Aufbruch und die helvetische Identitätskrise' in *Europäische Rundschau*, 2/91, p. 5.

16. Maurice, A. (1993) 'La Suisse ou la religion du petit' in *Trans-européennes*, no. 1, Fall pp. 20-4.

17. They refuse to consider the option of joining France and no political leader in the 20th century has tried to raise this issue. The French-speaking Swiss are also very reluctant to look for independence. There are still many differences between the Catholic and the Protestant areas of 'Romandie', between the rural and the more urban agglomerations.

18. Commission of the European Communities (1991) *The EEA Agreement*, Brussels, 24 October.

19. Krimm, R. (1992) 'Négociations EEE: un arbitrage limité. Le compromis juridique s'avère boiteux', *Journal de Genève*, 18 February.

20. Bradke, S. (1988/89) 'Plädoyer gegen den Beitritt der Schweiz unter dem Aspekt der Demokratie' *Praetor*, no. 3/4 and Meier, A. (1990) 'Schweizerischer Alleingang in Europa: Utopie oder Option?', *Neue Zürcher Zeitung*, 15 October.

21. During a Landsgemeinde, people vote for or elect their representatives by holding up their hands. The Landsgemeinde is seen by many Swiss Germans as the ultimate form of democracy. But it is also criticised for its lack of secrecy as everyone knows how his neighbour votes.

22. In Switzerland (as in Germany), federalism does not mean centralisation but the contrary. It is therefore considered as a value to be preserved.

23. Chr. Kr. (1991) in *Aktion für eine unabhängige und neutrale Schweiz*, Berne, June, p. 6. See also Thürkauf, P. (1991) 'Eigeninitiative statt Europa-Euphorie', *Basler Zeitung*, 12 August.

24. Fischer, O. (1990) 'EG/EWR: Schicksalhafte Entscheidung für die Schweiz', *AG Tagblatt*, 15 November.

25. Von Wartburg, W. (1992) *Gutachten zur Neutralität der Schweiz und ihrer Zukunft*, Basle: Unpublished, p. 9.

26. Schwok, R. (1990) 'The European Community and Switzerland: Fewer Frontiers but Continuing Neutrality' in Milivojevic, M. and Maurer, P. (eds) *Swiss Neutrality and Security, Armed Forces, National Defence and Foreign Policy*, New York: Praeger, pp. 217-31.

27. Intergovernmental Conference (1991) *Treaty on European Union*, Brussels, 10 December, article J.4, point 2.

28. Members of the Western European Union (1991) *The Role of the Western European Union and its Relations with the European Union and with the Atlantic Alliance*, Brussels, 10 December, Introduction, point 1.

29. Ibid, paragraph B, point 4.

30. Bütler, H. (1991) 'Neutralität am Ende?', in Riklin, A. (ed.) *Bewaffnete Neutralität heute*, Frauenfeld, p. 63.

31. Futterknecht, W. (1992) *La CE, une illusion*, Schaffhausen: Novalis Verlag, p. 27.

32. Hauser, H. (1991) *Traité sur l'EEE, adhésion à la CE, course en solitaire. Conséquences pour la Suisse*, Berne, 2 June, pp. 77-8.

33. Jacot-Guillarmod, O. (1990) 'Conséquences sur la démocratie suisse d'une adhésion de la Suisse à la Communauté européenne' in Jacot-Guillarmod, O., Schindler, D. and Cottier T. (eds) *EG-Recht und schweizerische Rechtsordnung*, Basle, pp. 41-79.

34. Germann, R. (1991) 'Pour une Constitution fédérale "euro-compatible"', *Revue de droit suisse*, I, p. 1.

35. Borner, S., Brunetti, A., Straubhaar, T. and Schweiz, A.G. (1990) *Vom Sonderfall zum Sanierungsfall?* Zürich, pp. 154-155.

36. Auer, A. (1991) 'La démocratie directe face à l'intégration européenne', *Société genevoise de droit et de législation*, *La Suisse face à l'Europe*, Geneva, p. 396.

37. Confédération et cantons suisses (1991) *Adaptation du droit cantonal au droit de l'EEE* Berne: Chancelerie fédérale, décembre, pp. 17-45. For a legal analysis: Jacot-Guillarmod, O. (1990) 'Conséquences sur le fédéralisme suisse d'une adhésion de la Suisse à la Communauté européenne' in Jacot-Guillarmod, O., Schindler, D. and Cottier, T., op. cit., pp. 7-38.

38. Intergovernmental Conference (1991), op.cit., article 3B.
39. *Agence Europe* (1991) 'Political Union: Franco-German Initiative on Foreign, Security, and Defence Policy', Europe Documents, Brussels, 18 October, and 'An Anglo-Italian Declaration on European Security and Defence in the Context of the Intergovernmental Conference on Political Union', Europe Documents, 5 October 1991, point 12.
40. Intergovernmental Conference (1991), op. cit., article J.4., point 4: 'The policy of the Union ... shall not prejudice the specific character of the security and defence policy of certain Member States.'
41. Member States of the Western European Union (1991) *Declaration issued on the occasion of the 44th European Council meeting*, Maastricht, 9-10 December: 'States which are members of the European Union are invited to accede to WEU ... or to become observers if they so wish'.
42. 'Neutralité, défense, Europe, Interview avec Kaspar Villiger', *L'Hebdo*, 6 February 1992. Kaspar Villiger is Switzerland's defence minister.
43. Straubhaar, T. (1991) *Schweizerische Ausländerpolitik im Strukturwandel*, Strukturberichterstattung, Rüsch, Verlag Rüegger, pp. 30-45.
44. There are more than one million foreigners in a population of around 7 million. This is the highest percentage in Europe after Luxembourg.
45. Intergovernmental Conference (1991), op. cit., Article 8b.
46. Flury von Arx, R. (1991) 'EEE: saisir la dernière chance', *Agri-Hebdo*, 12 October.
47. Federal Council (1992) *Rapport sur l'agriculture*, Berne: Office fédéral des affaires agricoles, pp. 318-319.
48. For a deeper analysis of the consequences of a solitary course, see Schwok R. (1992) *Suisse-Europe. Le choix historique*, Geneva: Georg, pp. 59-71.
49. For more details, see Schwok, R. (1991), op. cit., pp. 71-8.
50. Müller,U. *Bei einem Nein zu Europa fehlt der 13. Monatslohn*, Berne: Arbeitskreis Schweiz-Europa, June, p. 13.
51. Roth, J.-J. (1992) 'Sans l'Europe, la Suisse se prépare 60.000 chômeurs de plus', *Le Nouveau Quotidien*, 22 April.
52. Action pour une Suisse indépendante et neutre (1992) 'Conventions avec la CE', *Bulletin*, February, p. 7.
53. 'Positionsbezug der EG. Strassengüter- und Luftverkehr gegen freien Personenverkehr', *Neue Zürcher Zeitung*, 15 September 1993.
54. Moser, P. (1991) *Schweizerische Wirtschaftspolitik im internationalen Wettbewerb, ein Ordnungspolitisches Programm*, Zurich: Orell Füssli.
55. 'Pressekonferenz der Bankiervereinigung. Grundsätzliches Ja der Banken zum EWR', *Neue Zürcher Zeitung*, 19 September 1991.
56. The EEA agreement excludes EFTA countries from the 'comitology' on banking. See 'Les banques suisses mises sur la touche', *Journal de Genève*, 2/3 November 1991.

3 Austria: The Economic Logic of Accession

Karl Koch

The twelve EU Governments decided at the European Council in Edinburgh, in December 1992, that enlargement negotiations would commence in 1993 with Austria, Sweden and Finland. The decision was made before the full ratification of the Maastricht Treaty and signalled the end of the EU's endeavour to slow down the enlargement process.[1] This was contrary to what had been agreed at the Lisbon European Council of October 1992, which made negotiations on enlargement contingent on ratification of the Maastricht Treaty and agreement on the 'Delors II' package.

The Edinburgh European Council Summit marked a victory for those arguing for a wider EU. With the extension of Europe's free trade area early in 1994 to Austria, Finland, Iceland, Norway and Sweden, through the EEA, a significant step in this direction has been taken. The final step, which Austria should complete in 1995, is from EEA to full EU membership. Austria regarded this accession date as realistic and believed that it would be facilitated by Germany's term of presidency in the second half of 1994. For Austria, the EU-EFTA Agreement of October 1991, creating the EEA, was primarily a penultimate stage in the process of full EU membership. Whereas other EFTA participants will have to apply about two-thirds of the entire EU regulations, Austria has only to adapt approximately 140 federal and 70 *Land* legal provisions to comply with EU rules. This did, of course, simplify negotiations for Austrian membership of the EU. In fact, Austria's negotiations for full EU membership were in quite a different category from other EFTA countries. No other EFTAn had already achieved such a degree of economic integration with the Union or had so early on committed itself to applying a substantial part of the *acquis communautaire*.

This chapter argues that there are strong economic factors behind Austria's wish to join the EU and that there is a powerful economic logic to the further integration of the Austrian economy with that of the EU. In addition, despite the political constraints, for example Austria's permanent neutrality, the desire to influence the EU decision-making process has, without doubt, been a powerful force behind Austria's bid for full membership.

Political Dimension

Austrian politics were subject to a fundamental reassessment with the dramatic events in the late autumn of 1989 which were to lead to the disintegration of the eastern European order under the leadership of the USSR. The chain reactions released by these events were, in a historical perspective, no new experience for Austria. The collapse of Austro-Hungarian order, sparked by the events in Sarajevo in 1914, meant the destruction of centuries of political and economic stability in the Danube region. Once again, Austria is asked to reassess its potential as mediator between East and West in the new political landscape evolving in eastern Europe.

However, even before it was called to reassess its role in terms of East/West relations, it had already moved towards a policy with the aim of ultimate integration into the EU framework. It recognised earlier than Sweden, Finland or Switzerland that European evolution was accelerating towards a denser network of political, economic and social structures. It is worth pointing out that this realisation was converted into a European strategy when Alois Mock, the Austrian Foreign Minister, submitted a formal application for accession to the EU on the 17 July 1989, in Brussels. Austria was, at this time, the first member of EFTA formally to submit an accession request since the entry of the UK and Denmark in 1973. Circumstances then did not provide the options and flexibility which arose after 1990, and the changes in the old European political contours were not yet evident. In any case, the application for Austrian membership had been preceded by intensive deliberations from December 1988 onwards.

In fact, Austria's submission for accession was merely the expression of the concern for integration prevalent since the 1960s. In 1961, it made a decision to establish a relationship of association with the then European Community. The Governments of Julius Raab, Alrons

Gorbach and Josef Klaus all negotiated with Brussels over EU links. Before then, it had already evolved towards the principle of European cooperation; it participated in the Marshall Plan, was a founder member of the OEEC and, in 1956, joined the Council of Europe.

Austria's application at one level was an implicit understanding that its political locus was with the western pluralistic democracies, and also a recognition that it needed to link its economy to the European integration process. It had, as a founder member of EFTA, benefited from a free trade agreement with the EU since 1972 and was able to implement this with only minor changes in Austrian legislation governing economic activity. Developments since 1991 towards the present active involvement in the EEA, stem from a redirection of policy in 1985. Austria, with the other EFTA neutrals, Switzerland and Sweden, began to recast its policies of economic integration. This was stimulated by three events. Firstly, the EU passed the SEA in February 1986 to achieve the fundamental freedoms: free movement of goods, services, people and capital. This creation of an internal market posed problems of discrimination for the EFTA countries. Secondly, the global economy was characterised by the emergence of three blocs; Japan (with the Far East), the USA (with Canada) and the EU. For small open economies, such as the EFTA neutrals, strategic trade alliances became extremely important. Thirdly, companies operating in the small EFTA market (about 30 million people) needed to have full access to the EU (372 million people) in order to gain the full advantages of economies of scale. The initial approach of 1986 led Austria to a reorientation, in late 1989, after the collapse of eastern Europe.

Neutrality

The more complex question of Austrian neutrality, established after the Second World War, will not prove an insurmountable constitutional hindrance. In its letter to the Commission, of 14 July 1989, the Austrian Government had stressed its status of permanent neutrality: 'Austria submits this application on the understanding that its internationally recognised status of permanent neutrality, based on the Federal and Constitutional Law of 26 October 1955, will be maintained and that, as a member of the EC by virtue of the Treaty of Accession, it will be able to fulfil its legal obligations arising out of its status as a permanently neutral state and to continue its policy of neutrality as a specific contribution towards the maintenance of peace and security in Europe'.[2] The Council confirmed that this aspect of Austria's permanent status of neutrality '...

will be examined by the Community bodies in the framework of the existing provisions governing the institutions'.[3]

Clearly, Austria's permanent neutrality creates problems for both the EU and Austria. Military neutrality and Austria's autonomy are guaranteed through legislation, the *Bundesverfassungsgesetz*, passed on 26 October 1955, and moves towards EU common foreign and security policies would conflict with legal norms enshrined in this treaty. But Austria, as a result of German unification and the profound changes in the countries of central and eastern Europe, has reassessed its position.

The shift from neutrality to alignment was summed up as early as 1991 by the Austrian Foreign Minister, Alois Mock: 'It is also clear for Austria that the linkages of our time do not allow Austria to stand aside. The myth that one can find security on an isolated island is dead. Europe's security is our security'.[4] He referred, of course, to the European Union. The message is clear: neutrality cannot mean either dogma or isolation; there can be no interpretation which would obstruct cooperation between Austria and other nations. Integration within an enlarged EU would not be blocked by the constitutional resolution on neutrality. This does not, of course, mean that there could, nor would, not be problems. Neutrality means that Austria can never accede to any military alliance. But where does this place Austria in a politically harmonised EU imposing politically motivated embargoes?

Austrian foreign policy argues that as long as no clear collective security arrangements are in existence in Europe, as long as there is an appropriate EU security framework, neutrality remains an essential instrument of Austrian foreign policy. The EU Commission subscribes to the view that the political paradigm of Austria's neutrality principle has changed since the events of 1989.

The domestic political problem inhibiting Austria's accession to the EU is caused by the cleavage between internal consensus and the political decision-making apparatus and the disparity between foreign policy aims and domestic political developments. That the political establishment desires the integrative model with the EU is illustrated by the fact that the National Assembly voted 175 to 7 for accession to the EU. However, the uncertainty of popular support suggested that a premature referendum would have been a negative strategy by the Government; in February 1992, a significant 13 per cent of the population were uncertain and the fluctuating figures, coupled to Swiss rejection for EEA membership, seemed likely to make a 'Yes' highly questionable in the immediate future. Those who were undecided in their stance towards EU membership represented the crucial voters, as the gap between those for, just over 50 per cent, and those against, slightly under 40 per cent, was so narrow.

Article 44 of the Austrian Federal Constitution requires that any constitutional changes are subject to a referendum.[5]

Austrian Identity

Austrian *Neutralitätspolitik* is based on complex historical predispositions which have become an integral and emotive part of Austrian self-perception. This had already displaced the legacy of the Habsburg Empire before the Second World War. As Stourzh pointed out: 'A significant factor, which cannot be underestimated, is the change in Austrian attitudes. In fact, at the end of the 1930s and through the 1940s, the majority of Austrians converted to the idea of an independent existence. This will for independence clearly dominated over other traditions'.[6]

Austrian identity and neutrality are closely linked and have only emerged recently. Austria's history has been, and continues to be, influenced by its geographic location between the Germanic and Slavic cultures. Its antecedents were to be found in the multi-racial empire the Habsburgs created in central Europe. The demise of the Habsburg dynasty, the Napoleonic conquests of Europe and the rise of the German Empire created precursors for the existence of an Austrian identity and nation. The Austrian economic, social and other related factors necessary for the creation of modern nation states occured later than in many other European nations. Austrian democracy was also very late, in comparison with other European nations, in shaping the Austrian political landscape and was ultimately the result of global political constellations rather than self-determination. Perception of an Austrian identity was slow in coming. In 1964, 47 per cent of Austrians agreed that they belonged to a nation, in 1980 this had risen to 67 per cent and reached 74 per cent in 1990. The Austrian consolidation of a national perception is closely linked to its foreign policy activity and, in particular, to its neutral status dating from the late 1950s.[7]

But Austrian neutrality is different to, for example, Swiss neutrality. For the Swiss the refusal by a majority, at the end of 1992, to integrate with the EEA stems from questions of identity and the fear that this would be eroded in the EU. 'For anti-EEA people, Swiss neutrality is not directly challenged by an EEA membership. But as they assume that an EEA participation will lead automatically to EU membership, they fear that Switzerland's neutrality ... is not only a strategic, legal and economic element, it is also, in Switzerland, an instrument of political integration in a multi-confessional and multi-linguistic federal state. Neutrality is often viewed as one of the "deepest expressions of the essence of Switzerland"'.[8]

This cannot be argued for Austria; there, neutrality has different origins and is perhaps best expressed in its function as mediator between East and West. In any case, the ethno-cleavages so prominent in Switzerland do not feature in Austria.

On the other hand, anxieties concerning neutrality are balanced by expectations for EU membership. A recent survey reported that 55 per cent of Austrians would rather be outside the EU than relinquish their neutral status. On the other hand, 71 per cent of the survey sample expect that Austria's accession to the EU will eventually be realised.[9]

The 'Europe-ification' of Austrian citizens is presenting a severe challenge to those pushing for Austria's membership of the EU. Ultimately, the politicians can not make decisions without consensus. This places strain on Austria's distinctive domestic environment of centralised, cooperative politics dominated by the political parties and the major interest groups and their organisations.

Austrian Security Policy

Clearly the neutrality issue is intimately linked to Austria's security policy in the post-1990 world of multilateral politics. Austria's unique role as political mediator between the East-West power constellations had, in fact, already declined during the 1980s. The foreign policy role Austria's constitutional neutrality ascribes may, at times, have constrained its political manoeuvrability, but it also gave it an international political significance unusual for a small state. Austria's foreign policy and military strategies had rapidly to evolve new contours as the political order in Europe transformed itself.

Before the collapse of eastern Europe, Austria's security policy was clear. The threat posed by internal ideological differences from those states bordering it, and thus the threat of destabilising the *Pax Sovietica*, was always present. The second major security problem was the potential conflict between NATO and the Warsaw Pact. Austria's strategic position in geographic terms was such that any such conflict would have an impact; a constant foreign policy consideration for Austria. The fundamental changes since 1991 of the immediate political environment have required a reassessment of Austria's foreign policy. Particularly, the destructive armed conflicts in the former-Yugoslavia, the emergence of the Czech Republic and Slovakia and above all, the potential for further conflicts in the area have put pressures on Austria's concept of security.

Domestic parties made the question of Austria's security and neutrality a central issue during the 1991 election campaign for the Federal

Presidency. A distinct fissure between the Austrian People's Party (ÖVP) and the Socialist Party of Austria (SPÖ) manifested itself. Thomas Klestil, the ÖVP candidate, argued that the neutrality concept in its present form was no longer relevant in the new political landscape. Klestil conceived the idea of an aligned Austria, a state which might ultimately become a member of NATO. Rudolf Streicher, the SPÖ candidate, on the other hand, persisted with the continuation of Austrian neutrality: 'Neutrality is a natural element of our State Treaty which cannot be modified'.[10] This view reflected the perceived Austrian electorate's attitude. However, the subsequent, unexpected, landslide victory of Klestil in 1992 was a dramatic recognition that Austrian neutrality now operated within a new political framework. Klestil's success was in part due to his international experience as a diplomat; 71 per cent of voters gave his ability to represent Austria abroad as the reason for voting for him.[11]

Recognition that Austria's foreign policy needed readjustment was also precipitated by the now urgent necessity of completing the process of accession to the EU. Austria, like other EFTA states, for example Finland and Sweden, is well prepared, in military terms, to deal with small and defined conflicts. However, none of these countries could withstand a sustained military threat from a more powerful opponent, for example, Russia. Switzerland had already come to the conclusion that its neutrality was no substitute for security and that it had, in any case, lost its function.[12] In addition, the fear of isolation from developing EU politics provided a further stimulus to re-examine the neutrality position.

For Austria, the only realistic security option to have emerged is an integrated policy within a European security system which the EU will develop subsequent to the Maastricht Treaty. Federal President Klestil pointed out at the end of 1993 that Austria was more closely affected by the process of change in Europe than most other European countries and that given the proximity of existing and potential crisis regions, Austria was becoming increasingly aware of the importance of participation in effective agreements designed to strengthen European security. The Federal Government had thus fully accepted the terms of the Maastricht Treaty even with regard to security and defence.[13] Existing institutions, like the CSCE, the Council of Europe, NATO and the WEU are regarded as institutions which can contribute, by developing a cooperative network, to European security. However, these do not provide a substitute for a security framework stemming from EU membership.

Austrian Economy

The Austrian economy is distinguished by a relatively large public sector and by a high level of foreign capital. Partly as a result of privatisation policies, there has been a decline in the state's share of the total nominal capital of Austrian business; it fell from 32.6 per cent in 1978 to 25.8 per cent in 1989. The Austrian economy had, in the late 1980s, been in a phase of notable growth, with industrial production increasing by 6.6 per cent in 1989 and by 7.1 per cent in 1990. During this period, real growth in GDP was 3.7 per cent in 1989 and 4.9 per cent in 1990.[14] From late 1991, the Austrian economy weakened as a consequence of the slowing of the global economy. Nevertheless, the long period of prosperity and consensual economic management allowed the main macroeconomic equilibria to be controlled.

Because of the success of the economy, there is a significant body of opinion which regards the performance and structure of the Austrian economy to be endangered through membership of the EU. The distinctive decision-making structures within the field of economic policy-making are seen as incompatible with some of the developments within the EU. The Austrian Social Partnership, a form of voluntary incomes policy covering the entire economy, and supported by trade unions, the Council of Austrian Chambers of Labour, the Federal Chambers of the Economy and the Presidential Conference of the Chambers of Agriculture, is one system Austria wishes to preserve. This is despite serious changes and reservations regarding this institution; in particular the Parity Commission and its role in setting wages and prices. These institutions are seen as supporting Austria's positive economic growth, its traditional low unemployment record (5.8 per cent better than the EU average), solid export performances, controlled inflation, and minimal industrial conflict. These achievements should not, according to some interest groups, be put at risk by union with the EU.

In fact, the beginning of 1992 marked a certain loss of dynamism in the Austrian economy; this had been made worse in the first three quarters of 1991 when real growth in GDP declined to 3.2 per cent. Industry, notably exports, had already began to stagnate towards the end of that year. Industrial production declined from July 1992 onwards, as export orders fell; and this trend continued into the early months of 1993. In part, this reflects the negative economic domino phenomenon released by the disintegration of the USSR, combined with the economic stagnation of the USA. Western industrial nations were all affected by these trends. This suggested to some commentators in Austria that there were no fundamental changes in the economy, but that Austria was simply exposed to world economic uncertainties. This may be the case, but it has thrust the question of the economic consequences, and impact, of Austria's accession to the EU once again into the centre of the debate.

There is a strong opposing view, shared by the majority of producers, which sees the Austrian economy only flourishing if Austria becomes a full member of the EU. Estimates of Austria's benefits, in terms of annual GNP between 1992 and 1996 vary from 3.3 to 4 per cent, from 1992 to 1996. However, all estimates and predictions are based on two assumptions. Firstly, that the CIS continues to evolve peacefully and that the civil war in Yugoslavia ceases, with emerging nations quickly stabilising. Secondly, that Austria's participation in the EEA is formalised and that it moves towards full EU membership; and achieves this by 1995 at the latest.

Austrian integration policy, from the economic perspective, is clearly determined by the fact that it has developed close links with EU countries - in 1989, 67 per cent of total imports came from these countries and 64 per cent of total exports went to them. On this basis, it is not surprising that EU accession negotiations in the economic arena were relatively straightforward. A great number of issues, for example competitive legislation, consumer protection, fisheries, social policy and education, were agreed very quickly.

Transit traffic, even more than agriculture, was the most problematic area. It became something of a hard-core issue, with Austria insisting that the transit accord must retain full measures to ensure protection. Undoubtedly, the geographical location of Austria between EU member states and the proximity of eastern European borders, as well as Switzerland's restrictive policy, have made Austria the premier country of transit. Austria applies *dirigiste* measures to transit across its territory in an effort to resolve the problem. Thus, its policy has among its objectives the rediversion to Switzerland of traffic that has been passing through its territory as a result of the former country's restrictive measures. The remaining road transit traffic is to be brought into line with the requirements of environmental protection and conservation. The EU has responded to this by establishing a working group to discuss the adaptation of the road freight eco-point system and, possibly, extending this to the countries of eastern Europe, and bilateral lorry quotas.

The German/Austrian Currency Link

From economic considerations, Maastricht did not pose a fundamental problem for Austria's EU membership aspirations. The drive towards economic and currency union within the EU has been foreshadowed by Austria's intimate link with the German deutschmark (DM). Austria had decided, after the creation of the EMS in 1979, to bind the Austrian schilling (AS) to the DM. This 'hard currency' policy was based on classic Austro-Keynesian arguments of controlling imported inflation, stimulating productivity and fostering exchange rate stability.

From the beginning of 1982, Austria formed a *de facto* 'currency union' with Germany - with an annual average rate of 7.04 (AS per DM). It can be argued that these arrangements already contain many features of the European monetary and currency union staked out at Maastricht. Interest rate differentials between Austria and Europe have, since 1981-82, from up to 1 per cent difference, begun to converge.[15]

The participation of Austria in one of Europe's most stable economies produced a convergence of price stability. The elimination of exchange rate uncertainties and the resultant savings in transaction costs has had benefits for the Austrian economy. Between 1973 and 1981, Austria increased its exports to Germany from 21.8 to 29.1 per cent - an increase of 7.25 per cent. Since the AS-DM link, there had been a further 7.5 per cent increase to 36.7 per cent by 1990.

Effectively, the German/Austrian economic arrangements have also reduced Austria's advantage in terms of economic growth; between 1973 and 1981, Austria had an advantage of 0.5 per cent which in 1993 was reduced to 0.1 per cent - this means a 'cost' of the 'hard currency union' of 0.4 per cent of GNP growth. This needs to be balanced by a reduction in inflation, which fell in the same period from 1.3 to 0.5 per cent. If convergent indicators are taken into consideration on a global basis, then the 'hard currency' policy can be judged a success. The experiment of Austria's 'hard currency' union suggests that membership of an EU monetary and currency union could firstly be beneficial and, secondly, should not pose any significant problems. On the contrary, Austria contends that it has already demonstrated its ability to meet convergence criteria. Price stability, the retention of inflation at no more than 1.5 per cent above the inflation rate of the three EU members with the strongest price stability has already been achieved. Neither does it see a problem in retaining the +/- 2.25 per cent band in the ERM, or the long-term objectives of a ceiling on interest rates of no higher than 2 per cent above the three strongest economies within the EU.

The turbulence in Europe's ERM, between September 1992 and the beginning of August 1993, which was marked by the substantial depreciation of most European currencies against the deutschmark, had a moderate impact on Austria. It has not dissuaded Austria from retaining its

Prospective Europeans

currency link with Germany, and a monetary union within the EU is not out of reach.

But there have been costs to the Austrian economy. The monetary union with Germany has meant a certain loss of autonomy in monetary policy and, consequently, it has also had an effect on wage and incomes policies. Indeed, there has been a clear convergence of labour unit costs between Austria and Germany. There are, in addition, uncertainties. What of trading relations with important trading partners such as Italy? How would the Austrian economy be affected if such countries have to dampen the demand component in the economy to achieve convergence criteria?

However, the crucial question of whether or not the proposed monetary union of the EU is comparable to Austria's experience with its link to Germany is open. Would a unified European monetary system result in equal or higher economic growth rates and lead to macro-economic stability? There are no clear answers to these questions.

Austria and Eastern Europe

In contrast to Austria's close trading links with Germany and the EU, trade with eastern Europe in 1989 was 9 per cent of total exports and 6 per cent of imports. Before 1989, Austria's trade with Bavaria was higher than with COMECON, including the USSR.

The immediate effects of the changes in eastern Europe were that real GDP declined 16 per cent in 1991, and in 1992 a further reduction of 13 to 15 per cent was expected. There were signs that the economies in Czechoslovakia, Hungary and Poland were stabilising in the middle of 1992, but that East-West trade in general was declining. There were regional variations; trade between OECD countries and south-east Europe and the successor states of the USSR fell but the figures for Czechoslovakia, Hungary and Poland showed that, in 1991, OECD exports were up by 37 per cent and imports by 18 per cent. Future East-West trade developments will depend on the dismantling of trade barriers in the East and the realisation of western investment capital.

Austria has performed reasonably well in the three central European states; its market share in 1990 was +23 per cent (only Italy performed better, with a +32.5 per cent share); and in 1991 it was +16.8 per cent. The 1990 figure is undoubtedly partly explained by Austria's geographic location and its traditional association with these states. This would also explain Austria's giant slice of the export market, 69.8 per cent in 1990 in Czechoslovakia. However, this had declined in 1991 to a modest 10.8 per cent, substantiating the view that the dramatic collapse of the former GDR export economy was in part responsible. Nevertheless, as Table 3.1 shows, in absolute terms, there was, from 1988 to 1991, a doubling of exports to Poland, an increase of 35 per cent to former Czechoslovakia, with Hungary sustaining its previous level.

Table 3.1: Austrian Exports to Selected Eastern European Countries (AS bn)

Country	1988	1991
Poland	3.7	7.5
Czechoslovakia	6.8	9.2
Hungary	6.8	6.8

Source: *Der Spiegel*, No. 6, 1993.

The point has not been lost on Austria that the creation of a new 'Euro-region', such as the German-Dutch-Belgian example may be some way off. Logic may dictate a central cohesion along the line Dresden-Prague-Bratislava-Budapest-Zagreb with Austria well placed as mediator and trading partner. There has been a rediscovery of the concept of '*Mitteleuropa*', encompassing the former territories of the Monarchy as well as Bulgaria and the Ukraine: a natural economic area whose contours had already, in 1992, become visible after the collapse of the Iron Curtain. The Austrian construction industry has, for example, become the most significant foreign contributor in the Ukraine. But capital investment, infrastructure requirements, new management styles and, of course, political stability may all be some time in coming.

Despite the importance of eastern Europe, there is a contrary view of where Austria's trading future might be located. The geographic logic of EU unity dictated a core region, Germany, France and the Benelux states, and a periphery. The widening of the EU to the EEA has emphasised the importance of the periphery. The economies of the core region, taking inflation and economic growth indicators, have performed better than those of the periphery. Some economists count Austria, with Sweden and Switzerland, in the core. They argue that in a two-speed Europe, economic logic dictates that Austria's future lies with the core.[16]

This analysis suggests that Austria's economic destiny in eastern Europe is not that certain. Taking the traditional OECD export calculations, (excluding the ex-GDR), Austria showed a decline of -5.5 per cent in 1991; Germany had a small increase of plus 0.5 per cent in 1991. France, The Netherlands, Finland, Japan, and the USA all had greater success in eastern

Europe. However, even if Austria's progress in eastern Europe is slower than perhaps anticipated, it does have the expertise and commercial connections. 'Bridge-building' towards eastern European trade would contribute to the *Ostpolitik* of the EU.

Foreign Trade

Obviously, the Austria of the Second Republic has always been, and continues to be, highly dependent on foreign trade. It is a small country, of around 7.5 million inhabitants with limited resources, and it is therefore essential that it responds rapidly and effectively to political and economic changes. The composition of foreign trade has changed completely in the last 25 years; 25 years ago Austria's export structure was not very different from that of a developing country: 70 per cent of total exports were in timber, iron, steel, and paper. Since then, the composition has changed to finished and more sophisticated goods such as machines and electrical appliances.

The electro- and electronic industries offer a perfect illustration of this development. Internationalisation of the industry is fostered as products are cheap and easy to transport. In contrast to other industrial sectors, this branch has strong international connections through subsidiaries of international companies in Austria. Foreign investment capital doubled production from 1980 to 1989, to a value of around 67.6 billion AS. A further distinction, within Austria, of this sector is that of the 430 companies (with a combined workforce of around 75,000), 75 per cent are joint-stock companies; for Austria, fairly large companies. It is an export-oriented industry: two-thirds of total production is exported and nearly 75 per cent of exports, as Table 3.2 shows, are to the EU; and within that, 45 per cent to Germany.

At the same time, there has been a sharp increase in imports of manufactured goods and this reflects the growing international division of labour resulting from European integration. Austria is exporting manufactured goods in order to buy foreign manufactured goods. The export/import trend illustrated by the electro- and electronic industries is reflected by Austrian industry as a whole. Most importantly, as Table 3.3 shows, it emphasises the dominance of the EU as a trading partner. This high proportion of trade with the EU will continue and clearly indicates that Austrian industry and trade is already strongly integrated with the Union.

Table 3.2: Trade Values of Electro- and Electronic Industry, 1989 (%)

	Imports	Exports
EU	62.0	74.8
EFTA	5.2	8.1
Others	32.0	10.1
Eastern bloc	0.8	7.0

Source: *Statistischer Bericht, Elektro-und Electronikindustrie*, Institut für Unternehmensführung, Wirtschaftsunversität, Vienna, 1990, p.39.

Table 3.3: Austrian Foreign Trade by Economic Region

Region	Imports (%)			Exports (%)		
	1980	1990	1991	1980	1990	1991
EU	63.1	68.3	67.8	56.2	64.5	65.8
EFTA	7.6	7.1	6.9	12.1	10.2	9.2
Eastern Europe	9.7	6.0	6.0	12.1	8.5	9.0
OECD	77.4	84.6	84.4	72.6	81.2	81.1
Developing Nations	19.9	7.9	8.2	23.5	7.3	7.6

Source: *Austrian Central Statistical Office*, 1992.

In the past, Austria has usually had a deficit in its balance of trade and, mainly because of tourism, a surplus in its balances of services. Net receipts from tourism add approximately 6 per cent to GDP - and in some regions, such as the Tyrol, almost 25 per cent. Currency earnings from tourism increased by 9 per cent in 1991 to a total of 160 billion AS.

For Austrian tourism, there really is no alternative to EU membership; 90 per cent of all foreign nightly guests come from the 12 EU countries, 94 per cent from the EEA. EU membership would add 2 to 3 per cent per annum to the tourist economy. Non-membership would see, because of EU developments in bureaucracy and transport, a significant decline. Reliance on increasing the overseas market, especially the USA and Japan, is risky; outbreaks of terrorism have on occasion, demonstrated how easily tourist numbers from these countries can decline.

Austrian Industry

Austrian industry is closely linked to the EU in terms of export/import structure. Germany plays a central role in this relationship. The 1990 boost to Austrian exports, for example, was generated by the high level of demand in Germany as a result of unification. However, Austria has a marked deficit in high technology products, with a trend of imports in that area.

Austria's industrial sector produces 27 per cent of the country's wealth, and in 1990, according to some calculations, the productivity of Austria's industry equalled that of Germany. However, Austrian industry is presented with a number of challenges as it moves towards EU membership. There is a significant number of industries falling into the category of 'stagnating markets'. A further weakness for Austria is the cushioning of a large part of its industry, and productivity in those sectors is one-third lower than in Germany. Since the mid-1980s, structural changes have caused a decline in employment in the industrial sector. At the end of 1993, there were 8,800 industrial production units from a labour force of 632,000. But this sector contributes 96.5 per cent of total Austrian exports and, given spill-off, spill-over and multiplier effects, has a crucial impact on the economy.[17]

Steel and mining, common problem industries, had already evolved very close links with the EU. In many ways, these two Austrian industrial branches have moved considerably towards prevalent EU economic conditions. Austrian steel prices are already, in accordance with the free trade agreement concluded between the ECSC and Austria, aligned to EU rules. Austria's iron and steel industry is firmly part of the Union market; almost 40 per cent of its output is sold to the Union and almost 40 per cent of domestic consumption is covered by imports from the EU. But it produces only 3 per cent of total EU output, and, as it faces increasing costs, the industry will have a negligible effect on the EU's market. Membership, on the other hand, will bring additional advantages for the iron and steel industries in Austria. Rationalisation of administration and managerial structures and the dismantling of technical differences should provide efficiency gains. A further boost will be provided by better access to EU contracts and the overall simplification of cooperation with partner companies in the EU.

Not all industries would gain. Coal, for example, would lose present subsidies and be subject to great pressures. The transition of EEA membership does not remove discrimination against some industrial sectors. Agriculture is the obvious example, but textiles, dominated by small and medium-sized companies, will have a competitive disadvantage in the EEA.

A substantial structural problem which faces Austrian industry is a lack of corporate identity, coupled with a deficit of industrial leadership. Austria is dominated by small and medium-sized companies with 100 to 499 employees. There are no international companies and this has significant effects, such as a deficit in international and European management experience. For instance, German companies locating in Austria tend to appoint German managers to their Austrian subsidiaries. The structure of Austrian joint-stock and limited companies provide an additional constraint; their personnel are perhaps not sufficiently prepared to meet the challenges of increased international competition, accelerating market changes and innovative 'international' approaches.

This lack of international expertise somewhat dampens the positive expectations of Austrian industry from membership of the EU. Multi-national enterprises, particularly in electronics, transport equipment, machinery and chemicals, have targeted Austria as a location for production plants; a further uncertainty for Austrian industry.

In addition, the location of Austrian industry is highly concentrated, and consequently gives rise to regional disparities. As Austria is a federal republic, the powers of the state are divided between the Federal State and the 9 provinces. Although, compared with the federalism of, for instance, Germany, that of Austria is not that highly significant, it nevertheless has an impact on the economy; *Länder*, such as Styria and Upper Austria, with their heavy industries, were affected from 1992 by the global recession and structural changes. Salzburg and the Tyrol, in contrast, enjoyed high growth rates in tourism and were able to sustain positive economic policies. Regional concentrations of industrial production units cause further disparities. Vienna and Styria have over 80 per cent of their industrial production units consisting of a maximum of 9 employees; around 2 per cent have between 50 and 500 employees.

This problem of a massive dominance of small and medium-sized companies is acute in terms of their ability to innovate. Companies of this size do not have the financial capability to develop and produce high-technology products; funding for research and development is consequently a problem. Austria has long been aware of this and, in 1984, an *Innovationsagentur* was established to coordinate, assist and foster research, technology transfer and information for these companies. Austrian industrial policy is conscious that it needs to raise the present 1.5 per cent of national product invested in research to the international average of 2.5 per cent. EU membership would, in this case, bring enormous advantages.

Thus, small and medium-sized companies would benefit from the free movement of capital which would be a financial consequence of EU membership. These companies would gain from the more favourable credit and financial climate. Additional benefits from the free movement of capital would be a greater selection of insurance services, capital investments as well as a greater selection of credit institutions. Cash would be reduced for financial services because of an increase in competitiveness of financial markets. Overall, the EU would provide a far greater opportunity for Austrian industry and commerce for investment.

Conclusion

The consequences of not joining the EU are starkly spelled out by Switzerland's rejection of EEA membership. Swiss exporters will now be at a disadvantage compared to their competitors in the European single market. Perhaps more serious is Switzerland's exclusion from scientific and technological cooperation in the EEA. The prediction for 1993 from one source was very pessimistic: 'In the medium-term, higher unemployment is unavoidable, which will continue to stifle consumer confidence. In 1993, Swiss export and capital equipment investment will already begin to suffer form the country's limited access to the European market'.[18] These economic trends will persist and present a problem for Switzerland, and any other western state excluded from the EEA.

Austria has, in contrast to some EFTA countries seeking accession to the EU, been moving toward integrating with the Union for some years. This has provided dynamism, particularly in the business community, domestic political determination and convinced the EU partners of Austria's seriousness and resolve. Paradoxically, the major obstacle for Austria might have been the lack of consensus concerning EU membership in the population, a matter that had to be put to the test, because of the statutory provision within the State Treaty, via a referendum.

However, the economic arguments for Austria's accession to the EU are irrefutable. The monetary link to Germany has already provided a successful model of economic integration and created a climate for developing structures and processes with the EU. For Austrian industry, EU membership is by no means clear cut; as well as benefits, there will be costs. The relaxation of tariff barriers will be balanced by acceptance of tariffs on some raw materials. The innovation programmes which will enhance Austrian industry, through transfers and participation in research and development, will face the costs of harmonisation of technical standards and norms. In general, industry will of course have to accept the problems of liberalisation in terms of increased competition and subsidiaries coming to Austria.

But the economic consequences of Austria not joining the EU are far more detrimental than any costs incurred. For industry, there would be a loss of high technology and other research and development programmes. The costs are of such magnitude that EU cooperation is really a prerequisite. With such a loss there would be an inevitable decline in industrial skills, as well as a loss of supporting industries.

A worsening trade deficit, a further and vital consequence of non-membership, will have a negative effect on Austria's social structure. The obvious examples are the education and labour market sectors.

Does Austria have a realistic alternative to EU membership? Political stability lies to the west of Austria's borders. The transformation of eastern Europe will not provide a viable economic alternative to EU membership. Since 1992, there have been indicators that countries such as Poland, Hungary, the Czech Republic and Slovakia are providers of low labour-cost markets; this merely exposes Austria's weak industries. It is true that, in the field of small business joint ventures with former COMECON countries, Austria, in comparison with other western European countries, had top ranking. But in terms of the all important capital investment in these countries, it is Germany that comes out on top.

The thrust of this chapter has been to suggest that economic arguments can explain Austria's desire to become a full member of the EU. But economics is not the whole story. Austria is aware that despite its small size, it will, particularly with other small EFTAns, be able to exercise a significant influence on shaping the politics and future development of the EU.

Notes

1. *Agence Europe* (1992) 'European Council in Edinburgh, 11/12 December; Conclusions of the Presidency', 13 December, p. 5.
2. Commission of the European Communities (1991) *Commission Opinion on Austria's Application for membership*, Brussels, August, p. 6.
3. Ibid.
4. Alpbach Political Talks (1991).
5. In the event, of course, the Austrians voted in favour of EU accession by a substantial majority.
6. In Kreissler, F. (1984) *Der Österreicher und seine Nation*, Wien: Hermann Bohlhaus Nachf.

7. Kramer, H. (1991) 'Strukturentwicklung der Außenpolitik' (1945-1990) in Dachs, H. u.a., *Handbuch des Politischen Systems Österreichs*, Vienna: Mazsche Verlags-und Unibuchhandlung.

8. Schwok, R. (1992) *European Integration and Swiss Identities*, paper given at the British International Studies Association annual conference, Swansea, 15 December (unpublished).

9. Sozialwissenschaftlichen Studiengesellshaft reported in *Der Standard*, 13/14 February 1993, no. 128.

10. *Kurier*, 14 May 1992.

11. Plasser, F. u.a. (1993) 'Analyse der Präsidentenwahl 1992: Kandidaten, Medien und Wählerverhalten' in *Österreichisches Jahrbuch für Politik 1992*, Wien: Verlag für Geshcichte und Politik.

12. Report of the Study Group on Swiss Neutrality (1992) *Schweizerische Neutralität auf dem Prüfstand - Schweizerische Außenpolitik zwischen Kontinuität und Wandel*, Schweizer Bundesrat, 26 March 1992.

13. Lecture by Federal President Thomas Klestil, 'College d'Europe', Bruges, 28 September 1993.

14. Economic data calculated from *Statistische Übersichten, Österreichische Institut für Wirtschafsforschung*, 65, Jahrgang, 11/1992.

15. Detailed discussion in Breuss, F. (1992) 'Was erartet Österreich in der Wirtschafs- und Währungsunion der EG?' *Österreichisches Institut für Wirtschaftsforschung*, no. 10, pp. 536-8.

16. Seidel. H. (1993) 'Wirtschaftspolitik und Integration' *Wirtschafts Politische Blätter*, no. 1.

17. *Unternehmer* (1993) no. 10, p. 16.

18. Union Bank of Switzerland (1993) *Economic Trends in Switzerland*, February.

4 Sweden and Finland: From EFTA Neutrals to EU Members

Lee Miles

Sweden and Finland have traditionally maintained economically close, yet politically distinct relations with the EU. Both states are important European trading partners for the EU. Sweden, for example, was the EU's fourth largest trading partner in 1992.[1] Despite this, Sweden and Finland resisted the idea of becoming full members of the Union until 1991. Since then, they have reviewed their position and both Governments have now applied to join and, indeed, negotiated accession terms. Sweden formally applied on 1 July 1991 with Finland following shortly after, on the 18 March 1992.

The purpose of this chapter is to evaluate the changing rationales which governed Swedish and Finnish relations with the EU and why both Nordic nations have revised their policies and formally sought full EU membership. Through this structured analysis, three themes will be evident. First, that there are six common guiding factors that have influenced both Swedish and Finnish relations with the EU. It was the changes in these factors that made the original objections against membership outdated. Second, that economic priorities have overcome declining political ideology in favour of both states seeking full membership. Third, that the accession of these states will not be without difficulty.

Six Common Factors: A Theoretical Framework

It can be argued that relations between these states and the EU have been governed by six common factors which defined the limits of cooperation during the period of 1958-91. The level of influence differed between the two states in quantitative terms and timescale. The first four factors can be identified as 'internal/domestic' factors and the latter two as 'external/international' factors.

The Constraints of the Nordic Political Model

The Swedes and Finns are responsible for developing a Nordic consensual political model, built on the notion of national parliamentary democracy, combined with a highly successful corporate economic system. National sovereignty and political consensus were perceived as a winning formula which had allowed these states to develop high standards of living. Consensual democracy and a comprehensive welfare system remained sacred and integral parts of domestic political culture. Although there are distinct differences between the Swedish and Finnish parliamentary models, their success meant that there was little coherent political desire to want to join the EU. The argument that full EU membership would improve or consolidate the status of Nordic democracy was considered absurd.[2] Rather, the reverse was true. Both Governments feared that full EU membership could threaten their liberal democracies, given the accusations that the EU system remains undemocratic. Neither their parliamentary or comprehensive welfare state systems were to be compromised by external obligations. Many Swedes and Finns also remained unconvinced that joining the EU would increase their material standards of living. Sweden was particularly concerned that membership could lead to the dilution of its advanced but expensive welfare provisions, believing that it would be necessary to introduce lower EU common standards in order to maintain economic competitiveness.

The Dominance of Nordic Political Elites

Sweden and Finland were sustained by a limited number of elite political forces, which were dominant and unsympathetic to joining the EU. In Sweden, the long periods of domination by Social Democrats in government was an inhibiting factor since, until 1991, they opposed full EU membership. Ideologically, they viewed external infringements on national parliamentary sovereignty (incurred with EU accession) with suspicion, advocating that the Nordic economies had been successfully regulated by national authorities.[3] The ideology and political dominance of Social Democracy meant that Swedish membership of the EU was mainly off the political agenda. The main trade union organisation, the LO, was also against joining, clearly influencing the Social Democrats. In Finland, it was not the dominance of one party that was important, but the role of the President in maintaining order. The Finns have maintained complex and over-large coalition Governments.[4] Finnish coalition Governments have usually been built around the rural-based Centre Party, which traditionally opposed EU membership, making any application untenable. Yet, the complexities of Finland's multi-party system and the weakness of the parliament constitutionally have required a strong presidential role in domestic and foreign affairs.[5] The dominance of the Finnish President in foreign affairs was reinforced by the need to maintain good relations with the USSR. This placed the President in the position of having ultimate power in foreign affairs and made membership of the EU impossible, given the sensitivities of the Soviet Union. Finland's first post-war President, J. K. Paasikivi (1946-56) developed 'The Paasikivi Line'[6] where Finland was to be pro-Soviet, but non-communist in foreign affairs. Urho Kekonnen's long incumbency as President (1956-81) was also instrumental in maintaining a policy independent of EU membership, as nothing was to undermine the Finnish-Soviet relationship. This policy was continued by Kekonnen's successor, Mauno Koivisto, who showed a restrictive attitude towards debate on the EU until 1991.[7]

Common Nordic Preferences for Intergovernmental Cooperation

Politically, the Swedes and Finns share a common preference for pragmatic intergovernmental cooperation between nation states. Believing that the Nordic model of parliamentary sovereignty was a success, they favoured an intergovernmental approach to integration, in which the notion of national sovereignty could be protected. Revitalised proposals for a Nordic customs union failed between 1968 and 1970, due to Swedish and Finnish objections of its supranational overtones. Participation in the EU was unattractive for the same reasons.

Concerns Over the Nordic Economies

The economic infrastructure of both states is highly concentrated, containing powerful economic lobbies. In Finland, several of these influential economic lobbies remained fearful of complete market access and naked competition with the EU. Generally, both states were politically wary of the obligations of Union membership and sought to protect sensitive national economic interests. The Finnish Government was concerned that joining the EU would place too high a cost on its industry. The concentration of its economy in a few key primary products and high levels of government subsidy meant that Finnish industry feared that it would not be able to compete in fully liberalised EU markets. Equally, patterns of trade in Finland did not make EU membership conducive to Finnish companies. A large proportion of Finnish external trade was with the Soviet Union. The USSR remained Finland's most important single trading partner in the early 1980s, representing 25 per cent of Finnish exports.[8] As long as this trade was important, then EU membership was less attractive.

Potential Alternatives to Full EU Membership

There existed alternatives to the concepts of the EU and a supranational customs union. Nordic cooperation and the wider EFTA were seen by both states as more comfortable, but less ambitious frameworks for external relations until 1991. These two channels fitted Nordic preferences for intergovernmental approaches to European cooperation.

The chief institutional expression of Scandinavian cooperation has been the Nordic Council, founded in 1952. The organisation has been progressively upgraded. The 1963 Helsinki Treaty and a 1971 revision of the Treaty gave it a clearer procedural framework. These established key areas of cooperation including legislation, culture, social and economic policies. In some areas, the Nordic Council has been highly successful, even outstripping the level of integration in the EU, such as the Nordic Passport Union.[9] However, this has been generally restricted to limited economic areas. The Council has been selective about the levels of cooperation in order to reconcile them with concerns over maintaining national sovereignty.

Nordic cooperation with other western European states was preferred through the intergovernmental EFTA. EFTA remained a credible framework suited to Nordic preferences. Sweden and Finland benefited from participating in a wider western European free trade area in industrial products, without ceding large elements of national sovereignty. EFTA avoided sensitive issues such as agriculture and therefore excluded opposition from domestic lobbies. EFTA enabled them to enjoy a wider economic framework for greater trade and was compatible with neutrality. Until 1973, it also included the UK and Denmark, which were major trading partners for these states.

Neutrality, Strategic Concerns and the Legacy of the Cold War

The division of Europe into two political blocs until 1989 restricted these states' freedom of manoeuvre in foreign affairs. Both were unable to seriously consider joining supranational organisations until after 1989. Government priorities lay with the continuation of a credible foreign policy of neutrality. They needed to remain formally detached from the institutional make-up of East and West in order to maintain these policies. Initially, the EU was identified by the Soviets and the Nordic electorates as being economically associated with NATO and this made Swedish and Finnish membership unacceptable.

Swedish and Finnish Relations with the EU: Neutrality Policy and the Trading Dilemma 1958-91

Generally, the six factors illustrated had differing degrees of importance within each state. It can be argued that the Swedes and Finns faced a dilemma regarding their relations with the EU. This dilemma had two elements. The first consideration was the political constraints of maintaining a credible neutrality policy. These states needed to develop a distinct political relationship which would take account of neutrality policy. At the same time, their Governments had to deal with their growing economic interdependence with the Union, which meant ensuring that they maintained a close economic relationship. Policy was therefore directed at reconciling this dilemma between 1958 and 1991.

Their policies towards the EU can only be analysed within the context of neutrality policy. Sweden's relationship with the Union has been identified as 'the politics of independence' and was built around the concept of 'armed neutrality' and 'non-participation in alliances'.[10] It aimed at maintaining Sweden's position as a key European nation, which was not aligned to either of the two blocs in Europe. The Swedish Government needed to constantly reiterate its uncompromising neutral position throughout the post-war period until 1991. This was not an easy task. Sweden's status as a neutral state was voluntary and was not recognised in international law. Although she had been a neutral state since 1814, her credibility had been severely tested and weakened during the Second World War. The experience of the 'Engelbrecht Division' episode in June 1941 lead to Swedish post-war preoccupations that its neutrality was clear and transparent.[11] Her geographical position also heightened the primacy of neutrality policy. Sweden remained strategically sensitive to East-West friction, representing the northern hinterland surrounding the northern flank of the East and West blocs in Europe.

The primary foreign policy objective was to maintain an independent identity through non-alignment and a strong-armed capability. Its view of security was intrinsically linked to the maximisation of national sovereignty and a limited perception of international cooperation. To the Swedes, membership of the EU was viewed as politically inappropriate. Independence would be undermined by EU membership obligations, which inferred the ceding of national sovereignty to supranational EU institutions in key fields, such as commercial policy. The EU's common commercial policy was especially seen as incompatible with Swedish neutrality.

For Finland, neutrality concerns had even greater importance. Finnish relations with the EU were even more influenced by its neutrality policy than were Sweden's, being labelled the 'politics of security'.[12] Foreign policy was almost entirely governed by the legacy of the Cold War. Finnish neutrality was not recognised in international law and was more reactive and restrictive than Sweden's. Policy was governed by her long geographical border with the USSR and the fact that she had fought two unsuccessful wars against the Soviets in 1939-40 and 1941-44.[13] If the Swedes perceived neutrality in terms of maximising independent actions, the Finns viewed neutrality policy as the only effective way of preserving the state itself.

The cornerstone of Finnish foreign policy was the continuation of the 1948 Treaty of Friendship, Cooperation and Mutual Assistance with the USSR. Finland recognised the primacy of military-security issues and gauged all other relations against this dimension. The position of Finland was to preserve the 'status quo'. Her strict and passive view of neutrality ruled out any institutional obligations or supranational cooperation. Two crises in Finno-Soviet relations - the 'Night Frost' of 1958-59 and the 'Note Crisis' of 1961-62 - were taken as practical examples of the limits of Finnish neutrality and the extent of Soviet tolerance of Finnish independence.[14] For Finland, EU membership in any form was totally unrealistic.

Yet, both states needed to maintain sound economic relations with the Union. In particular, Swedish policy had to deal with her trading dilemma with the EU. The Swedish economy is export orientated. Its economic strength in manufacturing has been determined in large measure by its competitiveness *vis-à-vis* the rest of the world.[15] Sweden's manufacturing sector is large and its reliance on EU markets high. Economic indicators in Sweden favoured full EU membership. Swedish policy aimed at achieving a delicate balance of seeking liberalised trade without sacrificing neutrality.

Finland also shared this trading dilemma, but to a far lesser degree. It was bolstered by its substantial trade with the Soviet Union. Finland established a series of barter arrangements which allowed Finnish exports to find secure markets in the USSR. In 1989, the USSR's share of total Finnish exports amounted to 14.5 per cent. Finland was the USSR's second largest western trading partner.[16] Trade with the USSR also secured Finland's energy needs through cheap oil. Thus, for Finland, this dilemma was less noticeable or immediate. The Finnish economy was also highly concentrated in several economic sectors such as forestry, paper and pulp industries and farming (35 per cent of Finnish industry is still accounted for by the forestry industry alone). The main farming and forestry interest organisations such as, the agricultural MTK (Confederation of Agricultural Producers) were opposed to EU membership and still remain concerned about the possibility. The Finns did fear the effects of open EU competition on their highly protected industries. Finland's high-technology expertise tended to be in highly refined products which were not suited to EU markets, such as shipbuilding and icebreakers.

The 1960s

Although the dilemma facing the two states was similar, the differences in degree made their responses different in the 1960s. In 1957, both states initially viewed the negotiations on creating a European Economic Community with only partial interest. The (then) EC wished to establish a supranational customs union, which they found unacceptable. However, Sweden was quick to recognise the growing importance of the Community as an economic trading bloc in the early 1960s. Policy was directed at dealing with the growing economic influence of the EC on the Swedish economy, without having to become a member.

It can be argued that the Swedes adopted a threefold strategy using a 'triad' of trading relations. The first strategy was to maintain access to EC markets by securing a close relationship with the EC through trading agreements. When Britain and Denmark in 1960 and Norway in April 1962 applied to join the EC as full members, Sweden, fearing isolation, asked for association status with the EC, but only on the precondition of it being compatible with neutrality policy. The second was to provide an alternative pillar to strengthen Sweden's negotiating hand with the EC. It was a Swedish initiative that resulted in the 1960 Stockholm Convention and the formation of EFTA. Sweden favoured an intergovernmental free trade area which could facilitate free trade, without damaging political sovereignty or neutrality. In the 1960s, the Swedes tried to consolidate EFTA. Sweden was comfortable with EFTA membership as it also contained major trading partners such as the UK and Denmark.

The third strategy was to maintain sound relations with other Nordic states. The Swedish Government was conscious to maintain close ties with its Nordic neighbours and showed concern when any of them considered full EC membership. It paid keen attention to Norwegian and Danish desires of joining the Community.

The response from Finland was more relaxed. The dilemma for Finland was complicated, and lay in reconciling economic relations with the West without compromising strategic and economic relationships with the USSR. The solution, until the mid-1980s, lay in special measures and arrangements with the West, which indirectly took account of Soviet concerns. Finnish foreign policy became sophisticated, pragmatic and mature in balancing East and West. In 1961, Finland achieved associate membership of EFTA through its specialist FINNEFTA arrangement, while still guaranteeing rights to the USSR. The fact that within EFTA there existed other Nordic neutral states maintained Finland's credibility in Soviet eyes. EFTA also suited Finnish economic requirements. Her fragile economy needed a long transition to adjust to liberalised trade and FINNEFTA allowed for a period of adaptation.[17] EC membership was not considered important and Finland did not actively seek close contacts with the EC during the 1960s. The Cold War was at its height and the Soviet Union officially viewed the EC as the economic arm of NATO. Close relations between the EC and Finland were out of the question.

By 1967, Swedish policy had shifted to one that tried to consider how to gain conditions similar to full EC membership without paying the political price of damaging neutrality. The Swedes even considered a kind of flexible EC membership and approached the EC to open negotiations. This process failed when the French Government vetoed the applications of the UK and Denmark in 1967, shutting the door on the enlargement question.

The 1970s

During the 1970s, both states upgraded their relationship with the EC/EU. From 1970, Sweden was willing to seek closer trading ties, provided neutrality remained credible. The economic power of the EU was undeniable after the first enlargement and Sweden's dependence upon it ever growing. Swedish strategy altered to one that even contemplated EU membership, but only on its own terms. In 1970, Sweden tried to define a new agenda with the EU by submitting an 'open' application for membership, asking for extensive and close relations in a form compatible with Swedish neutrality.[18] When this failed, Sweden advocated a customs union between itself and the EU in 1971, allowing for full economic integration, but avoiding political integration with the Union. From the economic perspective, EU membership now made sense. The decisive reason for this change was the defection of the UK and Denmark to the Union. By 1973, the EU had enlarged to include most of Sweden's major trading partners, and the main constraints were now entirely political.

However, Swedish overtures were rejected, as the EU was formulating its own, more ambitious, agenda for future European integration and this would complicate obligations of EU membership at a time when enlargement negotiations were in full swing. In 1971, the Riksdag passed a virtually unanimous parliamentary resolution removing the issue of membership from the Swedish political agenda on the grounds that full EU membership would be incompatible with Swedish neutrality. This remained government policy until May 1990. In reality, *de facto* economic integration was intensified while political integration was studiously avoided.[19]

Equally, it was apparent to Finland that the EU was now a permanent and expanding entity. The process of realisation was slower but the outcome similar. Two of Finland's leading trading partners (the UK and Denmark) were to become full EU members. It was also the change in Swedish attitudes which influenced Finland. Sweden as both a fellow neutral and Finland's neighbour had a heavy influence on Finnish EU policy.

The diplomatic progress of the early 1970s was indirectly effective. Sweden signed a bilateral FTA with the EU on 22 July 1972, gaining the upgraded economic relationship with the EU it had been seeking. This Agreement established a free trade area in industrial products between the EU and Sweden. Yet, for the Swedes the results were disappointing. Sweden still faced restrictions on the major exports of aluminium and special steels.[20] The Swedish Government found the Agreement too small and stressed its evolutionary clause.

Finnish relations with the EU were only formally established in 1973. The 1973 FTA between Finland and the EU was essentially similar to that between the EU and Sweden. However, the EU-Finnish Treaty did not include an evolutionary clause (Article 32 of the Swedish Agreement), signalling that Finland would limit agreement to the specific conditions of the FTA. It was not politically committing itself to any related developments in the future. Finnish policy was still reactive, aimed at dealing with the growing economic power of the EU, whilst reconciling security interests. In 1977, the Government tentatively committed itself to developing a closer relationship with the EU. Finnish policy towards Europe gradually moved from one based on finite arrangements to one based on full EFTA membership. By 1984, the Finns had developed a comprehensive European trade policy, with EFTA membership remaining the cornerstone.[21] The free trade areas in industrial products between the EU and Sweden and the EU and Finland were completed in 1984. In 1986, Finland became a full member of EFTA.

The 1980s - A Dynamic Agenda

By the 1980s, both Governments realised that their relationship with the EU was radically changing. This was due to four elements.

The Obsolescence of Existing Arrangements

By 1984, both Governments were aware that the FTAs would be insufficient to provide continued access to EU markets. The EU's economic power became unquestionable after the second enlargement of 1981. Neither state could afford to remain too isolated from EU decisions. Therefore, both welcomed the upgrading of EU-EFTA relations with the 1984 Luxembourg Declaration. The main failing of this new shopping list of cooperation was its timing. It was signed just before the EU embarked on its ambitious Single European Market (SEM) programme, which made the Luxembourg 'process' too limited and superficial. It did not secure Swedish requirements of guaranteeing export shares into the EU, which could only practically be secured by a more formal and advanced institutional framework.

The Emergence of a Dynamic EU and the Single European Market

The EU started to formulate a more ambitious agenda, revolving around the revitalised concept of an internal market. It was feared that the SEM would have a direct impact on the competitiveness of Swedish and Finnish exports into the EU. Trade with EFTA and the other Nordics was now completely overshadowed by the economic importance of the EU. Neither state could avoid increasing economic interdependence with a larger Union, as it developed the internal market programme. An enlarged and more dynamic EU, a relatively weaker EFTA and a fear that the Union could turn into a 'Fortress Europe' were all factors to which both states needed to react, regardless of neutrality. The economic imperatives of securing trade with the EU were starting to override neutrality requirements.

Sweden's policy on the new SEM was evident by 1987. A key governmental policy paper given to the Riksdag[22] reiterated that it would be prepared to become an EU member in all respects, except for the common discussions on security policy. Sweden was informally shadowing internal market developments from 1987, clearly indicating that political as well as economic sovereignty was directly affected. Sweden implicitly recognised the threat of the SEM.

Attraction of New Areas of International Cooperation

In addition, Sweden became increasingly attracted to some of the EU's other new policy initiatives. Since 1983, the Union has launched its research and development programmes such as ESPRIT. For a small open economy like Sweden which is also home to a large number of multinationals, these programmes were an extra incentive. Moreover, both states were impressed by the Commission's decision to introduce a 'social dimension' to the SEM, which helped reduce worries over the protection of their social systems if economic cooperation was upgraded.[23]

Frustration with the EEA

The EEA seemed to initially provide the solution for both states. Jacques Delors' offer of a more structured EU-EFTA partnership, in 1989, seemed an attractive arrangement, especially as the EEA would extend the benefits of the EU's SEM programme to the EFTA states. As an advanced free trade area, the EEA allowed for closer economic integration, without imposing the political costs of EU membership. Neutrality would remain untouched, if economic factors could be divorced from the political.

However, advanced economic integration does impose a political cost. Sweden, by 1990, was frustrated with the prolonged nature of the EEA negotiations. This proved to be the catalyst for Sweden's application for EU membership. The EEA concept failed to provide the Swedes with practical influence on future EU decision-making on SEM proposals. It would be forced to accept large amounts of EU legislation, while only being permitted a consultative 'decision-shaping' role in determining future SEM legislation. This asymmetry in the EEA concept infringed Swedish economic sovereignty, without allowing proportionate political influence on

EU decisions. In practice, rather than pacifying political concerns, the EEA threatened Swedish concepts of independence.

By 1990, the Swedish Government had shifted in favour of full EU membership as the only practical way of securing Sweden's economic interests. In December 1990, the Swedish Parliament approved the decision that Sweden should follow Austria's example and seek full EU membership, with 90 per cent of the Riksdag supporting the motion. On 14 June 1991, the Prime Minister delivered a statement to the Parliament claiming that EU membership would bring considerable benefits to Sweden.[24]

Finland tentatively accepted the EEA concept and participated in the negotiations. Until late 1991, Finland still viewed EU membership as unviable and saw the EEA as providing a satisfactory alternative to full Union membership. Between November 1991 and March 1992, Finland moved quickly towards EU membership. The Finnish Government's original strategy was to wait until the conclusion of the EEA agreement, but two events changed its mind. First, the delays in the EEA's completion due to the European Court of Justice's criticism of the creation of a rival EEA court. Second, Sweden's decision to seek accession to the EU regardless of the outcome of the EEA negotiations tilted Finland in favour of full EU membership. In January 1992, the Finnish Government sought, and gained, approval from the Finnish Parliament to seek EU membership.

A Change of Perspective

Sweden formally applied for full EU membership on 1 July 1991 and Finland followed on 18 March 1992. The six factors which had previously made EU membership impossible had been reappraised.

The Asymmetry of Trade with the EU

The EU had become too large a trading partner to the extent that it had become impossible for non-member states like Sweden and Finland to deal with it adequately from the outside. The 1972 EU FTAs had functioned well, but had ironically heightened the economic interdependence between the Nordic states and the EU. Finnish exports to the EU between 1973 and 1978 rose by 85 per cent.[25] Swedish exports to the EU rose by 70 per cent in the same period. By 1991, Sweden's trade with the EU represented 55 per cent of exports[26] and 55 per cent of imports. Finland's trade with the

EU constituted 51 per cent of exports in 1991 and 45.9 per cent of imports.[27]

However, this interdependence is asymmetrical. In 1985, the EU supplied approximately 25 per cent of the Swedish home demand for manufactures. Yet, in 1985, Sweden supplied barely 1 per cent of the EU home demand due to the huge size of the EU's domestic market in relation to its imports.[28] Nordic economic sovereignty was rapidly becoming a myth and was in reality being heavily affected by the EU. The Swedes felt it necessary to copy EU legislation to maintain industrial competitiveness. By the late 1980s, trade was so intertwined that Nordic competitiveness was being damaged by exclusion from the EU structure.

The Weakness of the Nordic Economies

During the 1980s, Sweden and Finland experienced a gradual slowing down in their economies, raising fears of economic stagnation. Questions arose concerning the costs imposed on business by their highly corporate economies. Between 1990 and 1993, both states endured an economic recession, which was comparatively more severe than that experienced by the EU. In particular, Finland went into deep recession, with a decline in GDP of 8 per cent; industrial output fell by 6.5 per cent in real terms in 1991.[29] In Finland, GDP fell by 14 per cent between 1990 and 1993. In Sweden, real GDP declined by 6 per cent from 1990 to 1993 with a budget deficit envisaged to reach 15 per cent of GNP in 1994.[30]

Consequently, both states have become aware of the weakening of their economies. The Nordic model faces a crisis of confidence. Rather than being complacent about the success of their economic systems, their economic decline made both Governments regard EU membership as a way of reversing their economic problems. Instead of perceiving their corporate models as effective, they questioned whether welfare provisions were too extensive, placing too heavy a burden on their industries. Sweden is facing a severe structural crisis caused by the large size of the protected sector within the economy. Public spending represented 73 per cent of GDP in 1993. Both Governments now view EU membership more positively, believing it will reinforce the liberalisation of their economies, rather than dilute their welfare provisions as had previously been the perception. In addition, the Governments face greater pressure to ensure that their industries operate on equal terms within the EU, as these industries feel unable to withstand any costs of exclusion from the Union.

Moreover, the collapse in Finnish trade with the former USSR has forced the Finns to look towards the EU for new markets. Exports of

Finnish manufactures to the USSR fell by 65 per cent in 1991 alone.[31] Russian trade represented barely 2.8 per cent of total Finnish exports in 1992.[32] Soviet trade had protected Finland from the 1970s recession. That protection no longer exists in the 1990s. The future of both Finland and Sweden's economies now lies with EU integration.

Growing Criticism of the Nordic Political Model

The Nordic consensual political model has been openly criticised. It has been argued that the Swedish model of Social Democracy represented the most successful example of 'integrative democracy'.[33] However, the failure of successive Governments to deal with recession has led to further questioning of traditional Swedish economic policies. Sweden became more politicised. Social Democratic economic policy caused great divisions especially regarding their Labour-initiated reforms, such as employer investment funds. The regulated economy was perceived as not functioning effectively. The Carlsson Social Democratic Government submitted the Swedish application for membership partly as a means of reversing criticism of a stagnating corporate economy. The Social Democratic leadership changed to favouring EU membership by the time their Government ended in October 1991.

The Changing Views of the Dominant Nordic Political and Business Elites

Just as the dominance of domestic political elites had previously prevented full EU membership, it was the change in their views that facilitated the EU membership applications. The about-face of the Swedish Social Democrats in 1990 was led almost entirely by the party elites, with a complete lack of mass level involvement. However, it did reflect a heightened interest in the EU among business and labour leaders.[34]

The success of the SEM programme forced both Swedish and Finnish industrial lobbies to favour full EU membership as the only way to secure vital EU market shares. Their business elites had long since demonstrated their support for Union membership. The Swedish employers' organisation, SAF, had been openly critical of the potential economic costs of the neutrality policy. Companies like Stora, Tetra-Pak, IKEA, Ericsson and Volvo had enhanced their manufacturing facilities in the EU. In the last seven years, Swedish direct investment in the EU rose more than tenfold.[35] The conversion of the LO, with its close ties to the governing Social

Democrats, meant that both the leading sectoral organisations now favoured EU membership at a time when cooperation was critical to achieve stabilisation measures to tackle the recession. The LO was converted, as it believed that the Swedish welfare model could only be guaranteed by continued export growth. In Finland, business leaders realised that in order to survive in international markets, they had to establish their companies in the European market. From 1985 to 1990, Finnish net investments grew sixfold from 2.18 to 12.47 billion FM.[36] Business elites progressively demonstrated their support for EU membership by their investment actions. For both states, it can be argued that their applications for EU membership were part of the elite bargaining process indicative in Nordic consensual democracy.

Inadequacy of Intergovernmental Cooperation

Both states have increasingly recognised that supranational cooperation is necessary. Political separation from the EU was proving costly. The issue of European integration has been forced on the Nordic states due to impulses from abroad. The old process of intergovernmental cooperation could no longer guarantee Nordic access to the EU. The Union's decision to embark upon, and complete, its single market programme was critical in forcing both states to abandon intergovernmentalism. Intergovernmental cooperation could no longer suffice.

Failure of Potential Alternatives to EU Membership

Nordic cooperation failed to provide a credible alternative to the EU. The Norwegians refloated the idea of further Nordic cooperation after the rejection of EU membership in 1972, but there was little concrete response from other Nordic states. The Nordic Council's success has been limited to sectoral areas and did not provide the range of opportunities offered by the EU. For political and economic reasons, the attention of both states now looked firmly towards western Europe. Yet, even advanced frameworks such as the EEA were viewed as poor substitutes for EU membership. The problems with the EEA negotiations illustrated that only limited progress could be made with the EEA concept. Frustration with the EEA was a major reason why Sweden decided to apply for EU membership regardless. In addition, the EEA did not include the EU's post-1993 agenda and the implications of the Maastricht Treaty. By the time the EEA agreement was signed on 2 May 1992, the EEA could clearly not safeguard either state's long-term interests. The EEA was not an alternative to EU membership, but rather a step towards it.

Changes in the Strategic Environment

The disintegration of the Communist regimes in eastern Europe in 1989 and the eventual demise of the USSR in 1991 removed the major rationale for the neutrality policy. The break-up of the Soviet bloc and the eventual dissolution of the Warsaw Pact, in January 1992, has allowed greater flexibility in interpreting neutrality policy. Sweden quickly realised that the revolutions in eastern Europe removed the formal constraints of non-participation in economic organisations. In June 1991, in a statement to the Riksdag, Prime Minister Carlsson claimed that full EU membership was 'compatible with the requirement of our policy of neutrality'.[37] The bipolar world had disintegrated. For Finland, the break-up of the USSR removed the reason for her passive foreign policy. In 1992, the Finns signed a free trade agreement with the Russians, repealing the strategic constraints of the Finno-Soviet 1948 Treaty. Finland was free to follow Sweden in applying for EU membership. These post-1989 changes allowed both countries to adopt a more flexible interpretation of neutrality. Neutrality policy could now be compatible with full EU membership. The culmination of gradual 'internal/ domestic' circumstances favouring EU membership and a dramatic change in 'external' factors removed the traditional obstacles to EU membership. The possibility of EU membership was now too strong to resist.

From the Union's perspective, enlargement re-emerged as an issue. For the EU, the main reason for negotiating the EEA was initially to act as an alternative, which would deter the EFTA states from seeking EU full membership and allow the Union to concentrate on deepening integration. The 1991 Swedish application conclusively proved that this strategy had failed. It too realised that the EEA would be insufficient to appease the EFTA states over access to the SEM. The EEA concept accelerated the enlargement process rather than deferring it. By February 1992, the Union had finalised its integrationist agenda with the Maastricht Treaty. It had defined the parameters which all new applicants would have to accept. EU enlargement to encompass Sweden and Finland, was now appropriate, after January 1993, as the SEM was completed and the new deepening agenda relatively safe.

Eligibility for Membership

Finland and Sweden fulfil all of the preconditions for membership as laid down by the EU. This was confirmed in the Commission's Opinions on the Swedish (7 August 1992) and Finnish (4 November 1992) applications. The Commission's rapid response in issuing its Opinions on their applications also illustrates how seriously and favourably the EU now viewed their applications. It took 13 months and 8 months, respectively, for the Commission to reply to the Swedish and Finnish applications and issue its Opinions. This contrasts heavily with the time taken for the Opinions on Malta and Cyprus to be delivered. The accession negotiations also began relatively speedily with negotiations starting on 1 February 1993, only 3 months after the Finnish Opinion was published. The quick start to the enlargement negotiations illustrates the suitability of these states for membership.

Both states satisfy the three basic conditions of having a European identity, democratic status and respect for human rights.[38] Finland and Sweden are clearly European and are prominent members of European organisations, such as EFTA and the Council of Europe. They are advanced liberal democracies with excellent human rights and civil liberties credentials, having more advanced legislation in some areas than existing EU members. They also have functioning, competitive, market economies capable of dealing with EU membership obligations, being more economically advanced than the majority of EU states. Indeed, Finland and Sweden are almost ideal membership applicants as they are both relatively small in size and rich in terms of GNP. They will not pose big problems in integrating with the rest of the EU economically, especially as they already enjoy a large degree of integration with the Union. As part of the EEA, these states have adopted large parts of the *acquis communautaire*. Approximately 60 per cent, or some 12,000 pages, of the *acquis* had already been approved before accession negotiations even began. Both have also accepted the principles of the Maastricht Treaty and the EU. This includes the comprehensive acceptance of the political regime (*acquis politique*) and the ultimate political goals (*finalités politiques*). Therefore, the Commission believes their integration into the EU would not pose insurmountable problems.

The Accession Negotiations

It was originally envisaged that the EU accession negotiations would be relatively speedy and completed by the end of 1993. Both states would ratify the Accession Treaties formally in 1994, allowing them to become full members by 1 January 1995. This timetable was ambitious and in reality proved unrealistic as the conclusion of the accession negotiations was delayed until 28 February 1994 (and slightly later for Norway). Yet, there are incentives for both the Union and the applicants to ensure that accession is completed before 1996.

From the EU's perspective, the EEA agreement does provide a useful foundation which could pave the way for early Swedish and Finnish accessions. It was expected that both applicants would be flexible. The Swedish application was limited to one sentence with no reference to neutrality or any specific preconditions. The March 1992 Finnish application was short, including no reservations on neutrality.[39] Quick accession would also allow these states to participate as full EU members at the Maastricht Treaty review in 1996, reducing any complexities for the EU and incorporating Nordic perspectives. There seems little sense in embarking on the review before enlargement is finalised, otherwise another revision would be necessary almost immediately.

The accession negotiations also needed to be speedy for Finnish and Swedish domestic reasons. The time frame is limiting. First, a tight schedule is necessary in order to allow Sweden to ratify accession for 1995. EU membership may require amendments to the Swedish constitution, which must be endorsed by two successive parliaments with a general election in between. The whole procedure will take at least six months to complete. There is an alternative procedure which allows such legislation to be passed in a single session of parliament, but this requires a majority of no fewer than five-sixths from a quorum of no fewer than three quarters of all Riksdag members.[40] This would be politically difficult for the Swedish Government to achieve. Second, both Governments have committed themselves to conducting a referendum on the issue of accession. This will be an inhibiting factor, in terms of time, for ratification.

The accession negotiations cannot be compared to previous negotiations for several reasons. The EU has now entered a more dynamic phase and has adopted the Maastricht Treaty; a clearer future agenda to which all applicants must subscribe. This limited the amount of flexibility the Commission could provide in the negotiations. At the same time, this round of accession negotiations encompassed more applicants than any other previously, including states that are both committed to conducting referenda on the issue and have substantial minorities opposing EU membership. Thus, the deals struck at the negotiations needed to be acceptable to wider mass population concerns. This restricted the amount of flexibility that the Nordic Governments could offer in the negotiations.

Nevertheless, despite rather pessimistic assessments being made in 1993, when 'negotiations will last as long as they must', the accession negotiations were completed (more or less) on time (by the end of February 1994). Indeed, some of the more problematic issues, such as CFSP and social and environmental policy, were completed by the original December 1993 deadline.[41]

Turning to specific policy areas, several were vital to the success of the negotiations and are critical to the outcome of the successive referenda. For both states, the majority of their industrial sectors face few problems in the transition to EU membership. Most of the relevant *acquis* is in place by virtue of the EEA agreement. Despite manufacturing representing a large proportion of Swedish GDP (30 per cent) and of labour (31 per cent), most Swedish industry does not fear EU competition, having been used to operating in international markets and adjusting to EU directives since the mid-1980s.[42] In Sweden, there has been a substantial growth in research and development, due to a preponderance of large international firms in the chemical, pharmaceutical, electronic and telecommunication sectors, which give Sweden a strong level of competitiveness. They have accepted the EU's competition policy and anti-trust laws and changes in both Swedish, and Finnish, law are well advanced. Since 1 January 1992, foreign legal entities have been entitled to acquire shares in Swedish companies without permission from any Swedish public agency and all restrictions on company shares were repealed by 1 January 1993.

Problem areas for the negotiations proved to be the laws on restrictive practices and provisions regarding the usage and levels of state aid, as these have risen in recent years due to the deep recession in these states. The negotiations were tentative on reducing the number of state monopolies in line with Article 37. The issue of state control of alcohol monopolies proved a difficult issue for Finland and Sweden. These monopolies are sensitive areas for domestic public opinion as they are officially maintained on the grounds of public health. The negotiations found a crucial compromise, stipulating that on EU accession, both will have to abolish their monopolies on the import, production and wholesale distribution of alcohol, but both will receive a derogation.[43] They will be able to maintain a monopoly on the retail sales of alcohol, thereby reducing its impact on the Nordic populace and, hopefully, the outcome of the future referenda. The Commission has been flexible when interpreting Article 37.

Solutions to the inconsistencies between Finnish and Swedish commercial policy and the EU's common commercial policies were also important, and have been found. By October 1993, agreement on the customs union had been achieved. Sweden will increase its customs duties by on average 1 per cent and will adopt EU external tariff rates.[44] More importantly, both the Swedes and Finns were allowed to retain their free trade agreements with the Baltic states until the Union has negotiated similar agreements with these republics, establishing a large free trade area.

Agreement on agricultural questions was vital to the negotiations and the referenda. Three elements had to be addressed: the nature of Arctic and sub-Arctic agriculture within the CAP, the role of agricultural support within regional policy and the high levels of subsidies provided by Finland and Sweden. Agriculture was the most difficult aspect for Finland and will be the major issue in the later referendum. The EU has to accommodate Arctic and sub-Arctic agriculture into the CAP if the Finns are to consent to membership. Although the size and importance of agriculture is small in both states (representing only 3 per cent of Finnish GNP and 1.3 per cent of GNP in Sweden), its problems are unusual. In northern Finland, the summer growing seasons are short, being only 130 days in the north and 170 days in the south, compared with 220 to 230 days for Denmark.[45] Agricultural support plays a key role in maintaining populations in the north of these states, as agriculture represents the major economic activity and employment source. Generally, the Finnish problem is not the structure of agricultural policy, but the levels of subsidies. Agriculture is subsidised to a much greater level than in the EU. The level of support given by the Finnish Government is between 1.5 and twice the level of the EU.[46]

The Commission initially proposed that there should be an end to price support for farmers from the day of accession, when local prices would drop to EU levels. Governments would then be allowed to compensate farmers through state subsidies for a transitional period. The Finns recognised that national agricultural subsidies cannot be maintained at present levels, given the fragile state of the Finnish economy and the structural changes needed to comply with the 1993 GATT deal, but were still unhappy with the EU's proposals. For its part, the EU was aware of the need to be accommodating, as there are domestic political difficulties for the Finnish Government. The main coalition partner in government, the farmers-based Centre Party, is divided on the EU issue and agreement on agriculture is critical. As Heikki Haavisto commented in 1993, 'If the European Union rejects Finland's requests on agriculture, Finland will not become a member of the European Union'.[47] Ultimately, the EU insisted on the immediate alignment of agricultural prices (at CAP levels) on accession, but also agreed that it would compensate farmers in the new member states for the first four years. At the same time, it was agreed to create a new objective (number 6) for the EU's structural funds to help regions with a very low population density. It remains to be seen whether this will be sufficient to satisfy the Finnish and Swedish electorates, since the result for both states of CAP participation will be a downward pressure on prices, having harmful effects on domestic producers.

In Sweden, the system of support differs from the CAP. Since July 1991, her agricultural policy has been reformed, abolishing price regulations and export support. Therefore, it will be relatively easy for Sweden to adapt to CAP requirements, since its level of support is only 20 per cent higher than in the EU. In fact, it is perhaps questionable to what extent Swedes really need extra payments to cushion their farmers from the impact of lowering their prices to CAP levels. Indeed, it was claimed that 'what they [the Swedes] have won was a budget rebate disguised as a farm adjustment payment'.[48]

From an economic perspective, regional policy was perceived as an uncontroversial area. Sweden and Finland have GDP per capita levels near or above the EU average. However, for Finland, this was also seen as an important area. The main issue for EU regional policy was the political role of regional policy and the ability of the Nordic states to use high levels of regional subsidy to ensure that all remote rural areas are populated. Agreement was reached to designate one area in Sweden (Norbotten) and four areas in Finland (Etela-Savo, Pohjois-Karjala, Kainuu and Lapland) as Objective One areas for regional aid.[49] They agreed that CAP objectives should be widened to include a 'northern approach' and to add the aspect of low population density to its evaluation criteria for authorising state aid. Nordic accession will widen EU regional disparities. The agreement on regional policy in the negotiations was one of the major successes.

Regarding the 'Maastricht chapters' in the negotiations, these have also been viewed as a success, with agreement being reached in December 1993. Ironically, the issue of monetary policy and EMU which is one of the most divisive issues within the EU, did not prove difficult in the negotiations. Both Governments have accepted the principles of the Maastricht Treaty, its eventual goal of EMU and shown their commitment to a coordinated European monetary policy. The Swedes and the Finns linked the krona and markka to the ecu in 1991 and effectively operated as 'shadow' ERM members. Sweden claimed this was a practical illustration of the seriousness of her membership application. Hence, in 1992, Sweden raised her overnight interest rate to 500 per cent just to maintain her link with the ERM. It was only when the intense monetary instability of September 1992 made this policy impractical that both currencies were allowed to float freely. On 9 September 1992, the markka ceased to shadow the ERM after it had depreciated by 23 per cent since October 1991. This was followed by the krona on 19 November 1992. Since the pegged exchange rate was abandoned the krona has fallen by 20 per cent in value and the markka by 50 per cent.[50]

The Nordic states are perceived as credible EMU candidates in the long term, being viewed by the Commission as having a more viable chance of participating in the EMU timetable than the existing poorer members of the EU.[51] The Commission does not view the existing states of their economies as a barrier to accession. Indeed, division within the EU has caused problems over EMU, with the Spanish trying to insist that the first decision to move to EMU in 1997 should exclude the new Nordic members. Yet, their economies will need to recover if they are to fully participate in EMU in the future. If either state is to fulfil the conditions of EMU, then control on public financing must be stepped up. Sweden's budget deficit was SK 190.1 billion in 1993. The 1993 Lindberg Commission Report *'New Conditions for Economics and Politics'* estimated that Swedish public debt to GDP was rising rapidly and would reach 70 per cent by the turn of the century.[52] Finland faced a fall of 3 per cent in GNP, a current account deficit of 4 per cent of GNP and a foreign debt of 50 per cent of GDP in 1993.[53] Both are introducing austerity packages designed to restore confidence. The Swedish austerity package involves cuts of SK 40 billion in government expenditure.[54] The Finns hoped to shave FM 15 billion from public spending in 1993.[55]

However, the CFSP chapter was agreed in December 1993 and this is another vital success for the negotiations. The Maastricht Treaty provides in Articles J.1-10 for the creation of the CFSP, which 'shall include all questions related to the security of the Union, including the eventual framing of a common defence policy, which might in time lead to a common defence'. The EU was keen to ensure that Finnish and Swedish neutrality would not compromise its future and would be compatible with their neutrality. Although Finnish neutrality was always pragmatic, the changes in Europe since 1989 have allowed the Finns to be more flexible. On 9 January 1992, their Government issued the statement 'Finland and Membership of the European Community', declaring that EU membership would 'create a more effective channel for Finland's national aspirations and increase its importance'. Crucially, the Finns perceive EU membership from a security, as well as an economic perspective, viewing the EU as the stable strategic platform in which Finnish security concerns will be maintained. The Soviet successor states on its eastern border still remain unstable. Ironically, EU membership is now seen as a way of reinforcing Finnish security, rather than undermining it as in pre-1989. Finnish neutrality is pragmatic and could be slowly abandoned by them as the policy becomes increasingly irrelevant. Nevertheless, neutrality is important in defining Finnish post-war political culture and will need to be progressively phased out.

The Finns have developed a flexible interpretation of neutrality. Policy has been reduced to a core of military non-alignment, allowing them to develop an active foreign policy. They have taken a narrow view of the CFSP, stating that as it does not initially include a military alliance then it is not incompatible with neutrality. Any military role would be developed within the WEU and Finland would define its relationship with the WEU after EU accession. Hence, Finland could fulfil all initial CFSP obligations.

Sweden's reorientation of neutrality policy was even quicker than the Finns. Her traditional policy of armed neutrality and non-participation in alliances in peacetime has been subtly redefined. Prime Minister Bildt's policy statement (4 October 1991) marked a change in attitude to security questions, stressing the new policy as a foreign and security policy with a European identity. This was recognised by the Commission in the August 1992 Opinion. Like Finland, Sweden will decide whether to join the WEU after accession to the EU has been completed, as the defence dimension will not be operative. Until then, Swedish defence policy will remain one of military non-alliance.

In December 1993, the EU and the four applicant states agreed a common position on the CFSP. Sweden agreed to attempt to become 'a full and active member' of the CFSP as soon as it had obtained full EU member status. The Finns agreed to participate constructively and actively in the CFSP, but on the basis of a belief that their present policy of non-alignment was not in contradiction with the obligations resulting from EU membership, including the military aspect. Both states' positions on the CFSP still remain ambiguous, but this could be an advantage in the following referenda. Yet, this is not surprising given the lack of consensus within the EU itself on the CFSP. But there are question marks over their practical commitment to a fully developed CFSP.

Agreement over environmental and social standards was also a critical area. Given the high levels of environmental and social protection in Sweden and Finland, their Governments sought tacit assurances that membership would not mean a lowering of their standards. This is an important issue for the Nordic electorates and placed pressure on the Commission to be conciliatory on these aspects. The EU and the applicants agreed to a four-year transitional period from the time of accession, during which these countries could maintain their standards at present levels, while the EU would endeavour to raise its own environmental standards.[56] However, there were differing interpretations regarding the consultation procedure once this period had ended, with no guarantees for Sweden that it would not have to accept lower standards in 1999. In addition, the EU granted the Swedes a derogation from social policy regarding the 'snus' tobacco trade with Norway, which was an important cultural aspect for them. Both these are significant symbolic issues for the Nordics, on which EU concessions were essential.

However, enlargement has raised the issue of its institutional impact and the role of small states within a larger European Union. If all 4 states join, there will be 16 new votes in the Council of Ministers. Small members would then have 42 Council votes out of 90, despite representing only 81 million of the EU's 371 million people. Hence, the institutional impact has become a wider issue within the EU, including the role of blocking minorities in the Council of Ministers. Of course, the latter issue became contentious immediately after the accession negotiations had been completed and there was a major row about it in the EU.

Clearly, there were no 'insuperable problems of an economic nature'.[57] Moreover, any political difficulties faced by the Union are neutralised, to some extent, by the financial attractiveness of Nordic accession. Swedish and Finnish accession will have a positive impact on EU finances, as they will be net contributors to the EU budget, given their high levels of GNP per capita, and neither state should receive large amounts of EU aid. However, the very deep recession that they faced has made them less inclined to provide large amounts of finance for the EU; and the Finnish Government took a particularly tough line on its EU budgetary contribution, believing it had been previously generous with the EEA Cohesion Fund. The net result has been that, not only will Finland and Sweden receive substantial amounts of EU funds during their transition periods, but their net contribution even after that will be considerably less than originally anticipated.

The Domestic Popularity of Accession to the EU

However, the most difficult barrier to Swedish and Finnish accession was not the accession negotiations. Rather, the major obstacle is gaining the approval for accession from their domestic populations. Both states will be holding advisory referenda in 1994. Yet, in reality, a rejection by their populations would make it near impossible for either state to join the EU in 1995. In neither state does a resounding 'Yes' vote look a foregone conclusion. Six months after submitting the Swedish application, it looked like there would be few problems gaining a favourable referendum outcome for membership. In December 1991, twice as many citizens favoured membership as opposed it.[58] However, there has been a hardening of support for the 'No' campaign. Once the Social Democrats left office in

September 1991, they adjusted their strategy so as to reflect growing fears in their ranks on full EU membership. Recent opinion polls have suggested that there is real party fragmentation on the issue and that the population is sceptical towards the EU. According to a Sofio opinion poll in January 1994, 45 per cent of Swedes would reject EU membership and only 28 per cent would approve (27 per cent undecided). To many Swedes, opposition to the EU has become implicitly linked to the wider process of change, including cuts in the welfare state, rising unemployment and challenges to concepts of national sovereignty and neutrality.

In Finland, support for accession has been stronger and more clear cut. Despite there being a consistent majority in Finland in favour of EU membership, this majority has been declining dramatically. In January 1992, a Helsingin Sanomat poll stipulated that support had dropped from 65 per cent in 1991 to 51 per cent in January 1992. In August 1993, a poll conducted by the Taloustutkimus organisation indicated that 49 per cent were pro-EU, compared with 35 per cent against. The ruling Finnish Centre Party is split on the issue, with the Government actively attempting to appease the farmers. It is notable that Heikki Haavisto, President of the Finnish Central Union of Agricultural Producers and renowned Euro-sceptic, was appointed foreign minister in May 1993, sending a clear signal both to the domestic population and the EU that Finnish accession is not guaranteed. Thus, ironically, the actual accession terms are important in both states' domestic campaigns for EU accession. The EU must be seen to have been flexible and sensitive to Nordic concerns during the accession process if Sweden and Finland are to join. The chances of Finnish approval are more certain than a Swedish one.

Conclusions

Clearly, the rationales for defining both states' relations with the EU have changed. Economic imperatives of guaranteeing interdependence with the EU and its SEM overcame most objections to membership. Political events since 1989 removed the shackles of keeping a rigid neutrality policy. It was a reorientation in these 'internal/domestic' and 'external/ international' factors that allowed both states to formally seek EU membership.

The accession negotiations were completed, only slightly late, in 1994, although the accession process still includes many hurdles for the Nordic Governments to jump before EU membership is guaranteed. Much will depend on the perceived sensitivity of the EU in dealing with Nordic accession and the political effectiveness of the Swedish and Finnish Governments in convincing their electorates of the merits of EU

membership. The real problems for their accession will be gaining
domestic party and public support. This is not a foregone conclusion and
remains a growing challenge for the Nordic Governments.

Nevertheless, Swedish and Finnish membership of the EU does
seem inevitable, given economic trends. Their long-term impact on the EU
should be positive, but will contribute to changing the nature of the Union
itself. Neither country has a federalist tradition and hence they are likely
to resist future extensions of EU power, once full members. They will
strengthen the trend towards intergovernmentalism which has been apparent
since the problems with the Maastricht Treaty. As they are relatively small
states in terms of population size, they will also resist any institutional
reform which would reduce the powers of small states. Equally, the central
core, or axis, of the EU will return northwards once they are members and
will neutralise the Mediterranean bias within the EU since the 1980s.
Nordic accession should be viewed positively, but will have implications
for the EU of the 1990s.

Notes

1. Commission of the ECs (1992) *Eurostat Statistical Yearbook*, Brussels, p. 46.
2. Svasand, L. and Linstrom, U. (1992) 'Sliding Towards EC Membership: Norway in Scandinavian Perspective', *Government and Opposition*, vol. 27, 2, p. 332.
3. An analysis is provided in Tilton, T. (1991) *The Political Theory of Swedish Social Democracy*, Oxford: Clarendon, p. 257.
4. Anckar, D. (1992) 'Finland: Dualism and Consensual Rule' in Damgaard, E. (ed.) *Parliamentary Change in the Nordic Countries*, Oslo: Scandinavian University Press, p. 161.
5. Elder, N., Thomas, T. and Arter, D. (1988) *The Consensual Democracies?* Oxford: Blackwell, p. 170.
6. 'The Paasiviki Line' is succinctly analysed in Rhinehart, R.(ed.) (1993) *Finland and the United States Diplomatic Relations through Seventy Years*, Washington D.C.: Institute For The Study of Diplomacy, p. 59. 'The Paasikivi Line' described the conduct of Finnish foreign policy shaped by J. K. Paasikivi. He tried to convince the USSR that Finland's democratic institutions and liberal values did not threaten Soviet security, whilst convincing Finns that acknowledging Soviet concerns would not compromise sovereignty.
7. Arter, D. (1987) *Politics and Policy-Making In Finland*, Harvester Wheatsheaf: Hemel Hempstead.
8. See Anckar, D. and Helander, V. (1992) 'Finland In The Wake of European Change' in Crouch, C. and Marquand, D. (eds) *Towards Greater Europe, The Political Quarterly*, Oxford: Blackwell, p. 123.
9. Fitzmaurice, J. (1987) *Security and Politics in the Nordic Area*, Aldershot: Gower, pp. 55-7.
10. Oberg, J. (ed.) (1992) *Nordic Security In The 1990s*, London: Pinter, p. 19.
11. See Hadenius, S. (1985) *Swedish Politics During the 20th Century*, Stockholm: Swedish Institute pp. 53-5.
12. See Miljan, T. (1977) *The Reluctant Europeans*, London: Hurst, p. 38.
13. For a useful analysis see Singleton, F. (1989) *A Short History of Finland*, Cambridge: Cambridge University Press, pp. 127-39.
14. See Allison, R. (1985) *Finland's Relations with the Soviet Union, 1944-1984*, London: Macmillan, pp. 95-6.
15. Pettersson, L. (1992) Sweden in Dyker, D. (ed.) *The National Economies of Europe*, Harlow: Longman, pp. 160-87.
16. The Council of Economic Organisations in Finland (1990) *Mare Balticum*, Helsinki, p. 20.
17. Antola, E. (1991) 'Finland' in Wallace, H. (ed.) *The Wider Western Europe*, London: Pinter, p. 148.
18. Pedersen, T. (1991) 'EC-EFTA Relations: An Historical Outline' in Wallace, H., op. cit., p. 18.
19. Arter, D. (1993) *The Politics of European Integration In The Twentieth Century*, Aldershot: Dartmouth, p. 223.

20. The transitional periods for liberalisation was mid-1977. A longer transitional period for EU imports of aluminium and other metals lasted until 31 December 1979. See Commission of the ECs (1981) *Europe Information-External Relations*, 48/81, Brussels.

21. Laursen, F (1993) 'The Maastricht Treaty; Implications for the Nordic Countries', *Cooperation and Conflict*, vol. 28, 2, p. 116.

22. For further information see Hamilton, C. (1991) *The Nordic Countries' Options: Seeking Community Membership or a Permanent EEA-Accord*, Discussion Paper No. 524, London: Centre For Economic Policy Research, p. 6.

23. See several articles in (1992) 'Scandinavia and the New Europe', *Scandinavian Studies*, vol. 64, no.4.

24. Ministry For Foreign Affairs Information (1991) *Sweden, the EC and Security Policy Developments in Europe*, Stockholm, p. 13.

25. Commission of the ECs (1980) *Relations Between the EC and EFTA*, Europe Information, Brussels, p. 5.

26. Commission of the ECs (1992) *Sweden's Application For Membership: Opinion of the Commission*, SEC (92) 1582 FINAL/2, Brussels, p. 78.

27. Commission of the ECs (1992) *Finland's Application For Membership: Opinion of the Commission*, SEC (92) 2048 FINAL, Brussels, graph 21.

28. Stalvant, C.-E. and Hamilton, C. (1989) *A Swedish View of 1992*, RIIA Discussion Paper, No. 13, London: Royal Institute of International Affairs, p. 3.

29. Ministry of Finance (1992) *Finland, Economic Survey 1992*, Helsinki, p. 5.

30. National Institute For Economic Research (1993) *Sweden, The Autumn Report*, Stockholm, p. 1.

31. Finnfacts (1993) *Finnish Foreign Trade in 1992*, Helsinki, p. 1.

32. Organisation for Economic Co-operation and Development (1992) *OECD Economic Survey- Finland*, Paris: OECD, p. 14.

33. For a comprehensive critique, see Tilton, T. (1991), op. cit., pp. 257-61.

34. See several articles in (1992) 'Scandinavia and the New Europe', *Scandinavian Studies*, vol. 64, no.4.

35. McDonald, F. and Penketh, K. (1993) 'The European Community and the rest of Europe' in McDonald, F. and Dearden, S. (eds) *European Economic Integration*, Harlow: Longman, p. 178.

36. Vayrynen, R. (1993) 'Finland and the European Community: Changing Elite Bargains', *Cooperation and Conflict*, vol. 28, 1, p. 35.

37. Ministry For Foreign Affairs Information (1991), op. cit., p. 14.

38. The European Commission's criteria are outlined in Commission of the ECs, (1992) *Europe and the Challenge of Enlargement*, Bulletin of the ECs, 3/92, Brussels, p. 11.

39. Michalski, A. and Wallace, H. (1992) *The European Community: The Challenge of Enlargement*, London: Royal Institute of International Affairs, p. 89.

40. See several articles in (1992) 'Scandinavia and the New Europe', *Scandinavian Studies*, vol. 64, no.4.

41. *Agence Europe* (1993) no. 6134, 22 December 1993, p. 8.

42. Commission of the ECs (1992) op. cit. (*Sweden's Application...*), p. 43.

43. *Agence Europe* (1993) no. 6134, 22 December 1993, p. 8.

44. Ministry for Foreign Affairs (1993) *Press Release 5 October 1993*, Stockholm, p. 1.

45. Commission of the ECs (1992) op. cit. (*Finland's Application...*), p. 11.

46. Ibid, p. 10.

47. *Agence Europe* (1993) no. 6112, 24 November, p. 10.

48. *Financial Times*, 2 March 1994, p. 3.

49. *Agence Europe* (1993) no. 6115, 26 November, p. 7.

50. Financial Times (1993) *Survey- Finland*, 11 October, p. 2.

51. Branson, W. (1991) *Exchange Rate Policies For the EFTA Countries in The 1990s*, Discussion Paper No. 586, London: Centre For Economic Policy Research, pp. 2-32.

52. Ministry For Finance (1993) *Revised Policy Statement, 22 April 1993*, Stockholm, p. 2.

53. *Financial Times* (1993) *Survey- Finland*, 11 October, p. 1.

54. Ministry For Finance (1993) *Policy Statement*, 9 March 1993, Stockholm, p. 2.

55. Ministry for Foreign Affairs (1992) *Finland and Membership of the European Community, 9 January*, Helsinki p. 12.

56. *Agence Europe* (1993) no. 6134, 22 December, p. 8.

57. Commission of the ECs (1992) op. cit. (*Sweden's Application...*), p. 49.

58. For further details see Arter, D. (1993) *The Politics of European Integration In The Twentieth Century*, Aldershot: Dartmouth, p. 225.

5   Iceland and Norway: Peripheries in Doubt

Gunnar Helgi Kristinsson

Iceland and Norway seem to have all the main qualifications for membership of the EU. Besides being European states, they are mature democracies, economically prosperous and they were among the founding members of NATO. Few outsiders are as dependent on the EU market as Iceland and Norway. Around two-thirds of their exports go there, a higher share than half the member states. What may seem strange is that the two countries did not join the EU long ago. Actually, Norway rejected membership in a referendum in 1972, but in Iceland it has never been seriously considered. The reluctance of the two nations to join the EU is instructive in many ways, as well as important politically.

It will be argued here that two factors go a long way towards explaining the Icelandic and Norwegian reluctance to join the process of European integration. One is cultural attachment to autonomy, with deep roots in the history of the two nations. The other is economic distinctiveness - in other words peripherality - with economies based more on natural resources, and less on the production of highly developed industrial goods and services, than the neighbouring economies of northern Europe.

Attachment to Autonomy

There is no doubt that the populations of Iceland and Norway are deeply suspicious of the EU and what membership might do to them. Historically, this attitude may be traced to the northern peripheral position of the two countries in Europe. Along with the rest of northern Europe, Iceland and

86

Norway parted company with the Catholic church during the Reformation, to embrace national protestant churches instead. This rejection of the supranational authority of the Catholic church left the local state and its church in firm command over religious and cultural development.[1] The centralisation of state authority, which followed the Reformation, left the state as almost the only centre of significant political decisions. The supranational Catholic church was swept away by the Reformation and local autonomy was abolished by absolutism. The nation state eventually became a democracy, and its powers became the instrument of the popular will. In Iceland and Norway, democratisation took place parallel to the development of a fully independent nation state, which served to tie the two - democracy and the nation state - still closer together. Both countries were, for centuries, legally distinctive parts of the Danish kingdom. Norway later entered a union with Sweden, from which it did not escape until 1905, while Iceland remained in a union with Denmark until 1944. By the twentieth century, the state not only controlled the church and cultural development, but had also assumed a leading role in guiding economic development and social welfare.

History not only shaped a strong emphasis on the nation state in Iceland and Norway, but also a strong sense of reluctance among the populations at being drawn into the power politics played by the larger nations. Neutralist or isolationist attitudes tend to value national autonomy above the opportunity to make an impact through international commitments. Geographical location may have played a large role in shaping such views in Iceland and Norway. Through the centuries they were spared the agonies of war which large parts of Europe suffered. Icelanders and Norwegians grew accustomed to seeing isolation as a provider of security. So long as the British Navy maintained its predominance in the North Atlantic, it would grant almost automatic protection to Iceland and Norway. Neither country has a long experience in conducting foreign policy. Norway took over its foreign policy in 1905, when the union with Sweden was dissolved. Iceland obtained formal foreign policy powers on obtaining sovereignty in 1918, but the Danish Foreign Service took care of the administrative side until the Second World War. Both countries followed a policy of neutrality in the inter-war period, but developed strong relations with the United States and a commitment to the Atlantic Alliance in its aftermath.

The Second World War - when Iceland and Norway were occupied by opposing sides - drove home to their foreign policy elites that a peripheral location and neutrality were a poor substitute for security. Both countries were subsequently among the founding members of NATO, although Iceland had no military forces of its own. Both also, essentially, depended on the United States for their security. As a provider of automatic security, in fact, the protective shield of the United States was, for Iceland and Norway, the second best policy after continued neutrality.

In the post-war period there emerged, in both countries, a cleft between the foreign policy elites and those parts of popular opinion most sceptical of internationalisation. Various forms of international cooperation have been regarded with suspicion by parts of the public, not least military cooperation with the United States and economic integration in Europe. Such attitudes even reached into relatively 'harmless' issue areas, such as Nordic cooperation. The strength of the isolationist tendencies among the public has cautioned the national Governments and foreign policy elites to tread carefully in the area of international relations.[2] In Iceland in particular, this along with the extremely low population, has led to a reactive style of foreign policy making.

The privileged place of national autonomy in the political cultures of Iceland and Norway makes it unlikely that their populations will accept the general need for peace and cooperation in Europe as sufficient grounds for joining the EU as the populations of the original six member states did. As in Denmark, perhaps, economic considerations are likely to be decisive.

Peripheral Economies

Iceland and Norway are the most sparsely populated countries in Europe, the former with 2.5 inhabitants per km^2, the latter with 14 inhabitants per km^2. The population density of the EU, by comparison, is 145 inhabitants per km^2. Combined with a rather inhospitable climate, this has created special problems with regard to regional settlement and development, where agriculture and fishing play an important role. Regional development and support for agriculture are a greater priority in Iceland and Norway than in most neighbouring countries; and is costly, both to consumers and tax payers. Whilst the agricultural sector has been shrinking in recent decades, it remains an important symbol of the political commitment to regional development and the maintenance of settlements in rural areas. As the climate is rather inhospitable to agriculture, Icelandic and Norwegian agriculture is generally not commercially competitive, even with the limited range of products produced in the two countries. The level of support is far greater than in the EU. To the Icelandic and Norwegian farming communities, participation in the CAP of the EU could be disastrous.

Norway and Iceland are richer, however, in some other natural resources compared to the countries of the EU. These include fish and hydroelectricity in both countries, and oil, minerals and forests in Norway.

Both countries depend, to a larger extent than any other EFTA states, on the exports of low-technology products, where a few groups of products with very limited or no processing hold an important place.[3] This makes the economies more vulnerable, and in many cases more dependent on state assistance, than elsewhere.

Fishing has always been a particularly difficult issue in relations between the two countries and the EU. The fisheries industry has very little economic significance within the EU, and the fishery traditions of the EU countries are largely based on distant-water fishing. Iceland and Norway, by contrast, fish in nearby coastal fishing grounds. The gradual extension of fishing limits up to 200 miles, which gained international recognition in 1976, transferred the control over large parts of the stocks of fish to the coastal states. This was very beneficial to Iceland and Norway, but equally unfavourable to fishermen within the EU, who were cut off from their traditional fishing grounds. A major objective of the CFP of the EU has been to reduce overcapacity within the community fleet and gain access to new fishing resources for its fishermen.

Concern for the primary industries is among the major reasons why Iceland and Norway have found it difficult to accept the full *acquis* of the EU. The Union system has been shaped by the needs of less peripheral economies, and, to many Icelanders and Norwegians, the EU has appeared unwilling to make the kind of allowances which would make membership acceptable.

The Troublesome 1960s

Faced with the formation of two different trade blocs in Europe, the then EEC (1958) and EFTA (1960), Iceland and Norway responded differently. Norway became a founding member of EFTA, while pursuing membership of the EC until 1972. The Icelandic Government decided not to apply for EC membership, but joined EFTA in 1970. After heated domestic debates, however, the conclusion was the same for both countries: EFTA membership and free trade agreements with the EC in the early 1970s.

EFTA was primarily oriented towards free trade in industrial products, but not, for example, the products of agriculture and fishing. Despite almost all of Iceland's exports in 1960 being fishery products, the fact that its most important markets were within EFTA provided insufficient grounds to join the Association. Membership of the EC, at the same time, was regarded as incompatible with Iceland's insistence on a protected labour market, restrictions on capital movements and national control in the primary sector. Some politicians and officials realised, nonetheless, that isolation from the process of economic integration in Europe might create problems later.[4] After exploratory discussions with several European Governments in the early 1960s, the Icelandic Government - consisting of the conservative Independence Party and the Social Democratic Party - favoured association with the EC.

The mere idea, which never actually reached the stage of a formal application, met with _n extremely hostile response from the opposition, the socialist People's Alliance and the rural-based Progressive Party. The criticism directed against association was partly nationalistic and partly based on hostility to big business and the market economy. It seems likely that the Government would have had difficulties in convincing the public of the benefits of association. Thus, the plans for association were withdrawn when the British application was rejected by the then EC in 1963; and it was not reintroduced with the new British application of 1967. Instead, Iceland finally acceded to GATT during the Kennedy round, thereby improving its competitive position in the US market, and joined EFTA in 1970. The direct economic interests involved with Iceland's EFTA membership were minimal. As before, fishery products were not included and Iceland's most important trading partners were leaving the Association. However, there was an important political factor involved, namely the possibility of obtaining a free trade agreement with the EC through membership of EFTA. Such an agreement was concluded in 1972, parallel to similar agreements by the other EFTA states.

Norway's Rejection of Membership

Norway, with a more industrialised export structure compared to Iceland, was among the founding members of EFTA at the Stockholm Convention in 1960. This move was in accordance with its pattern of trade, in which the original EFTA countries weighed more heavily than the EC Six. It also suited the Norwegian preference for less institutionalised intergovernmental forms of cooperation. When the United Kingdom applied for membership of the EC in 1961 and 1967, however, Norway followed suit. Between 1962 and 1971, the Storting voted 4 times on the issue of application, each time passing the proposal with three-quarters of the votes or more. Thus, in 1962 and 1967 it was agreed to send in an application, and in 1970 and 1971 the Storting confirmed and reconfirmed its decision of 1967.[5]

While the Government was preparing for Norwegian membership of the EC during the 1960s, the public debate on the issue was muffled. There were several reasons for this, foremost of which was the sensitivity of the issue and the competition between the socialist and non-socialist blocs for governmental power. Only two of the parties were, on the whole, united with regard to the membership question, the Conservatives, who were for membership and the Socialist People's Party, which was against it. A majority within the Labour Party - which held a majority in the Storting from 1945 to 1961 - was in favour of membership, but a strong minority within its ranks, and among its supporters, opposed it. Similarly, the three so-called middle parties - the Liberals, Christian People's Party and the Centre Party - were divided. The rural Centre Party was undoubtedly deeply suspicious of the EC, but a majority within the party was willing to go along with the policy of application so as to maintain the cohesion of the non-socialist Government (1965-71), in which it held the prime ministerial post. As the non-socialist coalition broke down, the party turned wholeheartedly against membership. So, eventually, did the Christian People's Party.

All parties, except the Socialist People's Party, had something to lose by an open conflict on the membership issue. The non-socialist parties stood to lose the opportunity of establishing a credible non-socialist governmental alternative to follow Labour Party predominance since the 1930s. The Labour Party, in its turn, risked an open split within the party if a major debate developed. As late as the parliamentary election of 1969, the political agenda was still dominated by domestic politics, at the expense of the membership issue.

Formal negotiations on membership started at the end of June 1970. They took place parallel to the Danish, Irish and British membership negotiations. They were concluded in January 1972 with the signature of accession treaties. The Norwegian negotiations proved extremely difficult, particularly with regard to agriculture and fisheries; at the same time, the opposition movement in Norway was gathering momentum. The basic difficulty lay in reconciling the EC's CAP and the emerging CFP with Norwegian interests. The Norwegian position was that special consideration had to be given to its geographical and climatic position and the fact that an important part of its regional population was dependent on coastal fisheries and commercially uncompetitive agriculture. Interest groups in agriculture and fisheries throughout Norway wanted no part of the CAP and CFP. This put the negotiators in a difficult situation, given the insistence by the EC that new member states should, in principle at least, accept the Community *acquis*. In the end, the negotiations failed to come up with a solution which could satisfy the demands of rural and coastal Norway.[6] This played an important part in the debates prior to the referendum.

While the demands of the Norwegian primary industries may have been somewhat unrealistic, the Community's attitude was unhelpful. The day before the membership negotiations started, the Six reached an agreement on the first outline of the CFP. With their national interests clearly in mind, they agreed to make the principle of equal access to fishery resources the main principle. Thereby, their own fishermen would gain access to the much richer grounds of the applicant countries.[7] This was in direct contrast to the way international law was developing, giving control over fishing resources to coastal states to prevent their over-exploitation.

The membership deal with the EC was supported by an impressive section of Norway's political elites, including 70 per cent of the Members of Parliament, most of the media and a good many public officials.[8] Yet, the electorate rejected membership in the referendum of September 1972 by 53.6 per cent against 46.4 per cent. Electoral research has shown that opposition to membership was strongest in the primary industries, in peripheral regions, particularly in northern parts of Norway, and among left-wing voters. The issues which 'No' voters gave as decisive for their position tended to be autonomy and the primary industries above all, whereas the 'Yes' voters stressed economic factors along with peace and unity in Europe.[9] The membership issue left deep wounds in the party system, and many 'No' voters did not return to their old parties in the parliamentary election of 1973.[10] Moreover, the Labour Party suffered an open split, when a number of EC opponents formed the successful Socialist Electoral Alliance, together with the Socialist People's Party and the Communist Party. Similarly, the unity of the non-socialist bloc was broken, with the Conservatives for membership, the Centre Party and the Christian People's Party against, and the Liberals split into one party for, and one against. Not surprisingly, Norwegian politicians tended to regard the outcome as binding for a long time after the referendum.

The Free Trade Agreements and Their Aftermath

Having rejected the membership option, Norway in 1973 - like the other EFTA states before - signed an FTA with the EC/EU. The FTAs between the EFTA states and the EU were basically of a similar nature, although they were negotiated separately and contained special provisions applying to each of the EFTA states. Tariffs on industrial goods and some processed agricultural products would be gradually eliminated, according to the Agreements. The Norwegian Agreement stipulated a special relaxation of tariffs for the fishery sector and restricted access for sensitive products such as aluminium and other metals.[11] The Icelandic one provided a favourable arrangement for the adaptation of Icelandic industry, but more importantly, it gave substantial tariff concessions to the country's fish exports to the EU. The tariff concessions on fish, however, were made conditional upon a satisfactory solution of the Anglo-Icelandic dispute on fishing limits. Thus, they did not take effect until 1976, when Britain, the rest of the EU and other major states, accepted the 200 mile fishing limits.

Following the FTAs of the early 1970s, there came a period of some 15 years of peace and quiet on the issue of European integration in Iceland and Norway. The FTAs were, in many respects, satisfactory for both countries. They were followed by continued economic growth and prosperity, whilst the EU ran into economic difficulties and political stagnation. This seemed to suggest that membership was not required to secure national prosperity. Economic growth in Iceland and Norway was based on increasing access to natural resources. Greater catches of fish in Iceland and the development of an oil industry in Norway allowed the two states to postpone some of the difficult and painful tasks of structural rationalisation within their economies, which other European Governments had to undertake at this time.

To the extent that either state wished for closer cooperation with the EU, this could be done on a bilateral basis. It was, above all, Norway which pursued closer cooperation, e.g. through participation in the so-called 'snake' and an agreement on fishery policy cooperation concluded in 1978. Similarly, Norway, from around 1980, actively pursued close contacts with the process of EPC, and managed to obtain a privileged position - for an outsider - and access to the consultations of the member states. Iceland and the EU, on the other hand, failed to reach an agreement on fishery policy cooperation on account of differences over the division of quotas and catches. Even after the conclusion of the last of the Cod Wars in 1976, Iceland has continued to cultivate its reputation as a hard liner when it comes to defending its fishing interests and fishing grounds against foreign fishermen. Unlike Norway, there never developed in Iceland any serious interest in following the foreign policy and security aspects of the European integration process.

On the successful completion of the schedule for the implementation of the FTAs, the first joint ministerial meeting of the EU and EFTA countries took place in Luxembourg in 1984. The meeting resulted in a political commitment to further cooperation in areas such as trade, research and development, education, culture and the environment. This marked the beginning of a process of multilateral cooperation within a European economic space, including both EFTA and the EU. The pressure on the EFTA states to adapt to the integration process within the EU increased dramatically with the increased dynamism of the latter in the 1980s, particularly its internal market strategy. Left outside the internal market, the EFTA states - despite the FTAs - faced the risk of economic marginalisation, the introduction of new trade barriers and exclusion from important research and technological cooperation within Europe. This prospect provoked a strong response from important business interests in some of the EFTA countries, fearing discrimination in the EU market.

The Norwegian Government responded to these challenges through a policy of integration without membership. The membership issue still being too hot to handle in Norway, the Government opted for the less controversial strategy of economic integration, while leaving the larger political question to a later date. The goals of this economic integration strategy were in the first place, adaptation to the internal market of the EU, secondly, participation in scientific and technological cooperation and, thirdly, the establishment of a European economic space, including the EU and the EFTA countries.[12] Late in 1988, Prime Minister Gro Harlem Brundtland called for a meeting in Oslo of the EFTA leaders in March 1989, to discuss relations with the EU. Before the meeting took place, Jacques Delors, President of the Commission, declared his support for institutionalising and extending the cooperation with the EFTA states to new areas. For the Norwegian strategy of integration without membership, this was an important opportunity to continue the work of economic integration but postponing the question of membership. At the Oslo meeting, the EFTA leaders issued a declaration where they welcomed the Delors initiative and called for negotiations on a European economic space, based as far as possible on the four freedoms for goods, services, capital and people. In addition to this, the EFTA leaders expressed an interest in cooperation with regard to research and development, education, the environment and consultations on economic and fiscal policy.

The Icelandic Government took longer than the other EFTA Governments to realise the full significance of the changes within the EU. EFTA membership had been uncontroversial in Icelandic politics after 1970, and Iceland basically followed the lead of the other EFTA states in their adaptive process. It seems clear that at least some of the coalition partners in the Leftist Government only had a very vague picture of what was going on. Iceland's lack of enthusiasm for the main issues of the EFTA-EU process is reflected in the fact that the Icelandic Prime Minister expressed important reservations at the Oslo meeting, concerning three of the four freedoms, the exception being the free movement of goods.[13] The Icelandic Government did accept the joint declaration of the meeting, however, after its partners had agreed to introduce the principle of free trade in fishery products within EFTA.

The European Economic Area

Formal negotiations on the EEA, as the project was now called, started in June 1990, and the final agreement was signed in May 1992. Ratification in the EFTA and EU countries took place in 1992 and 1993. Through the EEA, those EFTA states joining the Area adopt large parts of the EU's legislation concerning the four freedoms in exchange for non-discrimination in the EU's markets. The agreement also covers a number of other areas for cooperation, including the environment, research and development, education, consumer protection and so on. Some important areas of the internal market of the EU do not apply within the EEA, however, including the CAP, the CFP and trade policy.

The negotiation process was by no means easy. Pressure on negotiators was created partly by multiple requests within EFTA for exceptions and special treatment and partly by reluctance within the EU to grant too generous an access for the EFTA countries to influence and markets without them paying the appropriate price. In the end, the EFTA countries obtained a general safety clause, which they could apply against parts of the agreement according to specified rules. On the other hand, they failed to secure any greater influence over EU decision making, and they agreed to establish a special fund for underdeveloped regions within the EU. Among the most difficult issues during the negotiations was the question of fisheries. The EFTA states originally insisted on free trade in fishery products, a demand which was incompatible with the CFP, and hence totally unacceptable to the EU. Some of the EU states insisted on greater access to EFTA waters in exchange for tariff concessions. In the end, the EFTA states received important tariff concessions for their fishery products, while Norway agreed to increase EU quotas within its fishing limits. Iceland, on the other hand, made only minimal concessions in accordance with its policy of not exchanging access to resources for access to markets. It did commit itself, however, to making an agreement on fisheries cooperation with the EU; according to which, a small amount of quotas will be exchanged.

The EEA received a mixed welcome in Iceland and Norway, marking the end to the general consensus over the issue of European cooperation prevailing since the early 1970s. In Norway the non-socialist Government, formed in 1989, had to resign the following year on account of the EEA issue, as the Centre Party turned against Norwegian participation. This left the road clear for a new minority Government of the Labour Party. Both the Socialist Left and the Centre Party were strongly against the EEA, along with a number of individual parliamentarians from other parties. The Christian People's Party was severely divided, but, in the end, it decided to support the agreement along with the Labour Party, the Conservatives and the right-wing populist Progress Party. The Storting accepted the agreement by 130 votes to 35 in October 1992.

The EEA agreement encountered strong opposition in Iceland as well. Although doubts may have existed within the Left-wing Government in 1989 on the suitability of the EEA process for Iceland, a concern for the cohesion of the Government and an unwillingness to break with the other EFTA states prevented an open dispute on the issue. Some government leaders were apparently not aware that the EEA was in form an Association Agreement of the same type their parties had opposed in the 1960s, and in content much more far-reaching. Before the parliamentary election of 1991, the only party which unambiguously rejected the EEA was the Women's Alliance. Following the election, the Left-wing Government was replaced by a coalition of the Independence Party and the Social Democrats, partly on account of scepticism among the Social Democrats on how far the People's Alliance and the Progressive Party would be willing to support the EEA process. In the end, the People's Alliance did turn against the Agreement, while a much divided party conference of the Progressive Party, late in 1992, failed to take a clear stance on the issue. Given the divisions within the opposition and the fact that the Progressives and the People's Alliance had backed the negotiations while in government, they tended to de-emphasise the contents of the Agreement during much of the debate in exchange for a demand for a referendum. Scepticism was also raised concerning its compatibility with the Constitution. As regards the contents of the Agreement, it was, above all, the exchange of fishery quotas, negotiated bilaterally, in the second half of 1992, which came under attack from the opposition during the last stages of the debate. The EEA Agreement was accepted by the Althingi in January 1993, after various delaying tactics by the opposition, by 33 votes to 23. Government MPs voted for it, with the exception of the three members of the Independence Party who were opposed to the Agreement. The opposition voted against, apart from 6 Progressives and 1 Women's Alliance MP, who abstained.

Association versus Membership

Although sometimes regarded as a mere waiting room for prospective members, there are also some who regard the EEA as a long-term solution, a way of avoiding membership by solving the economic problems of adaptation without political integration. It is indeed conceivable that Iceland and Norway will end up by making association, rather than full membership, their predominant mode of adaptation to the European challenge. Apart from the EEA, an association agreement has already been signed between the two countries and the WEU, and some form of association might also emerge in the sphere of monetary cooperation if the two countries decide to persist in their attempts to maintain a stable currency *vis-à-vis* the ecu.

Through the EEA agreement, the EFTA Governments have temporarily warded off the threat of isolation from European markets. They have also cleared many of the issues which would inevitably have to be dealt with in membership negotiations. In a number of ways, however, association is very different from full membership. Issue by issue, each state will have to weigh the advantages or disadvantages of membership against association. One of the arguments in favour of an application for membership is that the final summing up of advantages and disadvantages cannot be done except during and after a process of membership negotiations. This argument is not conclusive, however, in the sense that only a serious application, based on a clear conception of the issues involved, is likely to lead to a positive result. Among the decisive issues, when weighing the costs and benefits of full membership, are the questions of influence, security and foreign policy, monetary cooperation, agriculture, fisheries, trade policy, energy, the environment, the social dimension and Nordic cooperation.

Influence

The EEA Agreement does not secure an adequate measure of influence for the EFTA states within the Area. Nonetheless, the EFTA members will, in effect, have to adopt EU decisions if they wish to maintain parallel development with the EU and prevent new barriers to trade. Seen from the standpoint of responsible democratic politics, this is not a healthy state of affairs. Membership of the EU on the other hand would give them more influence. As a member of the EU, Norway would get a similar representation in EU institutions as Denmark, while Iceland might expect one not too dissimilar to that of Luxemburg. This will not normally give either country a decisive say in the way the EU develops, particularly if it moves in a more supranational direction. There is no doubt, however, that the difference between being a member and non-member is enormous, both with regard to the formal and informal aspects of decision making.

Security and Foreign Policy

If the Atlantic Alliance develops in the direction of a dialogue between a European pillar, represented by the EU, and a North American pillar, represented by the USA and Canada, Iceland and Norway face a difficult future unless they strengthen their ties with the European pillar. To strengthen NATO, and avoid a choice between its European and North American pillars, both countries have become associate members of the WEU. Association enables them to take part in the dialogue and activities within the WEU, but they do not have voting rights, and will therefore not be bound by its decisions. To Iceland, which has no military forces of its own and very limited foreign policy ambitions, this could turn out to be a satisfactory arrangement, so long as a choice between Europe and the USA can be avoided and there is no weakening of the US commitment to the defence of the country. To Norway, on the other hand, with a common border with Russia, nothing short of full membership of the EU and the WEU is, in the long run, likely to secure the kind of influence on foreign and security policies and commitment to joint security wished for by the Norwegian Government.

Monetary Cooperation

Although there are good arguments for maintaining stable currencies *vis-à-vis* Europe for Iceland and Norway, there may be reason to doubt the advantages of maintaining such stability too rigidly. Dependence on natural resources in the Icelandic and Norwegian economies distinguishes them from the more central economies in Europe, and could mean that there would be a tendency for their currencies to react differently to economic fluctuations. If Iceland and Norway as members of the EU would in addition have to accept ceilings on budget deficits, this could mean that the whole burden of economic adjustment had to be carried by domestic wages and prices, which could turn out less than satisfactorily.[14] Given the peculiar nature of the Icelandic and Norwegian economies, they might be better served by moving slowly towards the goal of full monetary union. Participation in a flexible system of monetary cooperation, on the other hand, would undoubtedly strengthen the Icelandic and Norwegian economies. If the EU, therefore, develops in the direction of a full monetary union, this could make membership less attractive for Iceland and Norway. A Norwegian Labour Government in the case of membership is likely to wish for greater involvement of the EU with industrial policy and a central bank system less autonomous from political considerations than in the Bundesbank model.

Agriculture

Broadly speaking, the EEA allows Iceland and Norway to maintain their agricultural policies intact. Other factors, such as the need of the domestic economy for structural rationalisation, or developments within GATT, may require some trimming of agricultural support in the future. But the EEA differs from membership in a decisive respect for farmers; a much higher level of support can be maintained compared to the CAP. Special treatment for agriculture, to soften the blow to farmers, is likely to be among the priorities for any Icelandic or Norwegian Government negotiating membership of the EU; and indeed was for the latter. The Norwegian formula is that the EU must develop special policies to deal with Arctic or sub-Arctic agriculture. The idea is that, whereas the EU might have difficulties in granting special treatment to individual states, the broader concept of the Arctic and sub-Arctic region, which applies to several states, makes it easier for the EU to accept special support for Scandinavian agriculture.

Fisheries

From the standpoint of the fishery industries of Iceland and Norway, membership of the EU is a threatening spectacle, although it is by no means inevitable that the EU would increase its catches substantially within Icelandic and Norwegian fishing limits if they were to join.[15] The fishery policy of the EU underwent considerable changes in the period up to 1983, where a system of national quotas in effect pushed the principle of equal access into the realm of theory. The main principle behind allocation of quotas has been traditional patterns of fishing. Membership is nonetheless widely opposed within the fishery industries of Iceland and Norway. This is partly because of the EU's poor record of fisheries management, partly because foreign firms might try to get a foothold in the domestic fisheries industry at the expense of the locals, and partly because the revision of the CFP, scheduled to finish by 2002, may be less advantageous than the present system. On top of all this, Spain and Portugal, nourishing a grievance against the allocation of quotas within the EU are likely to demand increased access, and fishermen fear the repetition of the

Norwegian story from 1972, when the Government accepted a conclusion in the negotiations which was clearly unfavourable to their own industry.

Foreign Trade

As the EEA is not a customs union, and free trade does not apply to agriculture and fisheries products within the area, border controls and customs documents cannot be dispensed with. This means that transaction costs are likely to remain a distortion and a barrier to trade between the EFTA states and the EU. Apart from the disadvantage for exporters, this will inevitably affect the decisions of both domestic and foreign investors, and businessmen, to the disadvantage of Iceland and Norway, so long as they do not join the EU. As more EFTA states join the EU, and as cooperation within the EMU deepens, the significance of the remaining trade barriers will be felt increasingly within those EFTA states still outside.

Energy

Norway is Europe's largest oil producer. Both Iceland and Norway, moreover, are rich in hydroelectric power resources, which have been used for the development of power-intensive industry domestically, but may increasingly be exported directly by submarine cable to European electricity networks. Their energy sectors are characterised by heavy state involvement and high sensitivity to the European market. The EEA naturally covers energy policy to a rather limited extent, given the embryonic state of this policy area within the EU itself. The emergence of a common energy policy and competition rules prohibiting national discrimination could make it difficult for Iceland and Norway to maintain the present level of state involvement in the energy sector. To secure market access in the long term and influence on the development of energy policies in the EU, Norway and Iceland may be better served by membership. On the other hand, they may need a considerable period of special treatment to adapt their energy sectors to changing conditions.

Environment

Both Iceland and Norway are vulnerable to environmental damage, on account of a sensitive natural environment and a reliance on natural resources. The EEA agreement states a number of general objectives of environmental policy, together with a clause on closer environmental cooperation. However, differences of opinion exist within the EU between some of its poorer and richer members on the priority of environmental protection. Even if the Maastrict Treaty has increased the competence of the EU in a number of environmental issues, the southern members together with Britain, for example, are still in a position to block decisions. Divisions within the EU could mean that the EFTA countries are not likely to be able to affect the direction and development of environmental policies within the Union to a significant extent, except by joining it. If the Nordic countries were to join, allied for example to Germany and several other members states, they could undoubtedly become influential actors in the development of environmental policies within the EU.

Social Dimension

With rising unemployment in recent years, the Icelandic and Norwegian Governments are likely to be increasingly sensitive to this issue. Especially to any Labour Government in Norway, the maintenance and further development of the social dimension within the EU is likely to be an important priority. A similar stance will be taken by the strong labour organisations in the two countries, where scepticism concerning European integration is not uncommon. The social aspect of the EEA is largely based on corresponding clauses in the Treaty of Rome and the SEA. In addition, the EEA agreement is accompanied by a declaration of the EFTA Governments that they wish to adhere to the Social Charter. While the EEA contains the minimum provisions for a joint labour market to operate, the EFTA countries will be excluded from other areas of cooperation, including such areas which are financed through the EU budget. This includes aspects of the social and labour market policies as well as access to the structural funds. As regards other areas of social policy, it may prove difficult to develop the cooperation within the EEA beyond the minimum which the EU twelve can agree, so long as the Union itself is divided over such policies.

Nordic Cooperation

European integration inevitably affects Nordic cooperation, partly by taking over some of the traditional tasks of Nordic cooperation and partly by creating new ones. The Nordic Governments are adapting to these developments through changes in the set-up of Nordic cooperation, e.g. by increasing the role of summit meetings of the Nordic prime ministers. In the future, its seems, the cooperation will be increasingly directed towards coordination and cooperation between the Nordic countries on the international political scene. With Denmark already in the EU, and Finland, Norway and Sweden well on the way to membership, it seems clear that Nordic cooperation will be focused to a great extent on EU issues, particularly after the achievement of an eventual membership for all four. For Iceland, or any of the Nordic countries deciding to abstain from membership, this could lead to exclusion from a substantial part of Nordic cooperation.[16]

On the whole, membership in the long run seems to have more advantages than association, provided an adequate membership deal can be negotiated. A favourable negotiation settlement, however, is a factor of some considerable uncertainty. Particularly in the Icelandic case, where the fisheries situation weighs more heavily than in Norway, there may be reason to doubt that an adequate solution can be found.

Norway Tries One More Time

At its meeting in Lisbon in June 1992, the European Council gave its blessing to the opening of enlargement negotiations with those EFTA states wishing membership of the EU. The membership negotiations took place separately for each applicant, but in a parallel manner as far as possible.

Norwegian political leaders realised of course that the issue of membership could not be avoided indefinitely. Not until all the other EFTA states except Iceland and Liechtenstein had applied for membership, however, did the minority Government of the Labour Party take the decisive step of applying on behalf of Norway, in November 1992. The opportunity of conducting membership negotiations alongside Sweden and Finland was a decisive factor in determining the timing of the application. In many respects, however, the circumstances were not particularly favourable, after a turbulent summer within the EU in 1992, with strong opposition within the Labour Party itself, and with confidence in the party being at its lowest for decades, according to opinion polls. The party leadership presented the issue in a cautious manner, underlining that an application was not the same as membership and that a favourable outcome of the negotiations would be essential. Thus, the party conference in November concluded: 'In the negotiations we shall emphasise in a conclusive manner the maintenance of Norwegian control over natural resources, and favourable solutions for the primary industries and regional development. When the Labour Party evaluates the final outcome of the negotiations, these issues will be of great importance...'.[17]

Despite the cautious formulation, the application proposal met with greater opposition at the party conference than expected. It was accepted by 182 to 106 of the 300 delegates, a smaller majority for membership than when the party last made up its mind on the issue in 1972. With regard to fisheries - which was among the most difficult areas in the negotiations - the Labour Party underlined the seriousness of its stance prior to the application by making an opponent of EU membership minister for fisheries. Similarly, during the parliamentary debate on the application, the Government tended to avoid expressing clear views on the issue of EU and the Maastricht Treaty. Even on the pro-membership side in Norway, there are substantial reservations about political union - let alone federation.

According to the Norwegian Constitution, membership of the EU would require a three-quarters majority in the Storting. After the parliamentary election of September 1993, it seems clear that no such majority exists. The election was a setback for the pro-membership side, which lost a considerable number of seats. The anti-EU Centre Party emerged as the great winner, increasing its share of seats from 11 to 32 in the 165 member Storting. Although the Labour Party improved its position slightly in the election, some of its MPs are opposed to membership, and the pro-membership Conservative Party suffered heavy losses. The pro-membership side obtained no more than around 90 seats, against 75 for the EU opposition, a far cry from the three-quarters majority required. As the Norwegian constitution does not allow a new election until 1997, the hopes of those in favour of membership lie with a referendum on the issue.

It has always been clear that the results of the 1972 referendum would not be changed except in a new referendum. Such a referendum will take place now that accession terms have been negotiated. Winning a referendum will not be easy, although the amount of difficulties depends partly on reactions to the accession terms. Opinion polls on attitudes towards membership tend to fluctuate greatly. This was the case before the referendum of 1972 and this seems to be the case in the present debate.[18] So far, however, the opinion polls have confirmed a strong opinion against membership in Norway. An opinion poll published by *Dagbladet* in August 1993, four months after the opening of negotiations, revealed that 35 per cent of the electorate were for membership, 13 per cent were undecided and 54 per cent against. The hopes of those who wish for Norwegian membership rest with a favourable interpretation by the population of the accession terms and that Swedish and Finnish acceptance of membership will suffice to sway public opinion in favour of Norwegian membership.

However, neither of these can be taken for granted, which makes the outcome of the referendum highly uncertain.

Even a majority in favour of membership in the referendum will not necessarily guarantee its acceptance in Norway, since the referendum will only be consultative, and the Storting has the final say. While it used to be assumed that the Storting would not go against the outcome of a referendum, this can no longer be taken for granted. The parties most opposed to membership, the Left Socialists and the Centre Party, have complicated the issue by stating that they will not necessarily abide by the results of a referendum, except on certain conditions. The Centre Party will evaluate the results according to a number of criteria, including the press' handling of the debate, and the Left Socialists will only accept a majority for membership which is also based on a majority in at least half the districts. This could lead to a constitutional crisis if a majority of the electorate accepted membership while the Storting failed to pass it. In that event, a change in the Constitution could be made with two-thirds of the vote, but even this is beyond the present pro-membership majority in the Storting. To obtain such a majority would require the support of a number of anti-membership MPs, namely from the Labour Party, and the neutralisation of others. Thus, even a referendum in favour of membership - in itself highly uncertain - could fail to lead to the acceptance of membership in Norway.

Iceland Going It Alone

When Norway handed in an application for membership in November 1992, it left Iceland alone among the Nordic states with no plans for membership of the EU. In fact, very little public discussion had taken place on the possibility of membership. No interest organisation and no political party publicly advocated membership, apart from the youth organisation of the Social Democratic Party. The Social Democrats and the Independence Party have not excluded the possibility of membership at some future date. Both parties hesitate to take up the issue, however, anticipating a negative response among the electorate, stretching - at least in the case of the Independence Party - well into their own ranks. In most of the other EFTA countries, sectoral interest groups have played a key part in promoting the cause of membership. This has not happened in Iceland. The politically influential organisations within agriculture and fishing are clearly opposed to any moves which might lead to membership. Some individual business leaders have expressed themselves favourable to membership and industrial manufacturers, as well as the Chambers of Commerce, are positively disposed towards European integration in a general way. Neither organisation, however, is decided enough, nor powerful enough, to become the catalyst of Icelandic membership of the EU.

The closest thing to an attempt to open up a discussion on the pros and cons of membership came in the Foreign Minister's report to parliament in March 1992. The report regards the CFP as the main obstacle to membership. Thus, even if the revision of the CFP would lead to a more rational system of fisheries management within the EU, the basic problem would remain, namely that the control of fishing and allocation of quotas within Iceland's fishing limits outside the 12 miles would lie with the Commission. The report also takes a pessimistic view of the EU's responsiveness to the needs of a small state such as Iceland. Given the administrative problems for the EU associated with Icelandic membership, it is considered unlikely that it would so be flexible in negotiations as to secure for Iceland satisfactory exceptions and guarantees for its fisheries.

Two things could work in Iceland's favour during membership negotiations, according to the report. On the one hand, it seems clear that the possibility of a favourable outcome would be much greater during the present round of membership negotiations with the other EFTA states, than in a subsequent round with the eastern European states. On the other hand, the EU might be more easy to deal with in about ten years, provided it had managed to deal successfully with the over-capacity of its own fishing fleet by then. The problem is that, by that time, the Nordic express into the EU will have passed long ago. Thus, the report concludes, somewhat ambiguously: 'Clearly, the weakening of Icelandic control over the utilisation of Icelandic fishing grounds would be too high a price to pay for some uncertain measure of influence within the EU. Nonetheless, it has to be considered that Iceland is now parting company with the other Nordic states, which have come to the conclusion that the present opportunity to join the EU is the most favourable one. Therefore, a detailed scrutiny must take place within the ministries and governmental institutions on what EU membership would entail. Only when such a process has taken place can the membership option be rejected, after due consideration'.[19]

The Foreign Minister's report, however, failed to instigate a major debate on membership in Iceland. This was partly because the Government itself decided to concentrate on seeing the EEA agreement through and to avoid any link between EEA and EU membership. The uncertainty which has surrounded the applications of the other Nordic EFTA members, the Danish hiccup in ratifying the Maastricht Treaty and negative public opinion in Norway and Sweden, further encouraged caution on behalf of the Icelandic Government.

The governing coalition of the Independence Party and the SDP, probably the only type of Government in Iceland which could conceivably apply for membership, has adopted a wait and see attitude towards membership. External events are likely to decide Icelandic policy rather than the dynamics of the domestic debate. Events which could trigger a debate on membership in Iceland within the next decade or so include a favourable outcome of the Norwegian membership bid, difficulties in adapting the EEA satisfactorily to continued desertions on the EFTA side, and a favourable development of the CFP. In the longer run, economic isolation and stagnation might force Iceland to reconsider its reluctance to join the EU, but that would mean entering membership negotiations from a much weaker position than today.

The fishery question would be a decisive issue of any membership negotiations between Iceland and the EU. Iceland would probably make rather far-reaching demands for exceptions from the joint resource management prevailing in the CFP. In the end, it might have to accept something less than legally binding and permanent exceptions in exchange for some system of real and renewable exceptions, periods of adaptation and a political commitment by the EU to recognise Iceland's vital fishery interests. The EU, in turn, would fail to increase its access to Icelandic fishing grounds. No deal on membership would stand a chance in a referendum in Iceland unless it was clear that its fishery interests were securely provided for.

Ratification of an eventual membership agreement in Iceland would probably require two steps. In the first place, it would need a change in the Constitution to allow for the transfer of legislative and judicial powers to a supranational institution such as the EU. To change the Icelandic Constitution, a proposal must twice receive a majority in the Althingi, with a parliamentary election in between. Secondly, a referendum would be held on the outcome of negotiations. Although there is no tradition of referenda in Icelandic politics, it is unlikely that a decision on membership would be made without a popular vote. This seems to be the view of the Independence Party as well as the Social Democrats - the two parties most likely to support membership should the issue arise. Thus in Iceland as in Norway a majority of a sceptical population must vote for a membership agreement before it can take effect. The results of recent opinion polls are not particularly promising for those who advocate membership. One carried out by the Social Science Research Institute, in June 1992, showed 44 per cent of the electorate to be opposed to a membership application, against 20 per cent in favour of it and 36 per cent undecided.[20] Generally, the opposition to membership is strongest outside the urban Reykjavik area, where fishing and agriculture play a large role, among supporters of the left-wing parties, and among older people. But it is strong among all other major population groups.

The alternative for Iceland, if it fails to come to terms with the membership option, is to accept the role of a peripheral micro-state in Europe. An often forgotten part of the European landscape consists of a number of small populations - much smaller than even Iceland - with varying degrees of autonomy, ranging from special status, through home rule to formal sovereignty. Several of these are not formally part of the EU. Examples in the Nordic region include the Faroe Islands and Greenland. Failing to become a member of the EU, Iceland may try to develop a free-rider strategy *vis-à-vis* its larger neighbours, offering foreign business interests some special advantages, not available in larger states. Although the free-rider market is already well supplied by, for example, Monaco, Andorra, San Marino, Liechtenstein and the Channel Islands, the idea has some following in Iceland that special relations with the trading blocs in North America and Europe might provide sufficient economic opportunities to avoid full membership of the EU.

Iceland and Norway in Europe

Iceland and Norway are peripheral states within Europe. Their populations have, over the centuries, grown accustomed to finding security in their relative isolation. Their economies are based on raw materials and low-technology products to a greater extent than those closer to the major centres of trade and industry in Europe, and their agriculture is largely uncompetitive compared to European agriculture. Both of these aspects of European peripherality have moulded a public opinion in Iceland and Norway which is less receptive to European integration than in most other states.

The opposition to membership in Iceland and Norway is composed, above all, of the rural and regional interests threatened by the EU and those most opposed to participation in the power politics of the larger countries and in favour of unlimited political autonomy. The former are represented in the party systems, in particular, by the Norwegian Centre Party and the Icelandic Progressive Party, the latter by the Norwegian Socialist Left and the Icelandic People's Alliance. Both the Icelandic parties are much stronger than their Norwegian counterparts, and the opposition towards membership is also stronger in Iceland than in Norway.

Isolation, however, is not easily maintained in the modern world, except at the cost of stagnation and backwardness. With improving technology and economic interdependence, the importance of geographical distances and state borders is steadily decreasing. Iceland and Norway will sooner or later have to accept the consequences of this challenge to the nation state. The EU plays a key role in the adaptation of European political structures to increasing interdependence. The choice which Iceland and Norway are faced with is that of becoming fully recognised member states of the EU or merely the northwestern territories of the EEA.

The EU itself will also play an important role in deciding whether Iceland and Norway can join or not. The reservations about membership in Iceland and Norway are partly based on economic distinctiveness, which the EU should be able to accommodate. Neither security policy, democratic stability nor economic backwardness provide grounds for the EU to block Icelandic and Norwegian membership. Politically and ideologically, it would be a setback for European integration if the EU proved unable to accommodate the fully legitimate distinctive economic interests of Iceland and Norway.

The reservations about membership in Iceland and Norway are, of course, also based on a preoccupation with autonomy, which is difficult to reconcile fully with membership of a European union. Such mind-sets can create difficulties and will not disappear at one stroke. But they do not exclude membership. Both Iceland and Norway, if they were to enter the EU, would, in the beginning, have to reckon with considerable domestic opposition to membership, which would not only complicate domestic coalition politics but also their freedom of manoeuvre within the EU. But it is not only the Icelanders and Norwegians who are doubtful of the more ambitious federalist plans for Europe - large sections of the population of the EU share such scepticism, as the debates on the Maastricht Treaty in 1992 clearly showed. Dealing with such attitudes is a joint European task.

So far, Norway has applied for membership, and has agreed terms, but Iceland has not. The Commission policy is that the EFTA applicants must subscribe to the Maastricht Treaty and accept the EU's financial perspectives for 1992-97. The negotiations settled Norway's special problems with regard to agriculture, fisheries and regional policy. While the EU has made it clear that the Danish solution with regard to the Maastricht Treaty applies exclusively to Denmark, and not to other existing or potential member states, it has shown the applicant states that it is possible to tailor membership to the needs of individual states to a greater extent than would have seemed possible before. The Icelandic road to membership will be a difficult one. Although the factors which have weighed against membership are in many respects similar to the ones in Norway, the effects of isolation and peripherality are stronger in Iceland. In the short run, only the combination of a number of factors, including an external stimulant and a receptive governing coalition in Iceland, is likely to lead to an Icelandic application for membership. Even so, once the present round of enlargement is concluded, the EU may not be particularly receptive to an Icelandic application, on account of the political and administrative difficulties associated with such a small population.

Notes

1. On the effects of the Reformation on nation-building in European peripheries, see Rokkan, S. and Urwin, D. (1983), *Economy, Territory, Identity*, London: Sage Publications.
2. Cf. Eriksen, K. and Pharo, H. (1991) 'De fire sirklene i norsk utenrikspolitikk 1949-61' in Due-Nielsen, C., Noack, J. and Petersen, N. (eds) *Danmark, Norden og NATO 1948-1962*, Kobenhavn: Jurist - og Okonomforbundets Forlag; Riste, O. (1985) *The Historical Determinants of Norwegian Foreign Policy in the 1980s*, Oslo: Norwegian University Press; Gunnarsson, G. (1986) *Icelandic Security Policy*, Reykjavik: Öryggismalanefnd; Johnsson, A. (1989) *Island, Atlantshafsbadalagio og Keflavikurstooin*, Reykjavik: Öryggismalanefnd.
3. Cf. Neil, P. (1990) 'EFTA in the 1990s: the search for a New Identity' *Journal of Common Market Studies*, vol. XXVIII, no. 4.
4. Cf., for example, Gislason, G. P. (1979) 'Island, Friverslunarsamtokin og Efnahagsband-algio', *Fjarmalatioindi*, vol. XXVI, no.3.
5. Schou, T. L. (1980) *Norge og EF*, Copenhagen: Forlaget Politiske Studier, p. 82.
6. The negotiations and their results are descibed in Dynna, B. (1972) 'Fiskerisektoren i EF-forhandlingene' and Froysnes, T. (1972) 'Jordbruksforhandlingene and med EF', both in Angell, V. and Holst, J. (eds) *EF - Norges vei?* Oslo: Universitetsforlaget.
7. The emergence of the CFP us described by Wise, M. (1984) *The Common Fisheries Policy of the European Community*, London: Methuen.
8. Schou, T.L. (1980), op. cit..
9. All the above is based on Valen, H. (1973) 'Norway: "No" to EEC', *Scandinavian Political Studies*, vol. 8, and Gleditsch, N. and Hellevik, O. (1977) *Kampen om EF*, Oslo: Pax forlag.
10. Valen, H. and Rokkan, S. (1974) 'Norway: The Election to the Storting in September 1973', *Scandinavian Political Studies*, vol. 9, 1974, p. 214.
11. Cf. Pedersen, T. (1991) 'EC-EFTA Relations: A Historical Outline' in Wallace,H. (ed.) *The Wider Western Europe*, London: Pinter Publishers.
12. See, for example, St. meld nr. 11 (1989-90), *Om utviklingstrekk i det internatsjonale samfunn og virkninger for norsk utenrikspolitikk*, p. 127.
13. Prime Minister Hermannsson's speech is reprinted in Europustefnunefnd (1990) *Island of Europa*, Reykjavik: Alpingi.
14. Melchior, A. (1992) 'Is there a case for a two-speed Europe?' in Angell, V. (ed.) *Norway facing a changing Europe*, Oslo: FNI, IFS, PRIO & NUPI.
15. Cf. Holm, P. (1990) 'EFs fiskeripolitikk og norsk fiskerinaering', *Internasional Politikk*, vol. 48, no. 2; Kristinsson, G. H. (1990) *Evropustefnan*, Reykjavik: Öryggismalanefnd; Sigurjonsson, K. (1991) *Hin sameiginlega sjavarutvegsstefna Evropubandalagsins*, Rekjavik: Alpjooamalastofnun Haskola Islands.
16. Cf. 'Norden og norkisk samarbeid i et Europa i forandring', *delrapport til Europautredningen*, Oslo, 1992.
17. Quoted from *Aftenposten*, 9 Nov. 1992.
18. Some data concerning this can be found in Heidar, K. (1983) *Norske politiske fakta 1884-1982*, Oslo: Universitetsforlaget and Saeter, M. and Knutsen, O. 'Norway' in Wallace (1991), op. cit..
19. Utanrikismal (1992) *Skyrsla Jons Baldvins Hannibalssonar utanrikiraoherra til Alpingis*, Reykjavik: Ministry of Foreign Affairs, pp. 17-18.
20. Data obtained from the Social Science Research Institute, University of Iceland.

Part 3

The Mediterranean

6   Turkey: A Crucial but Problematic Applicant

William Hale

The paradox of Turkey's relationship with the EU is that it has been waiting the longest for accession, but, among the present applicants,[1] it appears to be the furthest away from attaining it. Its recent history is also quite different from that of most of the present applicant states, except for Norway, in that it was not previously debarred from the EU by any commitment to neutrality. It has been a member of NATO since 1952, and is most unlikely to abandon that membership, unless NATO itself breaks up. Nor has it undergone the transformations which have affected the eastern European states, which may join the queue. However, the obstacles to its admission are long standing and substantial. The economic gap between Turkey and the Twelve is a wide one, though probably no greater than that which separates the present EU members from eastern Europe. Turkey's shaky record on human rights, the legacy of three military interventions since World War II, and a seemingly unending feud with Greece, do not recommend it to the EU. Its integration into the EU would be made more difficult by the simple fact that, with a population of some 60 million, it is far larger than any other likely candidate. Finally, in spite of the commitments which the EU has previously made to Turkey, the feeling among many western Europeans and their political leaders that it is not part of the European identity, has inevitably coloured western European reactions to the Turkish application, and will probably continue to do so. On these grounds, the problems faced by the Union in reaching a mutually acceptable relationship with Turkey are probably greater than in the cases of the other potential members. On the other hand, the costs of failure would be more far-reaching, given the Turks' crucial position in the international politics of the Middle East, central Asia and the Balkans.

Currently, the Turks cannot know whether they will eventually be admitted, or what the EU will look like when, and if, they are. Nevertheless, it seems most unlikely that they will abandon the goal of ultimate accession. To expand and explain this, this chapter summarises the evolution of the Turkish-EU relationship since the 1960s. It then looks at the pros and cons of developing the relationship, as they appear to each side. The final section assesses the current situation, and the effects of the end of the Cold War and the transformation of eastern Europe on future prospects.

Turkey and the European Union, 1963-92

Following Greece, Turkey signed an Association Agreement with the EEC in September 1963. This outlined a three-stage process, leading to an eventual customs union, together with the progressive alignment of economic and social policies. An Association Council, composed of representatives of the Turkish and member state Governments, was to oversee this process and settle mutual disputes. The Agreement was followed by an Additional Protocol, signed in November 1970. The Protocol provided for a series of staged tariff reductions and the abolition of import quotas, which were expected to lead to the establishment of the customs union by the end of 1985 (at the earliest) or the end of 1995 (at the latest).[2] Between 1973, when the Additional Protocol came into effect, and 1976, the two sides proceeded with its implementation, but the process then ran into serious problems. On its side, the EU imposed quotas on the import of cotton yarn and textiles from Turkey, to protect domestic manufacturers. More seriously, in 1978 Turkey relapsed into political anarchy and virtually total economic dislocation, which forced the Government to announce that it would suspend its undertakings under the Additional Protocol for the following five years. The anarchy was ended by a military coup on 12 September 1980. The military regime restored law and order and a degree of economic stability, but the coup also raised new political obstacles, since the EU was reluctant to draw closer to a country which was not under democratic government. Somewhat surprisingly, in June 1981, or over nine months after the coup, the EU ratified a 600 million ecu package of grants and concessionary loans to Turkey, known as the Fourth Financial Protocol. However, this package was later frozen, following the ruling military junta's decision to close all the existing political parties in October 1981. Thanks to Greek objections, it has remained frozen ever since.

Turkish-EU relations came out of the ice box after the re-establishment of elected civilian Government in December 1983 - a process aided by the fact that the new Prime Minister, Turgut Özal, was, in any case, committed to the deregulation of both foreign trade and the domestic economy. The planned reduction of import duties on industrial products was resumed, but Özal appeared to be jumping the gun in April 1987, when his Government submitted a formal application for accession to the EU. In response, the Commission prepared an official Opinion on the application. This was issued in December 1989 and endorsed by the EU Council of Ministers in February 1990.[3] In effect, the Opinion gave a measured rebuff to the Turkish application, by concluding that the Union could not enter into any negotiations for accession with applicant countries until after the completion of the single market in 1993. Nor would the EU commit itself to opening negotiations even after that date. However, in June 1990 the Commission sugared the pill by sending a Communication to the Council and European Parliament, unofficially known as the 'Turkey package'.[4] This proposed that the two sides should resume progress towards implementation of the customs union in industrial products by the original target date of 1 January 1996. In addition, there would be renewed cooperation in industry, technology, agriculture, transport and the environment, and the Fourth Financial Protocol would be belatedly implemented.

The 1990 package was potentially important, but for some time it was impossible to put it into effect, primarily due to Greek obstructionism. However, the British presidency, during the second half of 1992, began to loosen the logjam, mainly because the British had always been more supportive of the Turkish case than most of the other member countries, and were more appreciative of Turkey's enhanced international role following the Gulf War of 1991 and the collapse of the USSR. On 10 November 1992, at a delayed meeting of the Association Council, it was agreed that both sides would continue to work for the establishment of the customs union by the beginning of 1996, and that a timetable would be established for the eventual introduction of free movement of labour and economic cooperation. A regular political dialogue between Turkey and the EU would be established, at prime ministerial or presidential level. Turkish spirits were also raised by the reported remarks of British Foreign Secretary Douglas Hurd that 'we will include Turkey in the process of constructing [the new] Europe'.[5] Apparently, the Fourth Financial Protocol would remain blocked, since its release could constitutionally be prevented by a Greek veto, but the significance of this was largely symbolic, thanks to the vast improvement in Turkey's balance of payments position since the aid package was originally agreed to in 1981. While there was much ground which remained to be covered, the gradual implementation of the obligations, which had been accepted as far back as 1963, did seem to be in prospect at last.

Coinciding with this renewed movement in Turkish-EU relations, the Turks have also been managing to strengthen their links with other European institutions. Following the agreements between EFTA and the EU, (Turkey signed a trade agreement with the six EFTA members in December 1991, designed to synchronise the removal of trade barriers between Turkey and EFTA with the planned moves towards a Turkey-EU customs union) Meanwhile, the EU members were also signalling that, even if they felt serious reservations about the idea of Turkish accession on economic and, some, political grounds, its strategic importance was inescapable. Accordingly, they were anxious to incorporate Turkey in future European defence structures - in particular, the WEU. As a non-EU state, Turkey could not become a full member of the WEU, but it signed a partnership agreement in November 1992 and, like Norway, will apparently be included in future defence planning.

Goals, Opinions and Obstacles

Quite clearly, the range of questions raised by the possibility of Turkish accession has been enormously widened by the distance the EU has travelled since the Association Agreement was signed in 1963.[6] At that time, the main emphasis among the original six members was still on reducing trade barriers between them. Common economic policies, let alone eventual monetary and political union, were still only gleams in the eyes of the idealists. Today, all these issues are firmly on the agenda, even if the expected post-Maastricht process now shows serious signs of faltering. Turkey always had the problem of adapting to the EU, but it now has far more to adapt itself to than it once had. The possibility of a large number of new accessions - not just of the EFTA members, but also of the former Soviet satellites of eastern Europe - has also made the overall question of enlargement far more complicated. Some of these new issues are explored in the final section of this chapter. However, as a first step, it seems worthwhile to summarise some of the motives and obstacles which have been clear for many years, and which show few signs of vanishing.

In the main, Turkey's motives in seeking membership of the EU are similar to those of most of the other eastern European states - that is, that accession would give Turkish producers unhindered access to the western European market, and would reinforce, if not guarantee, the national commitment to democratic politics and the market economy. In the Turkish case, this incentive is strengthened by historical legacies. Since the reform movement which began in the Ottoman Empire in the nineteenth century, Turkish political leaders have treated acceptance into the western comity of nations (in nineteenth century usage, the Concert of Europe) as an axiomatic objective. As a sign of this, their anxiety to join NATO in the early 1950s was conditioned not just by the security threat from the USSR, but also by the assumption that NATO membership would symbolise their country's admission to the European club. By the 1960s, admission to the EU had come to be regarded as the next logical step.

This ambition is mixed with the realisation that western Europeans may be less than enthusiastic about the prospect; as Kemal Ataturk, the founder of the Turkish republic, put it in 1923, 'the West has always been prejudiced against the Turks ... but we Turks have always and consistently moved towards the West ... . In order to be a civilised nation, there is no alternative'.[7] To support his application for accession, the late President Özal produced a 370-page book, emphasising Turkey's European credentials, cultural, historic and political.[8] The ambition is opposed by Islamic conservatives, who would prefer Turkey to seek an identity in the Muslim world. This section of opinion is currently represented by the Welfare Party, which has 40 seats in Turkey's 450-member parliament. Traditionally, what could be called the nationalist left also opposed Turkey's membership of the EU, on the grounds that Turkey, as a developing country, needed to follow autarchic development policies which would be ruled out by membership. However, Islamic fundamentalism does not play a centre-stage role in Turkish politics, and much, though not all, of nationalist leftist opinion has generally come round to the opposite view that membership of the EU would strengthen the cause of political liberalisation.[9] Broadly speaking, the idea of accession appears to be supported by the leadership of virtually all Turkish political parties, as well as the professional foreign and economic policy-making elite (that is, the Foreign Ministry, the State Planning Organisation and the military chiefs). To put the case negatively, permanent and unqualified rejection by the EU would be regarded as a shattering defeat for almost everything the Turkish political leadership has claimed to stand for since the 1920s, if not the 1850s. In general, business leaders also favour accession, though there is probably more enthusiasm among the owners and managers of the bigger and more modernised firms, than among small manufacturers and traders.[10]

While there seems to be a consensus in favour of accession on the part of the political and business elite, it is far from certain that this enthusiasm is shared by public opinion. In Turkey, as in many member states, the elite may well be more pro-European (or perhaps more idealistic) than the people at large. Unfortunately, public opinion polling on broad issues of this nature is not likely to yield useful results, since the pollsters' art is still poorly developed in Turkey, and it is probable that the majority of ordinary people would not be able to give a considered opinion on what still looks like a remote question. However, a survey by Şahin Alpay, columnist on the Istanbul daily *Cumhuriyet*, gives a valuable insight into the views of fifteen of his leading fellow journalists, from a wide variety of newspapers, who are likely to be influential in moulding urban opinion. Predictably, their views on Turkey's links with the EU ran the gamut, from full support for the idea of Turkish accession, at one end of the spectrum, to outright opposition, at the other. However, the great majority favoured eventual accession, on the grounds that it would strengthen the country's commitment to secular democracy, rather than for economic reasons. At the same time, there seemed to be more realism among the journalists than among the politicians as to whether Turkey would eventually be admitted to the EU and if so how soon. Of the eleven journalists who favoured the idea in principle, only three thought it could be realised in the foreseeable future. Cultural and economic obstacles were the most frequently cited reasons for this.[11]

An overall assessment of western European reactions is far harder to give, since the question of Turkish accession is well down on the EU's agenda, and unofficial opinion is unlikely to be clearly or consistently expressed. However, it is probably safe to say that Europe feels that it needs Turkey far less than Turkey needs Europe. Viewed from Brussels, the obstacles to Turkish accession loom far larger than in Ankara. On the other hand, the debate is not entirely one-sided. On these grounds, a summary of the main arguments needs to be presented.

In the economic sphere, the wide gap between Turkey and the existing EU members was naturally pointed out in the Commission's Opinion, which concluded that, as a result, 'Turkey would experience serious difficulties in taking on the obligations resulting from the Community's economic and social policies'.[12] At the then current exchange rates, Turkey's per capita GDP in 1989 stood at $1,432 ($1,980 in 1991) compared with $5,399 for Greece and $4,623 for Portugal, the EU's poorest members. Recalculation at purchasing power parities reduces this disparity considerably, altering the per capita figures to $4,481 for Turkey, $7,253 for Greece and $7,360 for Portugal.[13] Nevertheless, however it is calculated, the economic gap is still a wide one, and will probably make it hard for Turkey to introduce, say, a universal social security system at anything like western European levels before the start of the next century (currently, about 30-40 per cent of the population is still outside the social security net).[14]

Although Turkey is undoubtedly far poorer than the present EU, its economy is growing faster. Between 1980 and 1988, GNP rose by an annual average of 5.4 per cent, compared with 2.0 per cent for the member states. Between 1988 and 1993, GNP can be estimated to have risen by an average of around 4.2 per cent per year. Total foreign trade volume has increased exponentially, from $10.8 billion in 1980 to $37.6 billion in 1992. Economic performance has been hampered by great volatility (GNP growth, for instance, registered 1.9 per cent in 1989, 9.2 per cent in 1990, 1.5 per cent in 1991 and 5.9 per cent in 1992) and high inflation, with consumer prices rising at an average of 66 per cent per annum between 1988 and 1991. On the other hand, it can be argued that even if the EU cannot admit Turkey to full membership, on economic grounds, they would be ill-advised to turn down the opportunity of free trade. Turkey has a rapidly growing market and an economy at roughly the same stage of, say, that of Italy at the beginning of the 1950s. As an example, sales of private cars increased from around 107,000 in 1987 to around 223,000 in 1991. Granted that automobile sales in western Europe have grown much more slowly in recent years, it is clear that Turkey offers a fast-growing market, even if it is still a relatively small one, judged against the size and population of the country. In 1991, Turkey still only had about 30 cars per 1,000 people, compared with 143 in Greece and 139 in Portugal.[15]

Apart from this general picture, two specific economic issues will undoubtedly overhang whatever accession negotiations eventually take place. The first concerns that hoary old chestnut, the reform of the CAP. Turkey is a substantial agricultural producer, and normally has a surplus of around $1.5 billion per annum in its agricultural trade. On these grounds, Turkish accession could lead to the further growth of European crop surpluses, particularly if the present price regime, or something like it, continues to encourage over-production. Fortunately, Turkey's agricultural exports to the EU consist mainly of specialist crops, such as dried fruits and nuts, for which the full system of intervention does not apply, but the budgetary burden of Turkish accession could be a serious one. Putting a figure on it is extremely difficult, since much would depend on the state of the CAP at the time of accession. However, a recent study published by the Turkish State Planning Organisation concluded that the annual gross cost to the EU budget under the CAP in 1995 would be around $3.4 billion, even assuming that the gap between EU and world prices has narrowed by then; since Turkey's agricultural imports from third countries are low, its contributions to the EU's agricultural budget would be slight, at around $350 million per year. This would leave a net annual support cost of around $3.1 billion, compared with an actual total guarantee expenditure by the EU in 1988 of $26 billion.[16] Another estimate, which takes in Turkey's possible demands on the regional and social funds, suggests an upper figure of 6-8 billion ecu per year (or around $7.5-10.0 billion at current exchange rates) and a lower figure of 3.6 billion ecu ($4.5 billion).[17]

The second economic obstacle is the commitment to free movement of labour which would be involved in Turkish accession. Under Article 36 of the Additional Protocol, the two sides pledged that free movement of workers between Turkey and the EU would be established in progressive stages between 1976 and 1986. In fact, when the first of these two target dates was reached in 1976, the EU restricted itself to improving the freedom of movement of those Turkish workers already in it, and undertook to accord priority to Turkish workers if a member state's manpower needs could not be met by other EU members. In effect, Article 36 has remained a dead letter.[18] Meanwhile, large-scale emigration from Turkey to the EU has ceased since the oil crisis of 1973-74, and the German decision of 1973 to ban further recruitment of workers from outside the EU. It would appear that the total number of Turkish residents in the EU has been virtually static since 1980, at just over 2 million, of which some 1.6 million are in Germany.[19] From German data, it can be roughly estimated that around 35 per cent are in regular paid employment, and the remainder are children or other family dependants.[20]

Given the current wave of xenophobia in Germany and France, and relatively high unemployment rates in the EU generally, it seems most unlikely that the existing member states would be willing to countenance free movement of labour until the disparity between Turkish and western European wage rates is reduced to around the levels currently obtained within the EU[21] – a target which is unlikely to be achieved until some time in the next century. Meanwhile, the most that Turkey would be likely to be offered is some arrangement whereby free movement could be phased in over a fairly long period after accession, assuming that the other obstacles to membership could be overcome. Since emigrants' remittances are now far less important in Turkey's balance of payments than they once were, it is possible that a future Turkish Government might be willing to accept this limitation, as a necessary price for admission.[22] In the meantime, the most worrying aspect of the large Turkish presence in Germany is the upsurge of neo-Nazi atrocities against Turkish, as well as other foreign, residents. This is bound to raise the temperature in the occasionally tense Turkish-German relationship. At the same time, the German authorities clearly need to halt the spread of racism for domestic-political reasons, quite apart from its effects on Bonn's relations with Ankara.

Politically, the two major hurdles to Turkish accession are the continuing disputes with Greece, and the continuation of human rights abuses inside Turkey. The first consists essentially of mutual conflicts over offshore oil rights and territorial waters in the Aegean, the treatment of Greek Christian and Turkish Muslim minorities in the two countries and the failure to reach a new constitutional settlement in Cyprus.[23] In early 1988, the then Greek and Turkish Prime Ministers, Andreas Papandreou and Turgut Özal, met at the Swiss resort of Davos, and agreed to institute a regular dialogue between the two countries. As a sign of the changed mood, Özal visited Athens later in the same year, the first Turkish premier to visit the Greek capital for several decades. Since then, however, virtually no progress has been made, despite changes of Government in both countries. At the EU's Lisbon summit on 26-27 June 1992, Greece lifted its previous veto on Turkey's participation in the EU's Mediterranean Programme, but has since shown no sign of dropping its opposition to implementation of the Fourth Financial Protocol. Two further rounds of talks between the then Greek Cypriot President George Vasillou and the Turkish Cypriot leader Rauf Denktash began in New York in July and October 1992, but the two sides appeared to have made very few advances towards a settlement, and did not seem to be under strong pressure from the two mainland Governments to do so. By the autumn of 1993, no further progress had been registered - in fact the peace process seemed to have moved backwards rather than forwards, following the election of Glafkos Clerides as Greek Cypriot President in February 1993, and Denktash's resignation as the chief Turkish Cypriot negotiator in August. Concerning the Cyprus problem, as in the bilateral disputes between Greece and Turkey, it appears that both Governments regard the cost of making mutually acceptable concessions to be greater than that of continuing the confrontation, given that their disputes are not likely to provoke a mutual war. In these conditions, it is difficult to see how they can break out of the stalemate.

The officially expressed Turkish view is that the Cyprus problem and other Greek-Turkish disputes should not be allowed to affect Turkey's relations with the EU, and that their settlement should be easier once Turkey has been admitted to the EU. It is hard to avoid the conclusion, however, that in this case the wish has been the father of the thought. The fact is that, whether the Turkish Government likes it or not, the Cyprus issue and other disputes do affect relations between Brussels and Ankara, and are likely to go on doing so. Similarly, Greece will argue that waiting to settle Greek-Turkish disputes until after Turkey has been admitted to the EU is putting the cart before the horse. The threat of a veto is the main weapon which Greece has against an otherwise far more powerful neighbour, and it is most unlikely that it would be discarded until after Greek objectives have been met. The outcome of the November 1992 Association Council meeting also implied that the remainder of the EU was aware of the importance of mending fences with Turkey, and was ready to do so, where Greek resistance could be ignored or circumvented. This tactic could be continued for some time, but in the last analysis it seems most improbable that the EU could begin accession negotiations with Turkey if Athens still objected. Sidelining Greek objections may help to soften the problem in the short term, but it cannot ultimately solve it.

Turkey's poor record in human rights is another long-standing obstacle to its admission to the EU, though it is worth pointing out that this is not its only significance, since there is also substantial internal pressure for wider civil liberties. Since 1945, the Turks have made a much more determined attempt than most other Muslim nations to establish a liberal democratic polity. However, there is a far greater commitment to the principle of rule by an elected civilian Government, than to the idea that, within a majoritarian system, the rights of ideological or ethnic minorities have to be protected. Restrictions on individual and collective rights, which would not be allowed in most democracies, and arbitrary and sometimes brutal behaviour by the police, have been inherited from earlier, less democratic regimes.

In recent years, there have been important advances on this score. In particular, in 1991, the notorious Articles 141 and 142 of the Turkish Penal Code, which prescribed long prison sentences for anyone deemed guilty of allegedly communist activities, were withdrawn from the statute book. Subsequently, the main cause of complaint was the length of time criminal suspects could be held by police without being brought to court, and the frequent use of torture and ill-treatment to extort confessions. During the election campaign of September-October 1991, the two ruling parties - that is the True Path Party and the Social Democrat Populist Party - both promised to eliminate torture. The Government programme which they issued after assuming office also undertook to reduce the period of detention without court supervision, and to allow suspects to appoint and consult legal counsel during police interrogation. After much delay, a bill for the reform of judicial procedures was passed by parliament, and signed by the President in November 1992. Under the new legislation, suspects may only be held for 24 hours (or 4-8 days in conspiracy cases) before being charged and can ask for the presence of lawyers during preliminary interrogation. In cases heard by the State Security Courts, which deal with charges alleged to affect national security, the time period may be doubled, and doubled again in areas where a state of emergency is in force (this covers most of the Kurdish-inhabited provinces of south-eastern

Anatolia).[24] If these reforms are put into practice, they should allay criticisms of the treatment of suspects, and at least curtail the use of torture. Just prior to the enactment of the new legislation, the human rights organisation Amnesty International reported that the police were continuing to torture criminal suspects, and that relatively few cases were being followed up by the authorities.[25]

The question of the treatment of the Kurdish minority, which probably accounts for around 15 per cent of the total population, is linked to that of civil rights, although it is more problematic, since collective - as distinct from individual - rights are hard to define. For example, the principle of national self-determination raises the question of defining the 'nation' and deciding how the right is to be implemented - assuming, indeed, that it exists in all cases. In recent years, there have been some official advances in recognising the Kurdish identity in Turkey. In April 1991, the previous law banning the use of the Kurdish language was withdrawn. Publications in Kurdish now appear in Turkey, although only Turkish may be used for government business and state education. After assuming office in November 1991, Prime Minister Süleyman Demirel and Deputy Premier Erdal İnönü both publicly recognised the separate Kurdish cultural identity, while urging that Turks and Kurds were 'brothers'.[26] These sentiments were repeated by Tansu Çiller, when she took over the premiership in June 1993. However, by the autumn of 1993 there was still no clear sign that her administration was willing to take definite political steps to end Kurdish grievances - by, for instance, withdrawing the special powers of the police and army in the south-east. In general, it seemed most unlikely that the Government would make any concessions to demands for Kurdish political autonomy. Separatist political activity and the formation of minority nationalist parties remain illegal.

The main Kurdish insurgency organisation in Turkey is the PKK, or Kurdistan Workers' Party. By August 1993, around 7,000 people had been killed since the start of the PKK's present campaign in August 1984.[27] The problem has been exacerbated by the strong-arm tactics adopted by the military, and the substantial number of unsolved murders allegedly carried out by undercover hit-squads which, it is claimed, operate with official protection. The Turkish authorities claim that these murders are part of internecine feuds between rival Kurdish militants, and this may well be true in some cases.[28] In pressing for the fuller application of human rights, European critics have to recognise that the Turkish authorities face a serious law and order problem in the Kurdish areas, and that the PKK frequently resorts to acts of brutal terrorism against unarmed civilians. On the other hand, it can be argued that two wrongs do not make a right, and that, however serious the menace of terrorism, it does not justify illegal actions by the security forces. For its part, the EU is right to press for respect for democratic norms by the Turkish authorities, but it has to be careful not to allow its criticisms to shade into implied support for the PKK or other terrorist groups.

The third political objection to Turkish membership of the EU rests on the assumption that the EU should be limited to countries with a European, or perhaps Christian, cultural and geographic identity, and that Turkey does not fit into either of these categories. These arguments are probably the most serious, since it is impossible to know how they could be overcome, even if the economic and other political obstacles could be eliminated. This point is occasionally referred to by Turkish commentators, who support the idea of eventual accession but who do not think it can be achieved in the foreseeable future.[29]

Against these objections, it has to be pointed out that, however deeply rooted, they are not easy to sustain in the light of Europe's previous undertakings. Those who argue that Turkey is not a European country have to explain why, in that case, it has been admitted to membership of both NATO and the Council of Europe, besides having associate membership of the EU and (since November 1992) the WEU. In practice, 'European-ness' is virtually impossible to define as a criterion for acceptance as a member of the EU - a fact recognised by the Commission in its report to the Lisbon summit in June 1992.[30] So far, the EU has consistently given Turkey the benefit of the doubt on this issue, at least in its official statements.

The vast majority of Turks are Muslims, but the Turkish Constitution specifically states that Turkey is a secular state. Nor is there anything in the Treaty of Rome to the effect that member nations must be Christian. On the concrete question of Turkey's eligibility to apply for membership, Article 28 of the Association Agreement commits the EU to 'examine the possibility of the accession of Turkey' once operation of the Agreement has advanced sufficiently far. Had the cultural and geographical objections been considered convincing, then presumably the EU should not have undertaken even to examine the question. To confirm this point, at the time of the signature of the Agreement in 1963, Walter Hallstein, the then President of the Commission, declared that 'Turkey is part of Europe'.[31] Nor did the Commission's Opinion of 1989 cite any doubts about Turkey's European identity as a reason for its conclusions. In fact, immediately after the publication of the Opinion in December 1989, Commissioner Abel Matutes confirmed that 'Turkey is ... eligible to become a member of the Community', and pointed out that there was no reference to religion in the Opinion.[32] Given these commitments, it is not likely that the cultural or geographical factors would be openly mentioned as the main reason for rejecting a renewed Turkish application; instead, the EU can be expected to refer to the economic and other political obstacles mentioned earlier. On the other hand, it has to be accepted that, whether they are openly admitted or not, considerations of this kind will probably remain influential in forming European reactions at the grass roots.

Current Prospects and Global Changes

By the end of 1992, it appeared that the Demirel Government was more realistic about Turkey's short-term chances of entering the EU than Turgut Özal had been in 1987, and this approach was continued by the Çiller administration in 1993. Even though the Government was still committed to working for eventual accession, it was apparently recognised that the more developed non-EU states, starting with Austria and Sweden, would almost certainly achieve membership some time before Turkey. The most immediate item on the agenda was the implementation of the customs union, to which both sides repeated their commitment. Unfortunately, the Turks had done little thinking about what would be entailed, or how they could best exploit the opportunity.[33]

For both sides, the customs union would offer some important advantages. For the EU it would keep Turkey in play, and would improve access to the Turkish market, without raising the huge problems of free movement of labour and full participation in the CAP, the regional and structural funds and the EU's political decision making machinery, which would be necessitated by full membership. For Turkey, also, there are important advantages to be won from free access to the EU market. Most importantly, the customs union would aid the modernisation and expansion of Turkish industry, since investors from both the EU and third states would be guaranteed that their products could enter the EU freely, and that they could import machinery, spare parts and raw materials from the EU duty free.

While the customs union seemed more achievable than full membership, its implementation would not be easy, particularly on the Turkish side. In the Additional Protocol, commodities were divided into a '12-year list', in which duties were supposed to be eliminated during the first twelve years of the implementation of the programme (that is, between 1973 and 1985) and a '22-year list', allowing for a longer period of adjustment. In February 1992, Turkish customs rates on both lists were reduced by 10 per cent, according to the prearranged schedule, and it was claimed that 70 per cent harmonisation had been achieved in respect of the 12-year list, and 60 per cent harmonisation for the 22-year list.[34]

However, while successive Turkish Governments, during the 1980s, were reducing customs duties, they were simultaneously increasing other charges on imports, such as stamp duty, wharf tax, municipality tax, and taxes for other 'extra-budgetary funds', which have the same effect. As a result, there is still a high effective rate of protection, estimated in 1990 at around 17 per cent for investment and consumer goods, and 7.5 per cent for intermediate goods.[35] [Although there has been an appreciable reduction in effective protection rates since 1989, and although Turkish industrialists now seem to be more confident of withstanding the challenges of free competition with the EU than they were in the 1970s, it is clear that they still have much ground to make up.[36] A particular problem is that of the nationalised industries, known in Turkey as the State Economic Enterprises or SEEs, which dominate heavy industry, but are renowned for their inefficiency, and regularly make large losses which are then made up by the public purse. Incoming Governments have regularly promised to reform and rationalise the SEEs, but so far very little has been achieved.)

Politically, the main objection in Turkey to the customs union is not that it would be bad in itself, but that it might become a permanent status, rather than a stepping stone on the path to eventual accession. It is argued that it would leave Turkey shouldering most of the burdens of accession, in the form of low tariff barriers, without the political advantages of membership. As a result, Turkey would be permanently condemned to riding in the second-class carriage of the European train, unable to help determine its progress. The perception that the EU does not want either to alienate Turkey or to admit it to full membership was quite widespread among the journalists interviewed by Şahin Alpay in 1990. According to Abdurrahman Dilipak, of the pro-Islamic Milli Gazete, the EU states 'will not accept Turkey in their house, but neither will they leave her outside of their garden'. Similarly, Hasan Cemal, editor of *Cumhuriyet*, suggested that the EU was saying to Turkey, 'For the time being, you are neither to become a full member, nor remain at the present associate member status. You will acquire a status of little more than associate member'.[37] It seemed likely that the majority of Turkish opinion would be reluctant to accept this status as permanent.

At the same time, the context within which the future of the Turkish-EU relationship will be decided has been profoundly altered by the end of both the Cold War and of the Soviet Union itself - neither of which was envisaged at the time Turkey's present institutional links with the EU were constructed. In Turkey, the immediate reaction to the end of the Warsaw Pact was that it would further reduce the chances of any movement towards eventual accession, since it removed the main reason the EU had for strengthening relations with Turkey, which derived from its crucial role on the south-eastern flank of NATO. Of all NATO's southern European members, Turkey seemed likely to be the biggest loser from any fundamental revision of Europe's security structures, since it was the only one which was not a member of the EU.

To some extent, these anxieties may have been lessened by Turkey's subsequent association with the WEU. More generally, it appears that the disintegration of Soviet power may have enhanced, rather than reduced, Turkey's strategic importance, and certainly changed its scope. As the traditional threat to European security from within Europe declines, so the West may have to cope with regionally more diverse challenges to its interests. If so, then Turkey's role in future western security is likely to prove crucial, since it is the only state in the Middle East which is a member of NATO, and it is also an important potential, or actual, political actor in the politics of the troubled Transcaucasian region of the former USSR, in the new republics of central Asia, and in the turbulent Balkans. Even before the last of these three theatres of conflict had emerged, the Gulf crisis of 1990-91 and subsequent western policy towards Iraq had underlined Turkey's significance to the West in the Middle East.[38] Almost certainly, it was their recognition of Turkey's potential importance in these regional problems which inclined the EU states to try to revive the EU's links with Ankara in the autumn of 1992.

Meanwhile, the possibility that several of the former Soviet satellites, such as Hungary, the Czech and Slovak republics and Poland, might be in a position to press for accession before, or contemporaneously with, Turkey has immensely complicated the whole project of enlargement, and Turkey's position within it. Granted the expected accession of the present EFTA members, the prospect is raised that by the time Turkey is ready to enter the accession process by the end of the 1990s, the EU could have a total of something like double the present number of member states. It is very hard to see how such a large number could be accommodated within the EU's institutions, as they are currently constituted, or how the new members could be brought into the planned process towards political and monetary union among the Twelve. Hence, it is sometimes suggested that the EU will have to adopt a much looser pattern of integration, characterised as the 'variable geometry' or 'dual-track' approach. The eastern European economies, along with Turkey, would be joined to those of the EU, but not necessarily committed to the same process of integration at the same speed. From Brussels' viewpoint, the main objection to such a solution is that it would constitute an unacceptable watering down of the uniform integration methodology urged by Jacques Delors.[39] From the point of view of Turkey (and, possibly of other eastern European applicants), its disadvantage is that it may not seem too different from the second-class status in Europe implied by permanent, rather than temporary, association. Whether it could be made more acceptable to Ankara by being made part of a package embracing the stronger eastern European economies as well as Turkey, which seems a likely tactic, is also open to question, though this could turn out to be the best way forward.

In view of all these difficulties, the proposal is sometimes made that Turkey might seek alternative regional alignments - specifically, with the other Muslim nations of the Middle East, with the Black Sea states, or with the new republics of Transcaucasia and central Asia. In fact, the institutional bases for such alignments have been in existence for some time, or have recently been constructed. Turkey is a long-standing member of the Organisation of the Islamic Conference, which includes all the Muslim countries, and the Economic Cooperation Organisation, which links it with Iran, Pakistan and the Muslim republics of the former USSR (that is, Azerbaijan, Kazakhstan, Uzbekistan, Turkmenistan, Kyrgyzstan and Tajikistan). Since 1990, it has taken the lead in forming the Black Sea Economic Cooperation zone which includes all the Black Sea states (that is, Turkey, Bulgaria, Romania, Moldova, Ukraine, Russia and Georgia) plus Greece, Albania, Armenia and Azerbaijan. Meanwhile, the Turks have been active in cultivating the friendship of the new Turkic republics of the former Soviet Union, with whom there have been frequent exchanges of official visits, and widespread commercial and cultural contacts.

The shortcoming of these new openings is that, although they have certainly raised Turkey's international profile, and boosted national morale after years of cold-shouldering by the western Europeans, they do not really serve as an alternative to Turkey's connections with the EU, either economically or politically. Although Turkey's trade with the other Middle Eastern and north African countries is still extremely important, with a total volume of around $5.7 billion in 1991, it accounts for a lower proportion of its total trade than in the oil-boom years of the early 1980s, and is far lower than trade with the EU, which in 1991 stood at over $16.4 billion. Politically, also, Turkey finds it hard to construct an overall alignment with the Middle Eastern states, which are themselves bitterly divided. Since Turkey is not an Arab country, and therefore ineligible for membership of the Arab League, there is no Middle Eastern club which it would be able to join.

To the north, the Black Sea Economic Cooperation project could promise useful gains in the expansion of trade, the alleviation of mutual political disputes, and the development of joint investments and environmental protection. However, almost all the other Black Sea states are undergoing internal political and economic upheaval, and are in several cases riven by internal or interstate disputes. It was also noticeable that in the declaration signed in their heads of state meeting in Istanbul in June 1992, the participating countries agreed that they would only work for freer trade between themselves 'in a manner not contravening their obligations to third parties'[40] - in other words, that progress towards Black Sea cooperation would not be allowed to obstruct the links of Turkey and other states with the EU. Similar considerations affect Turkey's relations with Transcaucasia and central Asia. The Nagorno-Karabakh dispute has serious implications for Turkey, since the Turks feel a natural affinity with their kinsmen in Azerbaijan. However, Turkey, as a state, cannot afford to alienate Armenia, given the presence of a large and influential Armenian diaspora in the United States and France. Expressions of mutual friendship with central Asia are all very well, but as a political programme, pan-Turkism does not seem realistic, and is, in any case, suspected in Turkey as the predilection of the ultra-right. For the central Asian states, the main advantage of friendship with the Turks is that Turkey is both a Muslim country and (unlike Iran) a member of the western alliance. Similarly for the Turks, one of the main advantages of the developing relationship with central Asia is that it increases Turkey's standing with the western powers. On these grounds, it seems fairly clear that the central Asian connection is supplementary to the western one, and far from being an alternative to it.

On their side, the EU members also have to consider the political effects of a breakdown of relations with Turkey. At the moment, the nightmare scenario that the country might be taken over by a Turkish version of Gaddafi or Khomeini does not seem likely, since Islamic fundamentalism is a much weaker force in Turkey than in most Muslim countries. On the other hand, if they perceived that the western powers were not prepared to pay any heed to Turkish interests, then the Turks might well retreat into a strongly defensive nationalism. Though Turkish politicians and diplomats are quite naturally disinclined to threaten their allies with what might look like veiled blackmail, the fact is that Turkey could adopt obstructive and uncooperative policies within the western institutions to which it is attached, without actually withdrawing from them. The implications of this could be far-reaching. Despite the end of the Cold War, NATO is neither dead nor useless, and Turkey still plays an essential role within it. In the Middle East, western attempts to rein in Saddam Hussein and protect the Kurds would be virtually impossible without Turkish cooperation. In central Asia, Turkey almost certainly has more political influence than any one of the western powers, and its alienation would mean the loss of an important asset to the West. Turkish opposition in either, if not both, these theatres could have serious consequences for western interests.

Under the Reagan and Bush administrations, this point seems to have been more fully appreciated in Washington than in most European capitals. So far, however, American pressure does not appear to have had much effect in Brussels. As François Heisbourg concludes, 'there is little purpose in US pressure on the EU to accept Turkey in its midst in the name of strategic imperatives - and they are by no means trivial - when the decision will be based on considerations of identity and common destiny'.[41] This expectation may well prove right, and the EU states may well decide that their common destiny does not include Turkey. On the other hand, they have to consider the political consequences of this option. At the moment, it is hard to disagree with Mr Dillpak's judgement that they prefer to keep Turkey in their garden, without letting it into the house. While the establishment of the customs union is still being completed, they may be able to put off the decision as to whether they should open the door, but they will probably not be able to go on doing so indefinitely.

Notes

1. That is, at the time of writing, Austria, Cyprus, Finland, Malta, Norway, Sweden and Turkey.
2. The English texts of the Association Agreement and Additional Protocol appear in Official Journal of the European Communities: Information and Notices, vol. 16, no. C113 (24 December 1973). For summaries of developments up to 1989, see Bourguignon, R. (1990) 'A History of the Association Agreement between Turkey and the European Community', and İlkin, S. (1990) 'A Short History of Turkey's Association with the Community', both in Evin, A. and Denton, G. (eds) *Turkey and the European Community*, Opladen: Leske and Budrich.
3. Commission of the European Communities (1989) *Avis de la Commission sur la demande d'adhésion de la Turquie à la Communauté*, SEC (89) 2290 final, 18 December.
4. See Redmond, J. (1993) *The Next Mediterranean Enlargement of the European Community: Turkey, Cyprus and Malta?* Aldershot: Dartmouth, pp. 49-50, and Cendrowicz, M. (1992) and 'The European Community and Turkey: Looking Backwards, Looking Forwards' in Dodd, C.H. (ed.) *Turkish Foreign Policy: New Prospects*, Wistow: Eothen Press, for Modern Turkish Studies Programme, SOAS, pp. 22-23.
5. *Milliyet*, 11 November 1992: Briefing, 16 November 1992, pp. 10-11. My wording of Mr Hurd's comment is a retranslation from the Turkish version.
6. This point is made by Cendrowicz (1992), op. cit., p. 11.
7. Quoted in Kilic, A. (1959) *Turkey and the World*, Washington DC: Public Affairs Press, p. 49.
8. Özal, T. (1991) *Turkey In Europe and Europe in Turkey*, Nicosia: Rustem and Brother.
9. See, for instance, Alpay, S. (1990) *Turkey and the European Community, as Viewed by Turkish Journalists*, Bonn: Centre for Turkish Studies, Working Paper no. 7, pp. 9-11,16-17, 23.
10. Ilkin, S. (1993) 'Businessmen: Democratic Stability' in Heper, M., Öncü, A. and Kramer, H. (eds) *Turkey and the West: Changing Political and Cultural Identities*, London and New York: I.B. Tauris, p.195 and Toksöz, M. (1988) *Turkey to 1992: Missing Another Chance?* London: Economist Intelligence Unit, Special Report no. 1136, pp. 77-78.
11. Alpay (1990), op. cit., pp. 6,13-15.
12. Commission of the European Communities (1989), op. cit., p. 6.
13. National income date from OECD *Economic Surveys: Turkey* (1992), end table. An alternative calculation of per capita GNP at purchasing power parities (PPPs) for 1990 gives the following figures: Turkey, $6,816; Greece, $7,382; Portugal $7,547 (using the OECD's PPP estimates); Güvenen, O. (1992), op. cit., p. 212.
14. In 1988, the proportion was 41 per cent, but it will almost certainly have fallen since then; Turkish Union of Chambers (1990) *Economic Report 1990*, Ankara: Turkish Union of Chambers, p. 93.

15. Data from OECD (1992), op. cit., pp. 145-46; Economist Intelligence Unit (1993) *Turkey: Country Report*, London: EIU, quarterly, no. 3, p. 3, and Annex to Commission of the ECs (1989), op. cit., Table 2.1.1.; IBS Research (1993) *Doing Business in Turkey*, Istanbul: IBS Research, Section 4.5.1.
16. Akder, H., et al., (1990) *Turkish Agriculture and European Community Policies: Issues, Strategies and Institutional Adaptation*, Ankara: State Planning Organisation, pp. 67, 93.
17. Estimates from Şen, F. (1989) 'Evaluation of the Possible Effects of a Turkish Accession to the EC', *Middle East Banking and Business*, vol. 8, no. 2, February, p. 17 and (1990) 'The EC View of Turkey-the Latest Report', *Middle East Banking and Business*, vol. 9, no. 2, February, p. 21.
18. Additional Protocol, Article 36, *Official Journal of the ECs* (1973), op. cit.; Association Council decision of 20 December 1976. For summaries, see Kadioğlu, A. (1993) 'The Human Tie: International Labour Migration' in Balkir, C. and Williams, A. (eds) *Turkey and Europe*, London and New York: Pinter, pp. 140-57; Ekin, N. (1979) 'Turkish Labor In the EEC' in Gumpel, W. (ed.) *Die Türkei auf dem Weg in die EG*, Munich and Vienna: R.Oldenbourg, pp. 88-91; and Ergun, I. (1990) 'The Problem of Freedom of Movement of Turkish Workers in the European Community' in Evin, A. and Denton, G., op. cit., pp. 189-90.
19. Eurostat (1991) *Demographic Statistics*, Brussels: Eurostat, p. 152.
20. This is the proportion recorded for Turks in Germany in 1988; Şen, F. (1989) *International Migration for Employment: Problems and Integration Constraints of Turkish Migrants in the Federal Republic of Germany*, Geneva: International Labour Office: World Employment Programme Working Paper MIG WP.44E, p. 40.
21. It would appear that it is the expectation of higher wages, rather when actual unemployment in their home country, which is the main reason for the migrants' decision to move. A survey carried out by the Turkish State Planning Organisation in 1971, at the high point of emigration, found that only 4 per cent of Turkish migrant workers abroad at that time had been unemployed before leaving Turkey; Paine, S. (1974) *Exporting Workers: the Turkish Case*, Cambridge: Cambridge University Press, p. 83.
22. In 1980, emigrants' remittances stood at $2,071 million, or just under 38 per cent of a total current account inflow (that is, exports plus services income and unrequited transfers) of $5,483 million. In 1992, emigrants' remittances were $3,147 million, or 10.7 per cent of a total current account inflow of $29,401 million. Data from OECD (1992) op. cit., p. 148 and *Briefing* (Ankara, weekly), 13 September 1993, p. 22.
23. For up to date summaries, see Bölükbaşi, S. (1992) 'The Turco-Greek Dispute: Issues, Policies and Prospects' in Dodd, C.H., op. cit., pp. 27-54 and Esche, M. (1990) 'A History of Greek-Turkish Relations' in Evin, A. and Denton, G., op. cit., pp. 106-116.
24. *Turkey Confidential* (London, monthly; now discontinued), December 1992, p. 5.
25. Amnesty International (1992) *Turkey: Walls of Glass*, London: Amnesty International, November, AI Index EUR 44/75/92, pp. 1-17.
26. In, for instance, a visit to Diyarbakir, the main city of south-eastern Anatolia, in December 1991; *Milliyet* (Istanbul, daily), 9 December 1991.
27. *Summary of World Broadcasts* (BBC, London, daily), 18 August 1993, ME/1770 C/1.
28. Ibid, December 1992, p. 8; Amnesty International (1992), op. cit., pp. 10-16.
29. See, for instance, the comments of Haluk Ülman, columnist of Gunaydin newspaper and a foreign policy adviser to former premier Bülent Ecevit, quoted by Alpay, Ş. (1990), op. cit., p. 14.
30. Balkir, C. and Williams, A. (1993) 'Introduction: Turkey and Europe' in Balkir, C. and Williams, A. (eds), op. cit., p. 18; Redmond, J. (1993) *The Next Mediterranean Enlargement of the EC: Turkey, Cyprus and Malta?* Aldershot: Dartmouth, p. 135.
31. Quoted by Kramer, H. (1987) 'Für und Wider einer türkischen EG-Mitgliedschaft', *Integration*, 10 Jg., 4/87, Institut für Europäische Politik, Bonn, October, p. 157.
32. Commission of the European Communities (1989) 'Press Conference by Mr Matutes on Membership of Turkey to the Community', 18 December: Ref: BIO/89/393, p. 2.
33. See, for instance, Sami Kohen, 'Yorum', *Milliyet*, 23 November 1992.
34. *Briefing*, 9 March 1992, p. 17.
35. OECD (1992), op. cit., pp. 80-81.
36. In 1988, a report by the Turkish State Planning organisation, which surveyed 70 per cent of manufacturing industry, concluded that 40 per cent of the industries covered were already able to compete freely with those of the Community, 58 per cent could become competitive if appropriate policies were applied, and only two per cent could not be made to survive. As Redmond (1993), op. cit., p. 33, suggests this conclusion may have been 'rather bullish'. However, there is certainly much more confidence on this score today than there was in the 1970s.
37. Alpay, Ş. (1990), op. cit., pp. 26-27.

38. Ibid, pp. 27-28: Sayari, S. (1992) 'Turkey: the Changing European Security Environment and the Gulf Crisis', *Middle East Journal*, vol. 46, pp. 10-14; Clark, I. (1990) 'The Military Aftermath of the Cold War' in Armstrong, D. and Goldstein, E. (eds) *The End of the Cold War*, London: Cass, p. 167; and Hale, W. (1992) 'Turkey, the Middle East and the Gulf Crisis', *International Affairs*, vol. 68, pp. 683-92.

39. Laurent, P.H. (1990) 'European Integration and the End of the Cold War' in Armstrong, D. and Goldstein, E., op. cit., p. 155. This conclusion is also suggested by Williams, A. (1993) 'Turkey: the Mediterranean Context' in Balkir, C. and Williams, A., op. cit., p. 64.

40. 'Declaration on Black Sea Economic Co-operation' and 'Summit Declaration on Black Sea Co-operation': texts kindly supplied by Ministry of Foreign Affairs, Ankara and by Mr İrfan Acar, Turkish Embassy, London.

41. Heisbourg, F. (1992) 'The European-US alliance: valedictory reflections on continental drift in the post-Cold War era', *International Affairs*, vol. 68, pp. 676-77.

7   Cyprus and Malta: Still the Mediterranean Orphans?

John Redmond

There is arguably little alternative to a close relationship with the EU for Mediterranean countries, particularly the smaller ones like Cyprus and Malta. Even if the need to have a healthy relationship with the dominant economic superpower in their region were not enough, pragmatic self-interest would drive Mediterranean states into the arms of the EU. The prospects of improved access to EU markets for exports which, together with financial assistance from the EU, could accelerate economic development and of access to EU labour markets for surplus labour are overwhelmingly attractive. Conversely, geographical proximity, mutual interests and colonial links have also compelled the members of the EU to take notice of the Mediterranean region. The region is of obvious political and strategic significance and there are many economic links, notably with regard to trade, tourism and oil.

However, this apparent mutual interest has borne little fruit other than for those countries which have managed to join the EU. Indeed, the EU has been described, with some justification, as 'having acquired its Mediterranean policy in a fit of absent-mindedness'.[1] The rush of bilateral agreements between the then EC and countries in the Mediterranean in the 1969-72 period created a patchwork of diversity. Efforts to standardise the process by the creation of a Global Mediterranean Policy (GMP) gave little comfort to the EU's Mediterranean partners as the EU's lack of generosity only served to increase the trade deficits of its Mediterranean partners. A subsequent relaunch of the EU's Mediterranean policy in the early 1980s[2] and a 'redirection' in the early 1990s[3] have done little to convince Mediterranean states that the EU's interest in their region in principle is ever likely to amount to much in practice.[4] In the face of the continuing inadequacies of the EU's Mediterranean policy, those countries which by dint of geography cannot apply to become members have become reconciled to a future at the margin of the EU, either accepting the continuation of the current relationship or turning away from the EU and promoting their own regional cooperation schemes.[5] Meanwhile, those in the north who can apply for membership have done just that, beginning with Greece; the applications of Cyprus, Malta (and Turkey) represent a continuation of this trend. Thus the failure of the GMP is the underlying cause for the Mediterranean applications for EU membership. However, the Cypriot and Maltese bids have doubtlessly been accelerated by two other factors. Firstly, Cyprus and Malta share widespread concern about the impact of the completion of the EU's market on their access to that market. Secondly, there is a feeling on both islands, probably based more on wishful thinking than on fact, that EU accession would solve their internal problems (which are economic in the case of Malta and political in Cyprus).

These introductory remarks have highlighted the similarities in the membership bids of Malta and Cyprus, but there are also important differences. The next two sections of this chapter focus on these and examine the history of each country's relationship with the EU and the key issues that accession would raise. These are followed by an examination of the EU's perspective (in the shape of the Commission's opinions on the membership bids) and some conclusions about how Cyprus and Malta might be accommodated in the future in an enlarged EU.

EU-Cyprus Relations: History and Issues

Cyprus was a British colony until 1960 and, consequently, did not react to the developments that culminated in the formation of the EU. This attitude might had continued for some time had not Britain decided to pursue EU membership. However, Cyprus had developed a typical colonial economic dependence on Britain and saw a close relationship with the EU as 'an economically rational step to ensure continued access for her traditional exports to her main trading partner, the United Kingdom'.[6] Not surprisingly therefore, an EU-Cyprus Association Agreement was signed just before Britain acceded to the EU in December 1972. The purpose of the Agreement was to create a customs union between the two (after a ten year transitional period) and not accession to the EU, and so there was no reference to the latter. It consisted of two stages, the first of which came into effect on 1 June 1973 and was to run until 30 June 1977; only this was agreed in detail. However, whilst no details of the second stage were discussed, the general intention was that 'the loss of the Commonwealth preference would be compensated by the entry into the second stage and the consequent gradual reduction and final abolition of duties in the whole enlarged Community for Cypriot exports'.[7] In fact, many of the concessions given to Cyprus by the EU were superficial and of limited value.[8] However, before this could become apparent, EU-Cypriot relations were effectively brought to a standstill by the Turkish invasion in 1974 and the *de facto* division of the territory thereafter.

The implementation, and further development, of the Association Agreement was now out of the question for political reasons; the EU wished to take a neutral position and could not risk accusations of favouring the Greek Cypriots by pressing ahead regardless. Moreover, the severe economic dislocation caused by the division of the island made a customs union with the EU impractical, even on the Greek side. Indeed, the Greek Cypriots accepted that an extension of the first stage of the agreement (in effect, a freezing of relations) was the only feasible way forward.[9] This is what was done, although financial protocols continued to be agreed and implemented, until 1987 when the EU finally felt able to move to a revised version of the second stage of association. This involved the gradual implementation, in two phases, with the first being of ten years duration, of a customs union between Cyprus and the EU. Progression to the second (five year) phase is not automatic but requires a decision by the Association Council.

The (Greek) Cypriot decision to apply for full EU membership in July 1990 was essentially a natural development of the movement towards an ever-closer relationship with the EU, accelerated by the single market programme. More generally, there has been a growing realisation that association, and particularly a customs union, represents an unsatisfactory half-way house. It puts Cyprus in a position whereby it has to obey EU rules which it plays no role in formulating and open its market to EU competition with no access to the EU's structural funds, agricultural subsidies and other benefits that only accrue to full members. The security guarantee provided by EU membership is also attractive and there is a belief that a resolution of the internal conflict in Cyprus would be accelerated. At his investiture, in March 1993, incoming President Clerides stated that 'Cyprus's entry into the EU will facilitate substantially the efforts to find a solution to the Cyprus problem'.[10] Not surprisingly, the Turkish Cypriot leadership opposed the application and has indicated that 'EU membership of Cyprus will not be considered until the Cyprus question has been settled'.[11] Such a position is in line with the 1960 Constitution of Cyprus which states that no decision in international affairs can be taken without both Greek and Turkish Cypriot assent. The Turkish

Cypriots were not consulted about the application to join the EU, therefore it is illegal (so the argument goes). However, it is clear that there would almost certainly be a highly beneficial flow of EU financial assistance to the TRNC, or whatever it became, should Cyprus join.

The political situation in Cyprus creates a difficult position for the EU and there is no doubt that the division of Cyprus is the greatest obstacle to the Cypriot application for membership. In fact, the partition of the island also has an economic impact, most obviously in the shape of the regional imbalance whereby the impoverished (Turkish) north has a GDP of something like a quarter of the (Greek) south. What the 1974 invasion did was to disrupt the Cypriot economy severely and to separate the Turkish segment and make it dependent on, and closely linked to, Turkey itself. This created a pronounced regional imbalance. The TRNC retains many underlying 'Cypriot' characteristics such as a dependence on tourism and a need for structural adjustment but, as a result of its Turkish links, which have had to be reinforced because of its isolation from the rest of the world, it has become dominated by a number of 'Turkish' characteristics, notably high inflation (through adoption of the Turkish lira) and a 'Turkish' level of GDP. There is no doubt that a significant injection of EU funds into northern Cyprus would be required if the island were to accede to the Union.

However, on the wider European scale this is probably a manageable problem. A more fundamental question relates to the virtual impossibility of both Greek and Turkish Cyprus belonging to the same single market. Implementing the four freedoms of goods, services, people and capital as required by EU membership would imply a completely open Cyprus. This is impossible to envisage in the present circumstances, particularly free movement of people. Even if an internal settlement were agreed, it would be many years before internal barriers were completely broken down. Much animosity and mistrust would initially remain. Greek Cypriots would fear the continued presence of the Turkish military but Turkish Cypriot sensitivities about personal security would make a swift withdrawal of Turkish troops unfeasible. Moreover, the Turkish Cypriots feel vulnerable economically and, specifically, fear that Greek Cypriots would buy up large amounts of land and property on the Turkish side of the island. Even if internal harmony could be achieved, the Turkish Cypriots would clearly be unable to compete in the EU's market. The Greek Cypriots are likely to fare better, particularly as they are widely considered to be adaptable and very entrepreneurial, but there may well still be a short-term problem; Cyprus's 'burgeoning trade deficit ... has been the one dark spot to emerge in Cyprus-EC trade relations since the signing of ...[the]... customs union agreement'.[12]

Beyond political and economic concerns, the relationship between Cyprus and the EU also has a security and strategic dimension. Cyprus itself is a security issue which must inevitably concern the EU, specifically because the antagonists are supported by a full member and an associate member of the EU and, more generally, because most EU member states are in NATO. The non-aligned status of Cyprus poses a question of a different kind. Indeed, it is a major cause of the only real Greek Cypriot political opposition to a close relationship with the EU - the Communist AKEL. However, the Cypriots are pragmatic and keen enough about membership to modify their status as required; and in any case, the issues are likely to be resolved in the framework of the accession of the EFTA neutrals currently negotiating with the EU. Finally, the smallness of Cyprus raises a variety of institutional concerns which also apply to Malta and are taken up in the next section.

Ultimately, the appeal of EU membership for the Greek Cypriots is irresistible and their economic credentials are impressive: a small island, with a GDP per capita (in Greek Cyprus) comparable to Spain's, which is already moving towards a customs union with the EU. The TRNC represents a trivial economic problem on a broad European scale which could probably be dealt with by EU funds and Greek Cypriot entrepreneurs. Unfortunately, however, no matter how strong the economic case, the political dilemma created by the partition of the island continues to appear to be insurmountable. There are three possible scenarios but they are all likely to be unacceptable to one or more parties:

(1)   The Greek and Turkish communities are unwilling to join the EU as one nation.

(2)   The EU will not accept the Greek Cypriots alone, despite the fact that the first principle on which it bases its bilateral dealings with Cyprus is that the Greek Cypriot administration is the only legitimate Government of Cyprus. This is because Greek Cypriot accession without the Turkish Cypriots would conflict with the EU's second principle, that the benefits from the EU should accrue to both sides.

(3)   A third possibility, that the Greek Cypriots and the TRNC join as independent states, is so contentious that it is unacceptable to all.

It is perhaps not surprising that the EU took three years to respond to the Cypriot application for membership and issue a Commission Opinion.

EU-Malta Relations: History and Issues

Malta[13] applied for membership of the EU in July 1990. This formally marked the end of a difficult phase in EU-Malta relations which had begun after the election of a Labour Government in 1971, shortly after Malta's Association Agreement with the EU had been agreed. For sixteen years, Malta was governed by a Labour administration with a decidedly ambivalent attitude towards the West in general, and the EU in particular. It was only when the (Christian Democrat) Nationalist Party was returned to power in 1987 that EU-Maltese relations thawed and were able to begin to develop. However, the Labour Party's hostility continues and has created a situation which is not unlike that in Britain and Greece at the time of their accessions to the EU: a ruling right of centre party strongly in favour of EU membership facing a left of centre opposition party against it.[14] Malta's close links with the EU make accession a logical objective but, on the EU's part, there are lingering doubts about Malta's suitability stemming, partly from the nature of its internal politics, but mainly from its size, the state of its economy and its neutrality.

Malta's Association Agreement with the EU was negotiated by a (broadly) 'pro-EU' Nationalist Government but then implemented or, perhaps better, tolerated by a (broadly) 'anti-EU' Labour Government for the next sixteen years. Whilst the Nationalist Party promotes (Christian) democratic values and is pro-western and pro-EU, the Labour Party is in favour of neutrality and non-alignment for Malta, with anti-western tendencies, and has been inclined to see the EU, at best, as one partner amongst many. Moreover, the island is truly divided as, since independence in 1964, the elections have been extremely close.[15] Because of this, Malta's relationship with the EU has been a troubled one. The Association Agreement was signed in 1970 and amounted to a customs union to be achieved through two five-year phases. Unfortunately, the newly elected Maltese Labour Government immediately made clear its intention to 'endeavour to amend the agreement in the Common Market ...'.[16] It is, therefore, not surprising that the Association Agreement remained stuck in an extended first stage and that EU-Malta relations deteriorated to a point of crisis in the early 1980s. Only after the return to power of the Nationalists in 1987, with their manifesto pledge to apply for EU membership, was normality and cordiality resumed. Nevertheless, the aftermath of the political divide in Malta over relations with the EU lingered. As recently as 1988, the European Parliament's Prag Report drew attention to the fact that a 'clearer indication of bipartisan support for membership might be regarded by the Governments of the Twelve as an important factor in their reactions to a Maltese application for membership'.[17] This was strongly criticised by Government and other sources in Malta[18] but it will be some time before the depths of EU-Maltese discord prior to 1987 are forgotten in the EU.

The political divide in Malta over the merits of joining the EU arises, in a large measure, from different evaluations of the nature and extent of the economic impact of membership. The major concern relates to the ability of parts of Maltese industry to cope with the increased competition that joining the EU would entail. The relative share of industry in the Maltese economy is similar to that in the EU[19], but an industrial sector was established unevenly and late in Malta, and did not really take off until after independence in 1964. Moreover, it was developed on the back of highly interventionist industrial policies which 'were the antithesis of those required to enable a country with a very small population ... to achieve a high degree of competitiveness on the basis of high and rapidly growing productivity'.[20] The net result has been a dualistic industrial structure with a great deal of very small-scale activity coexisting alongside a few large enterprises. There is a lack of diversity, with output and employment concentrated in a relatively small number of sectors,[21] and low levels of productivity and capital employed per worker. Furthermore, the public sector is large, with many industries subject to state control[22], which, quite apart from obvious potential conflicts with the EU's competition rules on state aid, has had the unfortunate effect on the workforce of encouraging 'the philosophy of trying to achieve a short cut to a contented life by ambling along on a low paid job which is afforded by the exchequer which tolerates an easy life and a guaranteed job for life'.[23] Such an outlook is obviously not conducive to meeting the challenges of EU accession.

Thus, not only is painful industrial restructuring necessary for Malta to be able to survive within the EU, but so too is a restructuring of attitudes. It is true, of course, that EU membership would allow Malta to benefit from the EU's structural funds and its enterprise policy (much of which is directed towards small and medium-sized companies) and that Malta could expect to attract more foreign investment. However, the essential point remains that the Maltese economy must shed its protectionism and must adjust; any attempt to evade this restructuring through a long transition period will only offer a temporary respite. Ultimately, as a small island economy on the periphery of the world's major trading bloc, Malta probably has to adjust its economy anyway and EU membership could therefore be seen as a useful catalyst.[24]

Beyond internal politics and economics, there are two other pressing issues raised by the prospect of Maltese accession to the EU. The first of these is Malta's neutrality. This was enshrined in the Maltese constitution as recently as 1987. Nevertheless, the current Maltese Government insists that its neutrality does not prevent Malta from aligning itself with common EU foreign policy positions.[25] It relates solely to military neutrality and simply prohibits the use or deployment of military bases, facilities or personnel in Malta.[26] However, whether a Labour Government would adopt a similarly benevolent view, particulary in view of their track record in government, is not clear. Perhaps solace is best sought in economic pragmatism; there is a view in some Maltese quarters (as in Cyprus) that neutrality is expendable and should, if necessary, 'be modified accordingly'[27] if it hinders progress towards EU membership (and the economic benefits that would bring). This would completely resolve any difficulties. In any case, Malta may well have to accept whatever form of neutrality the EU is willing to concede, since the neutrality issue is likely to be resolved in the course of the accession of the EFTA neutrals, with no reference to Malta.

Finally, the unique issue that is raised by Malta (and Cyprus) relates to the problems that arise from incorporating a micro-state into the EU. This is part of the general institutional problem raised by the forthcoming enlargement of the EU (which is examined in Chapter 10) but which would arise anyway, even if Malta were the only current applicant for EU membership. On the Maltese side, there is a need to address the administrative effects of EU accession which would severely test the quality of Malta's civil service and bureaucracy and their ability to increase their workload. The basic question is simply whether a small country such as Malta has sufficient technicians, professionals and bureaucrats to cope with what EU membership entails. Small countries have to negotiate, agree, implement and monitor the same number of EU rules and regulations as every other member. Furthermore, the financial benefits through the structural funds are not simply given to recipient members; acceptable programmes have to be worked up, monies have to be claimed and expenditure justified.

On the EU side, Maltese accession opens up the controversial issue of the role of small states in the Union and compels the EU to address it, because a micro-state, like Malta, pushes the issue to its extreme. In the current institutional framework, Maltese accession would imply an additional Commissioner, another national voice in the Council and the prospect of EU initiatives being blocked by a country with a population of only a third of a million, either by tipping the balance when majority voting was being used or by a veto when unanimity was required. It is not clear that the larger member states will be prepared to accept the ensuing dilution of their power. Finally, it has to be questioned as to whether a very small country like Malta (or Cyprus) could really take its turn at running the EU (Council) presidency. There must be great doubts on grounds of experience, availability of administrative and technical support and, most importantly, whether such a presidency would command credibility in the rest of the world.

The concern for the Maltese must be that the EU feels a need to reform its institutional framework to resolve these issues before it permits any micro-states to join. Such reform will not be easy, since the smaller countries already in the EU are keen to protect their current position which gives them a disproportionately large voting weight and general level of influence. The Benelux countries were very quick to react to a possible loss of this influence and submitted a memorandum on the matter to the Lisbon summit in mid-1992.[28] This basically insisted that the status quo continued and was prepared to sacrifice Maltese and Cypriot accession to this end (and offer them association instead).

The Commission's Opinions on Cyprus and Malta

The Commission's Opinions on the Cypriot and Maltese applications for EU membership eventually appeared at the end of June 1993. Both are generally positive but do not, in either case, propose the immediate initiation of accession negotiations.[29] Indeed, they highlight many of the concerns expressed in the two preceding sections. They also make it clear that, although the two islands are of similar size and raise similar institutional issues, it is misleading to think of the two applications as being closely connected or interdependent in any way. Both countries remain in the waiting room, but for quite different reasons and with very different conditions to fulfil.

The Opinion on Cyprus[30] begins by recognising that the adoption of the *acquis communautaire* should pose few problems (paragraph 9) but observes that the division of the island means that 'the ... freedom of movement of goods, people, services and capital, right of establishment and the universally recognised political, economic, social and cultural rights could not ... be exercised over the entirety of the island's territory' (paragraph 10). Much of the Opinion then focuses on a review of the situation in Cyprus and the prospects for a settlement (paragraphs 13-22) and of the history of the relationship between Cyprus and the EU (paragraphs 23-27). The next section, on the economic situation of Cyprus, is essentially very positive. Some concern is expressed about the (Greek) south's dependency on tourism and its level of industrial competitiveness and the (Turkish) north's decline, due to its isolation, and its consequent need to make up lost ground is recognised. Nevertheless, none of these problems is considered to be insurmountable and, indeed, accession to the

EU is seen as potentially economically beneficial (paragraphs 29 and 38). The Opinion does express concern in the penultimate section though, about the ability of Cyprus to participate fully in the EU institutions because of inexperienced officials, particularly on the Turkish Cypriot side (paragraph 41), and raises the related question of the ability to run a Council presidency (paragraph 42).

However, the key passages are contained in the conclusion (paragraphs 44-51) which, despite a positive diplomatic gloss, quite clearly makes Cypriot accession conditional on an internal political settlement, admittedly with one caveat. The Commission accepts 'beyond all doubt, ... [the] European identity and character [of Cyprus] and ... its vocation to belong to the Community' (paragraph 44). Indeed, it wants to send 'a positive signal ... that the Community considers Cyprus as eligible for membership' (paragraph 48) but it continues 'and that as soon as the prospect of settlement is surer, the Community is ready to start the process with Cyprus that should eventually lead to its accession'. What is actually on offer at the moment is therefore not accession negotiations but 'talks ... to familiarise the Cypriot authorities with all the elements that constitute the *acquis communautaire*'. The Commission is very clear about this (even if the Greek Cypriots may not be). Indeed, this verdict is hardly surprising, and there was considerable advance warning. For example, the then Council president (Ellemann-Jensen) stated quite baldly in January 1993: 'I do not doubt that some day in the future, when the unfortunate division has ended, Cyprus ... will be a member of the Community'.[31]

The caveat is in the last paragraph (51), which states an intention to review the Cypriot application in January 1995 if there is no internal political settlement. This is intended to prevent the Turkish Cypriots from effectively having the power of veto (in that they would be able to veto Cypriot accession to the EU by refusing to agree to an internal settlement with the Greek Cypriots). Whether this paragraph implies anything more, specifically an intention to go ahead with the accession of Greek Cyprus regardless of a settlement if the Turkish Cypriots are obstructive, is highly speculative and may have more to do with Greek Cypriot wishful thinking than Commission intention. At any rate, it is not clear that the Turkish Cypriots take that prospect too seriously. Within only a few days of the opinion being issued, their leader (Rauf Denktash) withdrew from the inter-communal talks being held under UN auspices.

The Council of Ministers endorsed the Commission Opinion in October and the Commission has thus been mandated to explain the *acquis communautaire* to the Cypriots in order to identify areas where the EU might help Cyprus adjust and to facilitate the Cypriots' preparation of their negotiating position. The first meeting was held in November 1993. The other significant step taken by the EU, initiated by Greece, has been the appointment of an EU observer to monitor and report back on the inter-communal talks. This may have an indirect bearing on the Cypriot membership bid, as the reconsideration in January 1995 has to 'be reassessed in view of the positions adopted by each party in the talks' (paragraph 51). Cyprus would thus seem to find itself in a position not unlike that of Turkey: eligible and, in principle, welcome - but not yet.

The Opinion on Malta[32] is structured in the same way as that on Cyprus, but there the similarity ends. The review of the situation in Malta focuses on two difficulties: firstly, the opposition of the Maltese Labour Party to EU accession and, secondly, the enshrinement of neutrality into the Maltese constitution in 1987. There is also a link between the two because the incompatibility between the EU's CFSP and Maltese neutrality may imply a need for an amendment to the Maltese Constitution which would require a two-thirds majority in the Maltese parliament. The review of EU-Maltese relations highlights the lack of progress resulting from the Maltese Labour Governments' hostility to the Association Agreement throughout most of the 1970s and 1980s. However, in sharp contrast to the opinion on Cyprus, the real difficulties are identified in the examination of economic issues. The Maltese economy is wholly unprepared for EU accession. To quote the Opinion (paragraph 34):

> The reforms which imply Malta's adoption of the *acquis communautaire* affect so many different areas (tax, finance, movement of capital, trade protection, competition law, etc.) and require so many changes in traditional patterns of behaviour that what is effectively involved is a root-and-branch overhaul of the entire regulatory and operational framework of the Maltese economy.

In the penultimate section, on Maltese participation in EU institutions, the same issues - shortage of skilled personnel and ability to manage a presidency - are raised, as in the Cypriot case.

The conclusions also echo those of the Opinion on Cyprus, although the route taken is economic rather than political and there is perhaps a greater degree of optimism, to the extent that Maltese economic problems may seem less intractable than Cypriot political ones. The EU's position is made clear in paragraph 44, in which reference is made to 'Malta's indubitably European calling' and the 'need to send a positive signal' but the Commission 'is [only] willing to open accession negotiations with Malta when conditions allow'. What the Commission is offering is 'an intensive dialogue with a view to establishing jointly the nature and timetable of the priority reforms needed to equip the Maltese economy to cope with international competition and to prepare the ground for integration with the Community' (paragraph 48). As already implied, the Maltese position may be somewhat better than that of Cyprus, as there is a strong incentive for them to reform their economy anyway, in order to be able to compete more effectively in their export markets. As in the Cypriot case, the Council of Ministers endorsed the Opinion in October. Discussions began later that month with a view to identifying areas of the Maltese economy that require reform, and also potential mechanisms for reform, in order that the Commission might be given the appropriate instruments to help.

Conclusions

After three years, the EU finally responded to the membership bids of Cyprus and Malta in June 1993. At first glance, the two Opinions were positive and were certainly constructive, in that they indicated what each applicant needed to do to move on to accession negotiations. Indeed, there is arguably a sense in which these countries are in a preaccession negotiations stage. However, careful reading of the Opinions indicates that if this is the case, then progression to accession negotiations is far from automatic. A cynical observer might even argue that the EU has done as little as it possibly could, and has effectively put off the accession of these rather awkward countries for many years to come by imposing conditions which are reasonable in principle, but extremely difficult to fulfil in practice.

Turning first to the Cypriot case: there is a view that the commitment to review the progress towards an internal settlement to the political divide in January 1995 is tantamount to the EU envisaging 'negotiating with only part of the island if responsibility for the failure is clearly incumbent on the other'.[33] The Greek Cypriots are certainly losing no opportunity to promote this interpretation. For example, President Clerides, in Brussels shortly after the Opinion had been issued, claimed that if the Turks were obstructive then 'the EU will certainly not penalise the Greek part by refusing to open the negotiations'.[34] However, the Opinion does not actually say this but merely that 'the situation should be reassessed in view of the positions adopted by each party in the talks ...'.[35] This would appear to leave all options open to the EU, including that of further delaying accession negotiations with Cyprus.

Similarly, the Maltese may yet have some way to go. Although the current Nationalist Government has done much to erase memories of the past, the lack of credibility in EU circles, engendered by the activities of the former Labour Government, is still not far below the surface. There is a fear that given the usual very close Maltese election results, a Labour Government could easily return to power and that this would herald a shift both in Maltese official attitudes to the EU and in Maltese economic policy away from reform. Both these trends would make Malta unwelcome in the EU. Paradoxically, the EU may have made this development more likely by refusing to move immediately to accession negotiations. The Nationalist Government has invested a great deal of political capital in EU membership and may require something more concrete to present to the electorate before the next general election in 1997. However, what the EU has done is to put the onus on the Maltese to come up with deeds rather than words - there has been some feeling in the EU that the Maltese are stronger on the latter than the former. It is now very clearly the case that the fate of the Maltese application for EU membership is firmly in their own hands.

The EU has explicitly signalled to Cyprus and Malta that they have a place in the European edifice and that this may take the form of full membership of the EU. However, it is over thirty years ago that similar signals were sent to Turkey which today is little nearer to EU accession than it was then. Things could easily go horribly wrong for Cyprus and Malta, particularly as these micro-states have little to offer the EU, which would equally lose very little (other than a small amount of credibility) if they were to turn their backs on Europe. Consequently, the pressure is very much on the applicants to change in order to become compatible with the EU. They have been given difficult conditions to fulfil and, although EU assistance is available, it is by no means certain that the Cypriots will be able to achieve an internal settlement and that the Maltese will be able to transform their economy, even in the medium-term. On top of this, both applicants will have to wait while the EU completes the enormously difficult task of putting together an internally acceptable reform of its institutions. Time is of the essence. The quicker the Cypriots and Maltese move to ready themselves, the more likely they are to win full EU membership. However, any delay, particularly if it allows the probable applicant states in central and eastern Europe to jump the queue (as the EFTAns did), may consign the Cypriot and Maltese membership bids to history and compel them to accept some form of associate or lower-tier EU membership.

Notes

1. Attributed to Alfred Tovias and quoted in Pomfret, R. (1989) *The European Community: Three Issues*, Malta: European Documentation Centre and the Chamber of Commerce, p. 12.

2. Commission of the ECs (1982) *Communication from the Commission to the Council of Ministers: A Mediterranean Policy for the Enlarged Community*, Brussels.
3. Commission of the ECs (1990) *Communication from the Commission to the Council: Redirecting the Community's Mediterranean Policy*, Brussels.
4. Independent critiques of the EC's Mediterranean policy are provided by Tovias, A. (1977) *Tariff Preferences in Mediterranean Diplomacy*, London, Macmillan; Pomfret, R. and Tovias, A. (1980) 'The Global Mediterranean Policy of the EEC' in Giersch, H. (ed.), *The Economic Integration of Israel in the EEC*, Mohr, Tubingen; Pomfret, R. (1986) *The Mediterranean Policy of the European Community*, Macmillan, London; Pomfret, R. (1992) 'The European Community's Relations with the Mediterranean Countries' in Redmond, J (ed.), *The External Relations of the European Community*, London, Macmillan; and Redmond, J. (1993) *The Next Mediterranean Enlargement of the European Community*, Aldershot: Dartmouth. Self-criticism is provided by Commission of the ECs (1982) 'The Community and the countries and regions of the Mediterranean', *European File* 19/82, and Economic and Social Committee (of the EU) (1990) 'Opinion on the Mediterranean Policy of the European Community', *Official Journal of the ECs*, vol. 33, no. C168, 10 July.
5. A useful summary of this development is provided by Pomfret in Redmond (1992), op. cit., pp. 86-8.
6. Gsänger, H. (1980) 'The EEC and Cyprus and Turkey' in Seers, D. and Vaitsos, C. (eds) *Integration and Uneven Development*, London: Macmillan p. 280.
7. Republic of Cyprus (1982) *The Association Agreement Between the Republic of Cyprus and the European Economic Community*, Nicosia: Press and Information Office, p. 6.
8. See Redmond, J. (1993) op. cit., pp. 67-8.
9. Tsardanidis, C. (1984) 'The EC-Cyprus Association Agreement: Ten Years of a Troubled Relationship, 1973-83', *Journal of Common Market Studies*, vol. XXII, no. 4, p. 359.
10. Reported in *Agence Europe* (1993) no. 5932, 4 March, p. 4. See also a speech of the previous president (Vassiliou), reproduced in *Cyprus News* (1990) no. 12, May, p. 3.
11. *New Cyprus* (1989) vol. V, no. 3, April, p. 16.
12. Ibid.
13. The Republic of Malta actually consists of three inhabited islands, these being from the largest to the smallest, Malta, Gozo and Comino.
14. The Maltese government's arguments in favour of EU membership are presented in Malta's Department of Information (1990) *Report by the EC Directorate to the Prime Minister and Minister of Foreign Affairs regarding Malta's membership of the European Community* (Valetta: Government of Malta). The disadvantages of joining the EU are highlighted in Malta Labour Party (1990) *Malta and the EEC: Economic and Social Aspects* (Valetta: Information Department). The two sides' arguments are summarised in Redmond (1993) op. cit., pp. 101-6.
15. In the last five elections, the Nationalist/Labour percentage share of the vote has been 48.0/50.8 in 1971, 48.5/51.5 in 1976, 50.9/49.1 in 1981, 50.9/48.9 in 1987 and 51.8/46.5 in 1992. The missing numbers in 1971, 1987 and 1992 are explained by (rare) votes for minor parties, notably, in 1992, Alternativa Demokratika, a new environmental pressure group. In all cases, the party with the most votes has formed the government with the exception of 1981 when the vagaries of the electoral system led the Labour Party to get more seats and, hence, to cling to power. Predictably, this caused outrage and the Maltese constitution was changed as part of a pre-election deal in 1987 (which also enshrined neutrality within the constitution) so that a party with more than 50 per cent of the votes would always form the government, by coopting sufficient additional members to form a majority if necessary. In fact, this was actually necessary in 1987 when the Nationalists, victorious in terms of votes cast, had to coopt three members to give them a majority of one.
16. Quoted in Malta Labour Party (1990) op. cit., p. 209. This is strikingly reminiscent of the British Labour Party's promise to 'renegotiate' British accession, if elected to government, when Britain joined in 1973.
17. European Parliament (1988), *Report on Malta and Its Relationship With the European Community* (Prag Report), PE 116.319/fin., Brussels, p. 18.
18. See, for example, Malta's Department of Information (1990), op. cit., p. 155 and Pace, R. (1987) 'A second class membership of the EC for Malta?', *Sunday Times* (of Malta), 13 December, p. 16.
19. Malta's industrial sector accounts for over 90 per cent of exports and approximately 30 per cent of GDP and of employment.
20. Malta Federation of Industry (1991) *The Effect of EC Membership on Industry in Malta*, (prepared by) Coopers and Lybrand Europe, Floriana, p. 22.

21. Nearly 50 per cent of output is produced by just seven sectors: clothing, construction, electronics, furniture, printing, tobacco and shipbuilding (Malta Federation of Industry [1991] *The Prospects for Industry in Malta in a Post 1992 Europe*, Valetta: Crest Publicity Ltd, p. 15).

22. See Redmond, J. (1993) 'Another Southern Enlargement: The European Community's Relations with Malta, Cyprus and Turkey?' *Bank of Valetta (Malta) Review*, no. 7, p. 32.

23. Malta Federation of Industry (1991) op. cit. (*The Prospects for Industry*.), p. 47.

24. Indeed, this very argument is used by the Maltese government. See Malta's Department of Information (1990) op. cit., p. 232-3.

25. European Parliament (1988) op. cit., p. 14 quotes the Maltese (Nationalist) Prime Minister as saying 'Malta has not adopted, in the technical sense of international law, a status of permanent neutrality'.

26. Malta's Department of Information (1990) op. cit., p. 153, quotes extensively from the constitution to make this point.

27. Mallia in Pomfret (1989) op. cit., p. 32.

28. *Agence Europe* (1992) 'The Community's Enlargement: the Benelux Memorandum submitted to the European Council of Lisbon', European Documents, no. 1789, 27 June.

29. This section of the chapter and the final concluding one draw on interviews conducted with officials in the European Commission and European Parliament in late November 1993.

30. Commission of the ECs (1993) *Commission Opinion on the Application by the Republic of Cyprus for Membership*, COM(93) 313 final, Brussels, 30 June.

31. Reported in *Agence Europe* (1993) no. 5903, 22 January, p. 13.

32. Commission of the ECs (1993) *Opinion on Malta's Application for Membership*, Bulletin of the ECs, Supplement 4/93.

33. *Agence Europe* (1993) no. 6078, 4/5 October, p. 7.

34. Reported in *Agence Europe* (1993) no. 6025, 19/20 July, p. 8.

35. Commission of the ECs (1993) op. cit., paragraph 51.

Part 4

Central and Eastern Europe

Part 4

Central and Eastern Europe

8 The EU and Romania and Bulgaria: Stuck between Visegrad and Minsk

Tony Verheijen

If one looks at the relative positions of the different candidate members of the EU, the situation of Bulgaria and Romania is particularly unclear. There seems to be a consensus among EU members that the Visegrad countries are among the next in line, after the candidates from EFTA. It is also becoming increasingly clear that membership for the republics of the former Soviet Union and Albania is not an issue for discussion. Regardless of the outcome of the Copenhagen summit, during which the EU confirmed that all associated countries, including Bulgaria and Romania, can, in principle, become EU members, opinions still differ on whether Bulgaria and Romania will finally be able to join the EU. One could therefore say that Bulgaria and Romania are, in a sense, stuck between Visegrad and Minsk as regards the likelihood that their ambitions for EU membership will be fulfilled.[1] The treatment of Bulgaria and Romania as a 'group' is one proof of the hesitant attitude of the EU towards the two countries. It also shows that the EU does not know the countries very well. In the first six months after the change in regimes, developments in the two countries were more or less comparable, but from the end of 1990, the two countries have chosen different roads towards the establishment of a democratic political system and a market economy. If one follows the logic of EU policy towards central and eastern Europe, this should lead to a difference in treatment of the two countries, while in reality the EU treats them as a bloc.

Bulgaria has, to a large extent, followed the example of Poland in trying to apply shock therapy for economic reform. Bulgaria tried hard to make up for lost time, especially between November 1991 and October

151

1992. Even though, during the last few months, the reform process has slowed down, Bulgaria generally follows the same type of reform strategy as the Visegrad countries, albeit with a one-year delay. According to the 'logic' of EU policy towards central and eastern Europe, Bulgaria should therefore not be treated much different from the Visegrad group.

Romania has followed a different type of reform process. Its way of dealing with economic and political reform is hard to classify. In no other country have reformist ex-Communists managed to win two free elections. There have been violent disturbances of the political and economic reform process which have it made clear that applying shock therapy is not a feasible solution. Therefore, the Romanian road to a market economy can be expected to be longer than for the other five countries. Two other differences between Romania and Bulgaria, as regards their relations with the EU, are found in their historical contacts with the EU. Bulgaria was a faithful follower of official CMEA[2] policy towards the EU, therefore contacts with the EU were hardly developed before 1988. In addition, relations with Greece, Bulgaria's traditional supporter, have cooled considerably because of the Macedonian question. Romania has developed individual contacts with the EU since the middle of the 1970s, and has a special relationship with France which often pleads the Romanian case within the EU.

Some explanations can be given as to why Romania and Bulgaria are treated as one group and why they are seen as being fundamentally different to the Visegrad group:

- The geographical proximity of the central European countries is one reason. Poland, Hungary and the Czech and Slovak republics are much better known than Bulgaria and Rumania. Bulgaria has been isolated for a long time because of occupation by the Ottoman Empire. The border between Croatia and Serbia was historically seen as the dividing line between the civilised world of western/central Europe and the 'barbaric' Ottoman Empire.[3] Psychologically, Poland, Hungary and the Czech and Slovak republics are considered to be close, while Romania and Bulgaria are seen as being far away.

- All three central European countries have a historical tradition of dissident movements under the Communist regimes. They were well known in western Europe, and their leaders made good use of their reputation when they finally came to power. The brutality of the totalitarian regimes in Romania and Bulgaria, combined with the limited interest of western Europe, which deprived possible dissidents of moral support, hardly permitted any opposition. The new political forces in those two countries needed support from the West more urgently, but did not get it.

The treatment of Bulgaria and Romania as a separate group whose fate is unclear has become a political fact. Regardless of the hesitant position of the EU towards Bulgaria and Romania, it is still important to assess their chances of becoming members of the EU. After the Visegrad Four they are, the most serious eastern European candidates for membership. Neglect by the EU could cause serious internal problems for the new political elite in Bulgaria and strengthen the conservative element of the governing party in Romania. Turmoil in one or two more Balkan countries will have a negative effect on the development of the EU itself.

This chapter will try to make an assessment of the chances for further development of EU-Bulgarian and EU-Romanian relations. First, it will examine the history of EU relations with both countries and the possible effect historical links can have on current developments. Second, there will be a short description of the trade and cooperation agreements and current EU assistance and the complicated negotiation process for the new association agreements will be analysed. In the last part, an attempt will be made to estimate the likelihood of Bulgaria and Romania becoming EU members in the near future, on the basis of an assessment of the progress in economic and political reform.

History of EU Relations with Bulgaria and Romania

In the past, Bulgaria and Romania have had a very different type of relationship with the EU. Bulgaria has faithfully followed the official eastern bloc policy, whereas Romania has played the role of the dissident, first in a positive, and later in a negative, sense.

Bulgaria: The Most Faithful Follower of the Soviet Doctrine

As a result of its faithful attitude towards the Soviet Union, Bulgaria has often been called 'the 16th republic of the Soviet Union'. The friendly attitude of Bulgaria towards the Soviet Union can only be understood from a historical perspective. Bulgaria owes its independence, to a large extent, to Russian assistance in the war of liberation against the Ottoman Empire. Other eastern Europe countries often had a negative historical experience with Russia and the Soviet Union. During the Cold War, Bulgaria followed the official CMEA policy, which meant that relations with the EU could not be established because of the EU-CMEA conflict. A brief analysis of the EU-CMEA conflict will make it clear why this was so.

The history of formal relations between the EU and the countries of central and eastern Europe is very short. It only started in June 1988.[4] The history of informal relations is a lot longer. The non-existent relations between the EU and CMEA did not cause a lot of problems until the 1970s. Problems started to emerge when the competencies and the number of members of the EU started growing. This growth was not balanced by a similar process in eastern Europe. The Soviet Union tried to extend the powers of CMEA, in order to give it a more supranational character. But the principle of unanimous decision-making blocked these attempts.[5]

The CMEA ignored the divergence between its development and that of the EU and wanted to negotiate with the latter on an equal basis.[6] The EU was not willing to accept this position. The CMEA had the possibility of concluding cooperation agreements, but all countries had to approve these agreements individually.[7] This meant that such competence was no different to the individual competencies of the member states. The EU has had its own unique competencies in the area of trade relations after the common commercial policy came into force. The EU wanted an agreement with CMEA in general fields of interest (like statistical harmonisation, etc.), and specific trade agreements with the individual countries.[8]

Moreover, the CMEA countries knew that even if they signed an agreement with the EU, this would not bring them many advantages. The CMEA countries fell under the restrictive trade regime established for state trading countries. The CMEA countries did not envisage changing their economic structure and knew that the largest part of trade restrictions would still be imposed. Reaching an agreement with the EU would not have changed their status of state trading countries. Only after the change in the Soviet Union's foreign policy doctrine, in 1985, was the CMEA prepared to negotiate on the basis of the parallel approach[9] proposed by the EU. Finally, this resulted in the common declaration of the EU and CMEA in June 1988.[10]

Only two specific issues concerning EU-Bulgarian relations are worth mentioning as regards this period. After 1985, most small European CMEA members started bilateral talks with the EU, aiming to conclude sectoral agreements. The new Soviet foreign policy doctrine allowed individual countries to start developing their own relations with western Europe. Bulgaria concluded an agreement on trade in textiles in December 1986.[11] By concluding this agreement, Bulgaria obtained the same treatment which applied to non-CMEA state trading countries after January 1975. The main effect of this agreement was a more flexible application of the quantitative restrictions and the setting up of a procedure to deal with perceived irregularities in the textile trade. Secondly, Bulgaria, like the other CMEA countries, had already recognised the authority of the European Commission *de facto* by conducting negotiations on the voluntary restraints of exports of goat and sheep meat.[12]

The lack of relations between Bulgaria and the EU in the past had a negative impact on current developments. There is little knowledge about the EU in Bulgaria, which puts the country in a disadvantaged position in its negotiations. This is one of the explanations for the lack of 'self-marketing' of Bulgaria in recent years. One of the reasons why Bulgarian foreign policy was, until recently, aimed more at the USA was a clear lack of information about what could be obtained from the EU. The lack of historical relations is, to a large extent, to blame for this situation.

Romania: The 'Traditional Dissident' in the East European Bloc

Romania is the only country which does not fit the general description of EU-eastern European relations. Romania has always been opposed to a lot of the ideas underlying CMEA cooperation. It never agreed to the role it was given in the division of labour, which was supposed to be set-up among CMEA member states.[13] Romania also declared its non-interest in or put its veto to any arrangement concerning an extension of the competencies of the CMEA, and did not agree with the CMEA policy towards the EU. Romania wanted to be able to negotiate its own trade agreement with the EU and did not want to be subject to CMEA discipline. After the EU's common trade policy came into force in 1974, Romania started to defy CMEA policy openly by looking for its own way to build up relations with the EU.

A separate agreement on trade in industrial products with the EU was concluded in 1980,[14] following limited sectoral agreements on textile and steel in 1978.[15] The 1980 agreement only dealt with commercial issues and the establishment of the institutional structure to manage the agreement. Issues concerning economic cooperation were not mentioned in this agreement. In the agreement, it was foreseen that the restrictions imposed on Romania as a state trading country would be brought back to such a level that they would no longer be in contradiction to Romania's Accession Protocol to GATT. Also, the EU was to suspend quantitative restrictions on certain industrial products and to loosen quotas for those Romanian products which fell under quantitative restrictions. A safeguard clause procedure was set and some limited trade promotion measures were announced. The most important effect of the agreement was that Romania was officially recognised as a developing country[16] and could, therefore, benefit from the GSP before 1990, the only eastern European country to do so. This agreement, even though limited in scope[17], gave Romania a competitive advantage over the other CMEA countries as far as trade with the EU was concerned. In other important areas like textiles, steel and agriculture, Romania concluded similar agreements to the ones concluded by the other CMEA countries.[18]

The initial advantage Romania had over the other countries since 1980 was almost eliminated by the EU measures against Romania at the end of the 1980s. Romania's negative human rights record led to the suspension of negotiations on the renewal of the 1980 trade agreement and to a non-ratification of the textiles agreement, which was only provisionally applied until the end of 1989. Nevertheless, even though relations between the EU and Romania stood at a very low level during the exact period that the other CMEA countries started to build-up their contacts, Romania still profits from its former status and experience. The EU as an organisation is better known in Romania and there is more experience in how to deal with it. This experience in dealing with the EU gave Romania an advantage over Bulgaria during the recent association negotiations.

From Trade and Cooperation Agreements to Association: A Difficult Process

At this point, it is useful to examine the content of the Trade and Cooperation Agreements between the EU and Bulgaria and Romania and the achievements of the PHARE programme, the main financial assistance programme for the central and eastern European countries. A discussion of this programme is relevant because, in the Association Agreements PHARE was supposed to continue to be the main framework through which financial assistance will be organised.[19] The coordination of aid between the EU and other multilateral organisations was also supposed to continue.[20] The negotiations for an Association Agreement with Romania and Bulgaria were concluded in November and December 1992, respectively. The trade provisions of the association agreements were put down in interim agreements which came into force earlier.

The Trade and Cooperation Agreements With Bulgaria and Romania: The Main Features

Trade agreements have been used in the past to express the support of western European countries for the reform process in central and eastern Europe. The TCAs served as a symbol of western support for the group of reform-oriented countries against the Soviet Union. Economic issues were only given any importance after the failure of the autumn coup in the Soviet Union in 1992, after which they became the main point for the negotiations on the Association Agreements. In this section, only limited attention will be paid to the content of the Trade and Cooperation Agreements. However, it is necessary to look at them briefly in order to discover what were the main issues left to be covered by the Association Agreement.

The three areas which are covered by the Agreements are trade and commercial cooperation, economic cooperation and the establishment of joint committees.

Trade and Commercial Cooperation

The main items concerning trade and commercial cooperation with the eligible countries were standard issues like:

- simplification of customs procedures and documentation;
- mutual accordance of the highest degree of trade liberalisation, with the standard exception of: steel and coal, textiles[21] and agricultural products.[22]

As regards abolition of quantitative restrictions, a distinction is made between general quantitative restrictions and specific quantitative restrictions (meaning: restrictions only applicable to state trading countries).[23] Under the TCAs, general quantitative restrictions were suspended for all countries. If the suspension of these quantitative restrictions caused problems within the EU, the restrictions could be reintroduced.[24] Specific quantitative restrictions would be abolished in the first few years after the Agreements entered into force. Under the trade provisions of the Association Agreements, the reintroduction of restrictions is no longer possible; the EU has, however, introduced safeguard clauses instead.

The abolition of tariffs is carried out in a non-reciprocal way. The EU would minimise its tariffs in five years for products covered in the

Agreements, while reciprocity would only have to be granted in ten years. The EU applies the GSP to the countries of central and eastern Europe for five years, although wages and capacity are bound to rise above the maximum level set for applying this status before the end of this period.[25] During these five years the countries of central and eastern Europe should start the process of granting the EU their most-favoured-nation tariffs.[26]

When the trade agreements were signed, Bulgaria and Romania were still seen as 'uncertain cases'.[27] This can be seen if we compare their TCAs to those concluded with the Visegrad countries. Later, most of the differences were eliminated.

Economic Cooperation

The aim of the provisions for economic cooperation is to reinforce and diversify the economic links between the EU and the central and eastern European countries. The different instruments which can be used to achieve this are listed in the Trade and Cooperation Agreements.[28]

Even though the provisions concerning economic cooperation contain little more than standard instruments, they are still important, especially for Bulgaria. Except for trade with Greece, which continued to be significant during the Communist period, Bulgaria had relatively little economic contact with western Europe and therefore needed ways to promote its economy.

Establishment of Joint Committees, Institutionalisation of Economic Contacts

The Joint Committees take care of the continuity and further development of the TCAs.[29] Furthermore, they serve, among others, as an exchange mechanism for information on legal changes affecting trade.

Further Development of the Trade Agreements: Points to Be Taken into Consideration While Negotiating the Economic Provisions of the Association Agreements

The TCAs had a limited scope and served as a political gesture towards central and eastern Europe. For several sensitive economic issues, especially for agricultural products, few provisions were made. These and the following technical issues have caused serious problems during the negotiations on Association Agreements with Bulgaria and Romania.

A first problem is the application of the principle of rules of origin. Normally the EU only treats products as originating from a certain country if they do not contain more than a certain percentage of elements originating from other countries (40 per cent). This conflicts with a different principle of the EU, stating that the trade potential of the countries of central and eastern Europe should be able to develop without too many hindrances, taking into account the old trade structure. This old trade structure will lead to violations of the rules of origin because of existing horizontal ties between the former CMEA countries. A solution could be to define 'local content' as central and eastern European content, including the European CIS countries. Until now, no such provisions have been made; cumulation of origin is only possible between the Visegrad countries and between Bulgaria and Romania.

A second problem is that many products originating in the countries of central and eastern Europe do not meet certain EU technical standards. They will have to conform to the minimum quality regulations set by the EU, regulations which they did and will not influence. Producers in the countries of central and eastern Europe need to be supplied with detailed information about technical standards to help them get access to the EU market.

A third problem is connected to the reciprocity which is expected in the field of competition. Government intervention in the former CMEA countries is no longer as intensive as it was under the centrally guided system. However, during the transition period the Government will keep on playing an important role in trying to avoid complete disorder in the economic structure. If the EU makes full use of the possibility to use anti-competitive government intervention as a motive for imposing trade sanctions, the establishment of a free trade area will, in fact, be a false undertaking.

Anti-competitive government intervention is also closely associated with the last problem: how to deal with dumping practices. Central and eastern European countries are not likely to qualify as market economies in the next few years. Therefore, the risk of anti-dumping measures being imposed on them is likely to remain. It has been suggested that those countries should be excluded from the category of non-market countries to give more explicit support to the development of their trading potential. A new category would be created which would lay down clear guidelines under which conditions anti-dumping measures could be taken. In this case, a more transparent anti-dumping procedure would come into being, based on a clear set of rules. Only when a violation of rules occurred would an anti-dumping procedure be started. At the moment, an arbitration procedure is being envisaged. The anti-dumping measures of the EU have not always been applied consistently.[30] The fear of central and eastern European countries of new, non-transparent, anti-dumping actions against them is understandable.

The PHARE Programme: A Framework for Financial Assistance, Now and in the Future

The PHARE programme was proposed by the G7 in July 1989 to support developments towards democracy and market economy in Poland and Hungary. Later, it was extended to Czechoslovakia, Bulgaria, Yugoslavia and Romania,[31] and, since 1 January 1992, to the Baltic States and Albania. The programme has been in operation since January 1990. Many difficulties have arisen during the implementation of the programme. There are three main reasons for this:

- the limited amount of financial resources available;
- the coordination problems caused by a lack of information about the member states' bilateral activities;
- the difficult decision-making procedure concerning the allocation of money to projects.

First, even though the amount of financial resources available seems at first glance to be reasonable (approximately 1 billion ecu for 10 countries in 1992), it is in fact very limited in relation to the real needs of the central and eastern European countries.[32] In addition, a specific financial problem concerning the PHARE programme should be stressed. The 12 non-EU countries of the G24 are supposed to bear 50 per cent of the expenses of the PHARE operation. If the European Commission decides to finance an action in the framework of the PHARE programme, this action can still not take place unless the other 12 countries commit their half of the necessary funds, something which they often fail to do. This means that in too many cases either between 50 and 100 per cent of the finance is provided, or implementation of the action is delayed until full financing has been assured.

Second, the EU is confronted with a number of difficulties in carrying out the internal and external coordination of the support programme. It has problems convincing the member states to coordinate their bilateral programmes with the EU. The member states feel that, unlike in the case of Trade and Association Agreements, they do not have sufficient influence on decisions concerning the allocation of PHARE funds. The individual wishes of EU countries are already brought forward in the pre-negotiation phase of Trade and Association Agreements. The different views of member states are exchanged in advance, and discussed in the Council, before the mandate is given to the European Commission.[33] In the case of the PHARE programme, the Commission has greater autonomy to decide the allocation of funds. In negotiations on the 'Europe agreements', the differing interests are of a smaller influence than in the implementation of the PHARE programme; trade matters are the exclusive competence of the EU and, even though individual countries can exert pressure on the Council on specific issues, the final agreement is a mixture of preferences and compromises.[34] In the case of assistance programmes, EU member states have an alternative; they can act unilaterally.

The external coordination of EU assistance has created additional problems. The Commission is supposed to be supplied with information about other aid activities by multilateral organisations. In practice, the Commission receives either no information or only receives it when projects are already running, which makes the coordination task very complicated.

Third, the complex decision making mechanisms concerning internal decisions in the EU and decision-making within the eligible countries in relation to the PHARE projects, causes further problems. The eastern European countries have to define a priority list, first determining the amount of money allocated to each main field and later, in a separate decision-making procedure, defining the division within the fields. The countries are advised by the Commission on these matters. One minister is made responsible for the composition of the priority lists. This often leads to numerous problems and delays within the countries as political coalitions fight to get their projects on the priority list. To avoid the difficulties caused by making one minister responsible for the programme, a PHARE Committee is always established, existing of ministry representatives. The decision-making process concerning the programmes in this framework is not very transparent. To this confusing picture, add the often dominant attitude of the PHARE Task Force, which has its own view on how the funds should be spent, and often persuades its counterparts to deviate from the chosen priority list. As the EU has a final say over the budgets, this means that further delays appear (ministers have to go back to their Governments to rediscuss priority lists, etc.). The whole procedure for approval of individual projects can thus take up to 18 months.

The procedure has an advantage as eastern European Governments are forced to face the realities of the choice between priorities. This improves the decision-making capacity of these Governments. In the short run, the EU approach creates a number of problems but it could well have positive side-effects on the decision-making capacity of the respective Governments in the longer term.

The Court of Auditors has made a critical evaluation of the role of the European Commission in managing the PHARE programme, stating that it has not met the initial objectives of the programme and has made serious misjudgements about the needs of the eligible countries. The slow decision-making process and the lack of response to defined urgent needs were also criticised.[35] The Court of Auditors' report follows earlier criticism by the European Parliament. The Commission defends itself by saying that a programme like this cannot be expected to run smoothly within one or two years, but that everything is being done to improve its management.[36] In fact, the problems quoted above could have been expected if one takes into consideration the lack of knowledge of the Commission's own personnel concerning central and eastern Europe; this is attributable to the non-existent history of EU-central and eastern European relations.

The Negotiations for the Europe Agreements: A Complicated Process

The Europe Agreement negotiations with Bulgaria and Romania have turned out to be more complicated than expected. Before and during the negotiations, a number of issues hindered a successful conclusion. This is one further reason why Bulgaria and Romania are worried that the door to the EU might still be closed to them after the entry of the Visegrad countries, even though, officially, the EU has promised equal treatment to Bulgaria and Romania.[37] The following issues caused the delay in the conclusion of the association agreements:

- The Yugoslav crisis, and especially the Macedonian question, received almost all the attention of the General Affairs Council in the first months of 1992. Even though the prenegotiation phase for both countries had been concluded at the beginning of January 1992,[38] it took over four months for actual negotiations to start. One could argue that the Council of Ministers has taken a big risk. The new reformist Government in Bulgaria was especially in need of external support.[39] As a result of the EU attitude, the UDF lost credibility in Bulgaria as it had rightly expected the EU to support a UDF-led Government more clearly than a socialist Government.

The lack of understanding of this situation by the Council of Ministers proves once more the incompetence of most EU politicians in dealing with Balkan affairs. A further proof of this is the current EU attitude towards Bulgaria and Romania in the case of the embargo against Serbia and Montenegro. Instead of assisting the two countries in dealing with the negative economic consequences of the embargo, which causes serious problems, especially for the Bulgarian economy, the EU has only insisted that the two countries maintain the embargo strictly and has offered no compensation. In addition, the start date of the interim agreements has been delayed repeatedly because of internal EU problems over Commission competences in the field of trade policy. This has further negative effects on the economic situation in the two countries.

- After the conclusion of the agreements with the Visegrad countries the EU member states were very reluctant to give further trade concessions to eastern European countries. France, Spain and Portugal, in particular, feared further internal problems if sensitive products from more east European countries entered the EU market. The volume of the trade concessions was the subject of long and difficult debates in the Council of Ministers. Spain, especially, wanted to get explicit guarantees that no cheap steel would do further damage to its steel industry and that increased financial assistance to Bulgaria and Romania would not be given at the expense of financial assistance to Latin America.[40] France had reservations about agricultural products and Portugal about textiles. As a result of these problems, the mandate to the Commission was postponed several times and the Commission was given limited manoeuvring space during the negotiations.[41] The Bulgarian agreement was concluded so late mainly because of problems concerning trade in textiles, steel, agriculture and wine.

- The foreign ministers of the Visegrad countries have, in their joint meetings with the EU Council of Ministers, stressed that there should be preferential treatment for the Visegrad countries as a group.[42] They see the developing relations between the EU and Bulgaria and Romania as a threat to their privileged position and fear that they will be linked with Bulgaria and Romania as a group of six; Bulgaria and Romania would slow down the integration process with the EU, for the Visegrad Four. The EU has stated that it is considering dealing with the six countries together as regards political cooperation meetings, but it is not clear whether it will keep this position under increasing pressure from the Visegrad countries. If Bulgaria and Romania do not succeed to become connected, in some way, to the Visegrad countries, this could have a negative effect on the reform process in Bulgaria[43] and to a lesser extent in Romania.[44]

- Even though the Commission resisted the inclusion of a political conditionality clause in the Association Agreements with Bulgaria and Romania, the Council of Ministers still decided to make an issue of this.[45] The Association Agreements with the two Balkan countries, unlike the agreements with the Visegrad countries, will be conditional on their respect for democratic principles and human rights. Even though the EU argues that this is a result of new competencies it will acquire under the Maastricht Treaty, it is fully understandable that the inclusion of this clause caused a lot of irritation in Bulgaria and Romania.

In addition to these problems, Bulgaria and Romania's bids for EU membership are hindered by the weakness of their lobbying at the EU. Romania's position is partly caused by the perceived instability of the country. This makes possible western allies, in particular France, reluctant to lobby for the Romanian case. If Romania is able to solve its internal political and economic problems it could, however, profit from the experience of its past relations with the EU to lobby the different EU institutions effectively itself.

Bulgaria is more advanced in its political and economic reforms but lacks experience in dealing with the EU; historically Bulgaria had the least developed relations. This leaves Bulgaria in a weak position as regards the EU. The fact that Bulgaria has remained relatively stable during the political transition period has increased the country's credibility in EU circles. However, it remains unclear whether Bulgarian politicians will be able to convince the EU to treat Bulgaria on equal terms as the Visegrad Four.

The conclusions of the Edinburgh and Copenhagen summits do not provide a clear answer to the question as to whether EU policy towards Bulgaria and Romania is going be fundamentally different to that towards the Visegrad countries. In the conclusions of the Edinburgh summit, positive references are made to the development of political dialogue with the Visegrad countries. In general, however, the conclusions of both summits mention 'the associated countries' which seems to indicate that no decision has yet been taken on this issue.

Results of the Negotiations

For Bulgaria and Romania, the main short-term benefit of the Association Agreements is political. They represent a recognition of the reform efforts undertaken by the two countries. Possible future membership of the EU is referred to in the preamble of the Agreements.[46] This type of political recognition of the reform effort is probably as psychologically important as trade concessions.

The main substantive areas of the Agreements are similar to the ones covered by the Europe Agreements concluded earlier with the Visegrad countries:

- Political dialogue.
- Freedom of movement of goods, people, capital and services.
- Economic cooperation.
- Approximation of laws.
- Financial cooperation.
- Cultural cooperation.

Just like the agreements concluded with the three central European countries, the Agreements with Bulgaria and Romania are mixed. This is not only the case for political cooperation but also, for example, for provisions on the freedom of movement of workers. Provisions in this area will, for the next few years, remain dependent on bilateral agreements between individual EU member states and Bulgaria and Romania, in which quotas are defined concerning the amount of workers eligible for work permits. Further extension of the freedom of movement of workers is conditional on the economic and social development in the east European countries. For the parts of the Agreements for which the EU has exclusive competencies, interim agreements will be concluded which will enter into force before the Association Agreements are ratified by all EU member states.

The content of the Agreements in the six above-mentioned areas can be summarised as follows.

The chapter on political dialogue contains elements directly linked to the Association Agreement itself (monitoring the development and, if necessary, adaptation, of the agreements) and provisions which will lead to a more common approach to world matters. The EU intends to deal with the Visegrad countries as a group in carrying out political cooperation. Joint summit meetings have already been held between the EU Council of Ministers and the political leaders of the Visegrad countries. The EU has hinted that Bulgaria and Romania will be able to join the joint political cooperation meetings once all Association Agreements have been ratified. A three-layer structure will be established to deal with political cooperation: a ministerial level committee giving the guidelines, an Association committee of top civil servants acting in a similar fashion to COREPER for the Association Agreement and a parliamentary committee acting as a discussion forum.[47]

The achievement of freedom of movement of goods, people, services and capital is a long-term process, and has also been the issue causing the main negotiation problems. The economic situation of the countries should improve before the four freedoms can be realised. Most of the provisions for the liberalisation of trade in industrial products are an extension of the provisions included in the Trade and Cooperation Agreements. They are set up in a non-reciprocal way. The EU will open its markets for most industrial products in 4-5 years, whilst reciprocity will only be demanded in 9-10 years.[48] For trade in agricultural products, only limited concessions have so far been made. This is hardly acceptable to the eastern European countries as agricultural products are, with textiles, and in some cases coal and steel products, the best potential export earners. A more flexible attitude of the EU in all those sectors could be of real help to the central and eastern European countries. As has been said before, Bulgaria and Romania are getting more restricted access to the EU market than the Visegrad countries as far as sensitive products are concerned. In the case of wine exports, it was even necessary to conclude a separate agreement with Bulgaria, outside the Association Agreement.[49] During the Copenhagen summit, however, EU leaders committed themselves to speeding up the breaking down of trade barriers, including in sensitive areas.[50]

The other two freedoms will only be relevant in the long run. The EU should first concentrate on helping the countries to restructure their service sector, develop a capital market and stabilise their currencies. The PHARE programme and EIB loans will be the instruments to give this assistance. The provisions concerning economic cooperation will use the framework set in the Trade and Cooperation Agreements to help the eligible countries bring their economic structures up to world market standards. The concept of economic cooperation is widened in relation to the Trade and Cooperation Agreements. The part on approximation of laws covers many relevant areas. Without this approximation, progress in most of these areas would be impossible. The training of specialists in this field has already been made a priority in Poland and Hungary, but not yet in Romania and Bulgaria.

A main question concerning the Europe Agreements with Bulgaria and Romania is whether they will give both countries the possibility to catch up with the Visegrad countries. Even if they manage to narrow the gap with the Visegrad countries sufficiently, by speeding up reforms, it remains unclear whether the EU is really willing to keep its promise of similar treatment to that given to the Visegrad countries to Bulgaria and Romania and to face the consequences of this policy; the EU will be confronted with six membership applications, all based on similar agreements, which will make it more difficult to discriminate between one country and another.

The State of the Art in Economic and Political Reform in Bulgaria and Romania: A Sufficient Basis for Further Development of Relations with the EU?

The state of affairs concerning political and economic reform in Bulgaria and Romania is the main reason quoted for the current difference in treatment between the two Balkan countries and the Visegrad countries. As indicated in the introduction, this difference in treatment emerged after the outcome of the first general elections in central and eastern Europe became clear. Romania and to a lesser extent Bulgaria are still less advanced in political and economic reform. To analyse the possibility of EU membership, however, it is more relevant to make a comparison of the trend of political and economic development in the two countries than to just take a picture of the current situation.

Bulgaria: Isolated but still Making up for Lost Time

Bulgaria's desire to become an EU member is clear, and no major political force in the country opposes this policy.[51] Bulgaria still has the reputation of being a slow reformer because of the hesitant start to economic reform under the first, socialist, Government after the first free elections. Following the strikes which paralysed the country in the second half of 1990, the Government resigned and a technocratic interim Government was formed which had as its main tasks to start the economic reform process, to write a new constitution and to prepare for elections in the autumn.

The interim Government speeded up reform considerably in the first half of 1991.[52] Bulgaria applied shock therapy similar to that used by Poland, but it received much less support from international organisations. The economic starting point was worse than that of the other associated countries. The economic reform strategy could only be applied because of the change in the political composition of the Government in December

1990. The Socialist Party was not willing to take the unpopular measures connected with the austerity programme and a coalition Government, mostly composed of technocrats, had to do the job.

After the start of the reform programme in February 1991, little progress was made until the elections of October 1991. The attention of most politicians was focused on the development of the new constitution. This constitution was finally adopted in July 1991 after long debates between the UDF[53] and the BSP.[54] The approval by a majority of both parties was needed in order to obtain the two-thirds of the votes required for the adoption of the constitution. Differences in opinion on this issue finally led to a split in the UDF. Ironically, the group that opposed the constitution won the October 1991 elections which gave Bulgaria a polarised parliament in which the MRF[55] held the balance. The MRF initially gave full support to the UDF Government,[56] but withdrew this support at the end of October 1992 for three main reasons:

- the unwillingness of the UDF Government to develop industrial and social policy instruments to support economically depressed regions;
- the extremist attitude of the UDF to decommunisation;
- the problems concerning the military-industrial sector.

First, even though the UDF Government had passed most of the necessary legislation to back up the macro-economic stabilisation programme,[57] it had failed to develop the necessary policy instruments to provide a kind of safety net for the victims of the austerity programme and a development programme for depressed regions.

Priorities for economic development were set by the Ministry of Industry, but nothing was done to stimulate development; especially in economically depressed regions, some government policy to attract foreign investment should have emerged. The creation of free economic zones would be one of the ways for development. Without any stimulation policy, economically depressed regions are only likely to continue to deteriorate.

No social policy for retraining factory workers has been developed. Especially in regions which were to a large extent dependent on one industry, training programmes supplied by government are a necessity. The quality of the workforce, combined with relatively low wages, is one of Bulgaria's main competitive advantages. If the quality of the workforce is not improved, or at least preserved, this will clearly have a negative influence on development possibilities.

A lack of attention for the above-mentioned policy areas is the first reason for the political crisis of October 1992. Most ethnic Turks live in areas which are most affected by industrial and agricultural decline. The

MRF could no longer support an economic policy which mostly impacted on its own voters. The UDF was deaf to the demands of the MRF for more influence in economic policy.[58] Second, the extremism of the UDF, in dealing with decommunisation, threatened to split the country. The UDF even alienated its own former leader, President Zhelev, who repeatedly pressured the overnment to take a less radical position on this issue. Third, the continuous turmoil around the future of the military-industrial sector destabilised the Government internally.[59] Together, the three issues brought down the Government on 28 October 1992.

After the unsuccessful attempts of the UDF and the BSP to form a Government, the MRF proposed a Government composed mainly of technocrats. The UDF distanced itself from the proposed Government, but the majority of UDF parliamentarians abstained in the vote in parliament. A minority of UDF parliamentarians, the MRF and most of the BSP deputies voted in favour which resulted in an approval of the Government led by Ljuben Berov, President Zhelev's former economic adviser.

From January 1993, however, the UDF turned first against the Berov Government and later against President Zhelev. The UDF has used all possible means to force Berov, and later Zhelev, to resign. Apart from a brief period in June 1993,[60] the UDF has fought its battle with political means. Three consecutive attempts to oust the Government by means of a vote of no confidence failed. Because of the tough UDF position towards the Berov Government, several UDF parliamentarians left the movement and formed a centrist political faction. The Berov Government can now count on the support of this centrist faction, the MRF and the greater part of BSP deputies. Even the Prime Minister, however, expects that new elections will be held during 1994.

The difficult position of the Berov Government (unsure of the continuing support of parliament) has led to a slowing down of the economic reform process. In general, however, the economic situation is more or less stable, inflation is high but under control, the Bulgarian lev is remarkably stable, the limited privatisation programme has almost been completed and a settlement with Bulgaria's commercial creditors seems to be within reach.

Bulgaria suffers from its current geographic isolation because of the Yugoslav conflict. It can only try to attract positive attention by fulfilling political and economic reform criteria. It is up to the Berov Government to fulfil these criteria in the current fragile situation and to leave its successor a stable basis on which to build. This would boost Bulgaria's credibility both with the EU and with the Visegrad countries. Consequently, this could give Bulgaria similar opportunities to join the EU to the Visegrad countries. It will surely take a few more years for Bulgaria to reach the economic level of the Visegrad countries; this is logical if one looks at Bulgaria's starting position. Assuming the trend continues, the EU should give some assurance that Bulgaria will be next in line after the Visegrad countries, otherwise the EU will put at risk the fragile stability in what is still the most promising Balkan country.

Romania: Difficult to Define

Romania is the only country in the process of becoming associated with the EU where the desire for membership is still an issue. In two of the three largest Romanian political parties, the DNSF[61] and the NSF,[62] there are important forces opposing integration with Europe beyond association; and nationalist forces within parliament are also against Romania's association.[63] The former Romanian Government, which mostly comprised experts with limited party affiliations, had a clear pro-Europe policy, but the policy of the new Government is generally more cautious.

The EU's approach to Romania has been more hesitant than its policy towards other countries, and progress in EU-Romanian relations can, in the next few years, be expected to be slower than that with Bulgaria and the Visegrad countries. The main reason for the EU to start negotiations for association was to support reform-minded forces and not to alienate Romania.[64] Most of the progress in economic and political reform can be accredited to the Stolojan Government, which pulled Romania out of a situation of indecisiveness and internal division. His predecessor, Roman, had tried to start radical economic reform in the spring of 1991, but parliament and the President halted his reform policy; this led to a steady deterioration of the economic situation. Roman was made a scapegoat during the miners' uprising in September 1991, and had to step down. The conflict over the reform policy led, in the end, to a split in the NSF between liberal (led by Roman) and conservative forces (led by Iliescu).

The Stolojan Government had more manoeuvring space because of its limited political affiliations, and was expected to pave the way for a Government to be led by the Democratic Convention (DCR), Romania's democratic opposition. The Democratic Convention, however, failed to make use of the split in the NSF and lost the September 1992 general election, mainly because of gross tactical blunders.[65] After initial protests, the DCR finally acknowledged defeat. The DNSF and the NSF are not likely to try to halt political reform. The latest elections brought a relatively broad spectrum of political parties into parliament which will now have to start working on the basis of compromise.

Further progress in economic reform is however at stake. The largest political force in the new parliament, the DNSF, is known to be a supporter of a slower economic reform process to alleviate the situation for the population, and the new Prime Minister has already announced that he favours slowing down price liberalisation,[66] and he is likely to slow down other economic reforms. There had already been a considerable delay in Romania taking the necessary reform measures. The various Governments have not managed to bring inflation down to an acceptable level, while price liberalisation has not yet been completed. Most of the necessary framework legislation has been passed, but this is less liberal than the legislation in place in other countries. The starting position of Romania was, however, more favourable than Bulgaria's. Ceaucescu's policy of limiting dependence on foreign countries and institutions had the positive side-effect that Romania does not have a foreign debt burden, thus giving the country more manoeuvring space in defining economic and social policies. Romania is less dependent on the international financial institutions than Poland and Bulgaria and can therefore afford, to some extent, to define its own policies.

It is likely that Romania will continue its economic reform programme at its own pace, and that it will not let itself be overly influenced by pressure from international financial organisations. Romania's policy is aimed less at 'competition' with other countries in the region. There is a strong belief in finding its own solution to the current economic problems. In addition, Romania is not likely to give up part of its sovereignty as easily as Bulgaria and the Visegrad countries. This attitude is again likely to put Romania in a special position in eastern Europe and to make it even more difficult for the EU to define its policy towards Romania.

Conclusion: A Need for a different EU Policy Towards Bulgaria and Romania

Even though the EU persists in treating Bulgaria and Romania as one group there are in reality few reasons for doing this. As regards economic and political reform strategy, Bulgaria is much closer to Poland than to Romania. Bulgaria is still suffering from its late start, but can be expected to keep on following the pace of the Visegrad four, with a slight delay. In contrast, Romania has a reform strategy which is different from the other countries and which is likely to lead to a further delay in development. It would help Bulgaria's internal stability if the EU would end its differentiation between the Visegrad countries on the one hand and Bulgaria and Romania on the other. If Bulgaria continues to be placed in one category with Romania, it will not help reform-minded forces to persuade the population of the necessity for a tough reform policy. Romania will continue to follow its own economic reform strategy, a more gradual transformation of the economy with as much compensation as possible for the population. It is clear that Bulgaria could not afford this type of gradual transformation (the Government's options are limited because of the debt burden). More explicit EU support, including some kind of compensation for losses incurred due to the Yugoslav embargo, would help the Government convince the population of the need for tough policy measures.

It is not yet clear if EU membership will have the necessary political support in Romania. Romania's commitment to economic and political reform will have to be confirmed in the next four years. As long as the leading political party and the President remain hesitant about economic reform measures, the EU should not extend its policy towards Romania and should consider the Association Agreement a final stage, and make its implementation conditional on progress in economic reforms.

On balance, it appears probable that EU membership for Bulgaria not long after the Visegrad countries is a feasible option, considering the current developments. To say the same for Romania would not be realistic at the moment. There are indications that there is a trend towards a slowing down of the economic reform process in Romania. In this situation, the EU should revise the basic division it has made between the Visegrad countries on the one hand and the two Balkan countries on the other hand. Looking at the progress the two countries have made on the policy issues on which the EU normally bases its judgements, there are very few reasons why Bulgaria should be treated much differently from the Visegrad countries. Such reasons do exist in the case of Romania.

The European Parliament has been the first EU institution to make distinctions between Bulgaria and Romania after the conclusion of the Association Agreements. Reviewing the Agreements, the European Parliament did not impose further conditions on Bulgaria, even though the importance of the continuing respect for human rights was stressed. In the case of Romania, however, the European Parliament only wants to give its assent after the Romanian Government has given an adequate response to the European Parliament's request for clarifications on four main issues related to human rights guarantees and progress in economic reform.[67] Regardless of this distinction, the European Parliament did not call for a change in the policy of treating the two countries as one group.

Only by making a clear distinction between Bulgaria and Romania (as long as the two countries develop in such different ways) can the EU live up to the expectations it raised by promising Bulgaria and Romania equal treatment to that of the Visegrad countries. Bulgaria has clearly aimed at meeting the EU's requirements. Romania has given preference to an approach which brings less risk of domestic upheaval, but which does not meet EU requirements. It is now up to the EU to take this into consideration in the development of its policy towards Romania and Bulgaria after the conclusion of the Association Agreements.

Notes

1. The Visegrad Treaty established formal cooperative links between the then Czechoslovakia, Hungary and Poland; the Minsk Treaty formally established the Commonwealth of Independent States (CIS).
2. Council for Mutual Economic Assistance, better known as COMECON.
3. Poulton, H. (1991) *Balkans, States and Minorities in Conflict*, London.
4. *Official Journal of the ECs* (1988), L157/35, mutual recognition of EC and CMEA.
5. Bloed, A. (1978) *Comecon en Socialistische Economische Integratie*, The Hague, pp. 12-15.
6. Ibid, pp. 194-7.
7. For a review of the external competencies of the CMEA, see Bloed, A. (1988) *The External Relations of the CMEA*, Dordrecht, or Schiavone, G. (1981) *The Institutions of COMECON*, London.
8. Ibid.
9. Signing an agreement on procedural and organisational matters with the CMEA and substantive trade agreements with individual CMEA member states.
10. *Official Journal of the ECs* (1988), L157, p. 35.
11. *Official Journal of the ECs* (1987), L287, pp. 1-40.
12. *Official Journal of the ECs* (1982), L43, p. 12.
13. See Schiavone, G. (1981), op. cit., p. 9.
14. *Official Journal of the ECs* (1980), L352.
15. See Dijmarescu, E. (1989) 'Trade Relations between Romania and the EC', in Maresceau, M. (ed.) *The Political and Legal Framework of Trade Relations Between the EC and Eastern Europe*, Dordrecht, pp. 39-49.
16. See the preamble of the agreement on establishing a Joint Committee in *Official Journal of the ECs* (1980), L352.
17. Most of the exports of Romania were still in the non-liberalised category.
18. See *Official Journal of the ECs* (1981), L137 and (1987), L318.
19. See the association agreements with Bulgaria (Articles 99-103) and Romania (Articles 100-105).
20. Ibid.
21. In autumn 1991, the Bulgarian and Romanian textile quotas were increased with 8 per cent and 2 per cent respectively.
22. *Official Journal of the ECs* (1990), L 291 and (1991), L79.
23. Van Bael, I. and Bellis, J.-F. (1985) *International Trade Law and Practise of the European Communities*, Bicester, pp. 385-7.
24. Pinder, J. (1990) '1992 and Beyond', *International Spectator*, no. 3, pp. 172-83.
25. Supra 21.
26. Ibid.
27. Ratification of the trade agreements with Romania was blocked by the European Parliament for nine months after the democratic process was disturbed by the miners' intervention in Bucharest in June 1990.
28. *Official Journal of the ECs* (1990), L291 and (1991), L79.
29. Ibid.
30. Horovitz, D. (1991) 'The Impending Second Generation Agreements between the European Community and Eastern Europe - Some practical considerations', *Journal of World Trade*, March, pp. 55-80.
31. *Official Journal of the ECs* (1989), L 257/1.
32. For example, the cost of German unification far exceeds 50 billion ecus.
33. Brinkhorst, L. J. (1988) *Grondlijnen van Europees Recht*, Brussels, pp. 174-7.

34. Ibid.
35. *Agence Europe*, 22/23 June 1992.
36. *Agence Europe*, 24 June 1992.
37. *Agence Europe*, 13 May 1992 and 22 April 1992.
38. *Agence Europe*, 7 January 1992.
39. See *Reuters News Service*, 11 November 1991.
40. See *Agence Europe*, 22 April 1992.
41. *Reuters News Service*, 7 October 1992.
42. See *Reuters News Service*, 5 and 6 October 1992.
43. See *Reuters News Service*, 13 November 1991.
44. Romanian Foreign Minister Nastase already gave an explicit warning about what the consequence on further EU indifference towards Romania could lead to, see *Reuters News Service*, 11 November 1991.
45. *Reuters News Service*, 6 March 1992.
46. See COM(92) 511 final and COM(93) 45 final.
47. *Agence Europe*, Europe Documents, no. 1646/1647.
48. See, for more specific information, *Together in Europe*, 1 July 1993, pp. 3-4.
49. An agreement on reciprocal protection and control of wine appellation and reciprocal tariff concessions was reached in June 1993. Bulgaria was, in general, satisfied with the result of these negotiations (unlike in the case of agricultural concessions). For more detailed information see *Bulgarian Economic Review*, 2-15 July 1993, p. 3, and 21 May-3 June 1993, p. 3.
50. See, for more specific information, *Together in Europe*, 1 July 1993, pp. 3-4.
51. The BSP even has a strong pro-Europe faction.
52. For an analysis of expected and real effects of the shock therapy see, Wyzan, M. L. (1992) 'Bulgaria: Shock Therapy followed by Steep Recession', *RFE/RL Research Report*, 13 November.
53. Union of Democratic Forces: originally a platform for most anti-Communist forces, the UDF has increasingly become a right-wing party, opposing substantial government intervention in the economy.
54. Bulgarian Socialist Party, the 'reformed' Communist Party.
55. Movement for Rights and Freedoms, mainly representing the Turkish minority.
56. This is a logical consequence of the policy towards ethnic Turkish under the Communist governments. The Socialist party still has the 'Communist' image, even though it has carried out a rigorous internal reform.
57. See, for more information on this point, OECD (1992) *Bulgaria, an economic assessment*, Paris. The OECD has made a very positive assessment of the achievements of Bulgaria's first completely non-Communist government, especially concerning the very liberal type of economic legislation which it has developed.
58. See *The Insider, Bulgarian Digest Monthly*, 'DPS (=MRF) claims new role', p. 2, October 1992.
59. The problems around the military industry form a microcosm of almost all the current political and economic problems of Bulgaria. They were the subject of a study of the Erasmus University (Department of Industrial Economics), the Bulgarian Industrial Association and the European Institute of Public Administration in the framework of the ACE programme of the EU. The scientific report is available from DG XII of the Commission of the EU or from Erasmus University.
60. One parliamentarian went on hunger strike for several weeks; during this period the UDF tried to destabilise the situation in Sofia by blocking the centre of the city.
61. Democratic National Salvation Front, representing the conservative wing of the former National Salvation Front.
62. National Salvation Front, the remaining, reform-oriented wing of the former National Salvation Front which decided to keep the name.
63. See, for a more elaborate discussion of this issue, Shafir, M. (1992) 'Romania's Election Campaign, The Main Issues', *RFE/RL Research Report*, 11 September, p. 31..
64. This could have made Romania take a more friendly attitude to Serbia in the Yugoslav conflict.
65. See, for more information, Shafir, M. (1992) 'Romania's Elections, Why the Democratic Convention Lost', *RFE/RL Research report*, 30 October, pp. 1-7.
66. See *Reuters New Service*, 11 November 1992.
67. *Agence Europe*, 26/27 April 1993, pp. 13-14.

9 Conditions of Enlargement to Central Europe: Social Market Economy, Pluralist and Federal Democracy

John Pinder

Until 1989, Poland, Hungary and Czechoslovakia belonged to the Soviet-dominated Council for Mutual Economic Assistance (COMECON). The Soviet Union, viewing the EU as a rival, capitalist organisation, kept the central Europeans from making trade agreements with it; and the EU refused to make a trade agreement with COMECON, fearing it would merely reinforce the Soviet hegemony over these countries. Trade continued, despite the lack of formal trade agreements and the inconveniences of relations between such divergent systems. But the command economies of the Soviet bloc were poor trading partners for the EU. Their system inhibited the production and marketing of goods and services that would sell in the competitive western market economies; and the EU restricted the import of many of those products that the COMECON countries could sell, because of the unfair competition due to their arbitrary pricing systems. Trade remained at a fraction of the level that would be expected between the EU and neighbouring economies with market systems.

From 1989 onwards, as the central Europeans began the process of transformation to pluralist democracies and market economies, their relations with the EU were also transformed. The EU reacted rapidly by according them tariff advantages under the Generalised System of Preferences (GSP), removing many import quotas and launching, along with other western countries, the PHARE programme of aid for economic reconstruction. It then proceeded to conclude Europe Agreements with the central Europeans. But, although it quickly became clear that these countries were aiming beyond such agreements, to becoming full members of the EU, the EU was slow to welcome the prospect of their eventual accession. In the Europe Agreements, it did not go beyond 'recognising the fact', in the Preambles, that the associates' 'ultimate objective is to accede to the Community'. It was only towards the end of 1992 that the Commission proposed, in a Report to the European Council of heads of state and government, that the EU should adopt the goal of eventual membership for the central and eastern European associates,[1] followed in June 1993 by the decision of the European Council that those of them as so desire should become members as soon as they are 'able to assume the obligations of membership by satisfying the economic and political conditions required'.[2]

The Aim of Enlargement

There has been an element of particularist egotism about the EU's hesitancy. The enlargement to include Spain and Portugal was held up for several years while French farmers, who feared the new competition, were appeased by the French Government; and then the Iberians themselves, as well as the French, had similar motives for reluctance about the central Europeans. But there is also a more respectable motive. France and other member states set great store by the strength of the EU and its institutions and they fear that premature enlargement would sap this strength by undermining the institutions and the capacity for action. Fear that enlargement to central Europe would shift the balance of the EU eastwards, away from France, may also have contributed to President Mitterrand's initial reaction to the idea of such enlargement: that it would take 'decades and decades'.[3] This reaction was reflected in the Commission's proposal to the Council for the negotiation of the Europe Agreements, which stated that future membership was 'not among (their) objectives'.[4]

There was a warmer welcome from some other quarters. The British Government was seized with the idea of consolidating the central Europeans' escape from Communism and stabilising their democracies, and saw membership of the EU as a contribution to this. But others suspected, with some justification, that the British hoped, in this way, to prevent any movement of the EU towards a federal union, and indeed to reduce it to a kind of EFTA. Against this, many federalists held to the principle that the European Movement had already enunciated at its founding Congress in The Hague in 1948, that the 'Union or Federation should be open to all European nations democratically governed and which undertake to respect a Charter of Human Rights'.[5] This could be seen to serve the EU's interests in a number of ways. The reconciliation of France and Germany had demonstrated that membership of the EU was a guarantee of peace among the participants. Security should also be enhanced by the greater stability that membership should bring to the relations between its members and other states: Hungary and Romania could be cases in point if Hungary joined while Romania remained for a time outside. The problem of minorities such as the Hungarians in Slovakia could also be alleviated when minorities as well as majorities become subject to EU law and contained within the EU's wider political process. The addition of new market economies to the Union would, moreover, enlarge the single market and should provide an impulse towards further economic development. Politically, membership could be expected to bolster the stability of the new democracies, as it had done in the case of the southern enlargement.[6] The area over which interdependence is subject to effective management would be extended and the EU's weight in world politics and economics would be increased, with the addition of some 60 million central Europeans. All this would depend on the proviso that the EU's institutions and powers would be strong enough to contain the new members successfully, which for federalists would imply federal institutions with powers over security-related foreign policy as well as the economy. Such considerations doubtless influenced President Delors when he said in 1991 that the year 2000 was a realistic target for membership of these central Europeans.[7]

The argument of this paper is that present policies are far from adequate to ensure that either the central Europeans or the EU will be prepared for such an enlargement by that date. The central Europeans may not have sufficiently competitive market economies or stable democracies and the EU's institutions, powers and policies may not be up to the task of embracing an enlargement of this scale and character. What has been done so far leaves room for serious doubt in these respects.

The Europe Agreements

The Europe Agreements are the most advanced arrangements that the EU has so far devised for the central and eastern Europeans. The agreements were to be offered to 'those countries giving practical evidence of their commitment to the rule of law, respect for human rights, the establishment of multi-party systems, free and fair elections and economic liberalisation with a view to introducing market economies'.[8] These would, of course, also be conditions for membership of the EU; but in view of the EU's reservations at that time, they should doubtless be seen rather as conditions for the likely success of such a close association. Hungary, Poland and Czechoslovakia were selected as the first to measure up to the criteria (the latter agreement being subsequently split into one for the Czechs and one for the Slovaks). Bulgaria and Romania were next in line; and other Balkan and Baltic states will doubtless follow.

The backbone of each Agreement is the establishment of a free trade area between the EU and each associate. The EU was to remove its tariffs and quotas from imports from the associate progressively over a period of five years, with the exceptions of agricultural products, for which quotas were fixed, and textiles, for which the tariffs were to be removed in six years and the quotas over a period to be determined in the light of the results of the Uruguay Round. The associate was to reciprocate over a period of ten years. Both sides retain the right to impose safeguards, usually quotas, to restrict imports of a product should they cause, or threaten to cause, injury to domestic producers. The associate is to prepare to enter the single market by applying EU law on competition and state aid and by adopting single market legislation. While this is, with the critical exceptions of agriculture and textiles, a comprehensive and structured arrangement, it did not in the first two or three years offer much more than what all the central and eastern European countries had already obtained from the decisions taken by the EU in 1989 and 1990, when most quotas were removed and tariffs were widely suspended with the offer of the EU's GSP.[9] Over the medium-term, however, foreign investors should be attracted by the assurance of an open EU market for exports from the factories that they establish in central Europe, provided that they also have sufficient confidence in the health of the central European economies and polities.

The agreements also provide for the free movement of services and capital, for the right of establishment and for equal treatment for the small number of workers from the associates who are to be allowed to work in the EU. Beyond that, the agreements provide for what is called co-operation, and which is in fact help from the EU for the transformation that the associates are undergoing, including the formulating of legislation and market institutions required for the single market. Such cooperation lacks content, however, if not underpinned by financial resources; these come from the PHARE programme of aid for the central and eastern European countries, not as part of the Europe Agreements, although the associates have received the lion's share of the PHARE assistance. The PHARE funds are provided by the EU itself, its member states, the other twelve members of the Group of Twenty Four countries (G24, comprising the OECD industrialised states), and the European Bank for Reconstruction and

Development (EBRD), the European Investment Bank, the World Bank and the International Monetary Fund (IMF), with the EU and its member states being the principal source. Whether all these states and organisations provide enough to give the transformation a fair chance of success is considered later.

The agreements establish three main institutions for each of the four associates: an Association Council, comprising the relevant ministers from each side and the relevant Commissioners; an Association Committee comprising high officials; and a Parliamentary Association Committee, with members of parliament from the associate and from the European Parliament. 'Political dialogue' is envisaged on both domestic and external affairs. As a step towards cooperation among the four associates, their Foreign Ministers attended the first extended Association Council in October 1992; and a summit of all four, with the Presidents of the European Council and the Commission, was held at the same time. The associates raised the question of their future membership, pressing the EU to fix a date, which the latter declined to do.

The Europe Agreements did not offer the associates much more, in the short run and in practical terms, than the decisions that the EU took on trade (GSP and quota liberalisation) and aid (PHARE) in 1989-90. But they provide a framework that could be the basis for a good deal more. The Commission, in its Report to the European Council of December 1992, made a number of proposals to further liberalise the trade and generally strengthen the economic and political links;[10] and the European Council in June 1993 agreed to 'accelerate the Community's efforts to open up its markets' and to take other measures so that cooperation with the associates 'shall be geared to the objective of membership'.[11] What more may be needed? The answer depends on a judgement as to the conditions that have to be satisfied before the central Europeans enter the EU, and as to what must be done to ensure the fulfilment of those conditions.

Conditions for Central Europeans: Social Market Economy

Member states must have properly functioning market economies in order to take part in the EU's single market and to compete with businesses in the other member states. Thus the central Europeans have to complete a successful transformation from the central directive economies, under which prices, wages, production, investment and external economic relations were centrally controlled, enterprises were state-owned and politically directed, capital was allocated through the state budget and the laws required for markets to work were absent. All this must be replaced by new laws, institutions, skills, behaviour and physical structure of the economy: an enormous task, even where, as in Hungary and to a lesser extent Poland, significant changes in this direction had already been made under the previous regime.

Central to the efforts of transformation have been programmes for macro-economic stabilisation of the economies, including monetary control, containment of budget deficits, price liberalisation and steps towards currency convertibility.[12] The IMF has provided the central Europeans with financial support, on condition that they carry out agreed stabilisation programmes. Such programmes are a necessary basis for a successful transition to market economies. But these weak economic systems received severe shocks. Production and incomes fell by one-third between 1988 and 1992, including 10 per cent in the latter year, across central and eastern Europe as a whole; and although it could, by the end of that period, be said that the central Europeans showed 'signs of improvement', there were still 'widespread feelings of disappointment and anxiety about the future'.[13] Stronger terms, such as 'crisis of disillusion', have been used.[14] In these still fragile democracies, such a mood is a threat to the reform programmes, because the electorates may not allow them to be sustained. This threat to the economic transformation, and perhaps to democracy itself will remain until the citizens are confident that their economies are becoming dynamic enough to deliver some prosperity over the medium and longer-term. But such deep recessions, the likes of which have not been seen in the West since the early 1930s, create a poor climate for the investments essential for economic dynamism. So it is important to consider what can be done to encourage investment and entrepreneurial behaviour.

In addition to the macro-economic stabilisation, the central Europeans have programmes for removing enterprises from political control, particularly by privatisation, for weaning them from dependence on state subsidies and replacing it by access to a capital market, for cleaning the balance sheets of the banks so that they are not bogged down by bad debts and for enacting the legislation required for a market economy, including that for the EU's single market. The PHARE programme provides technical assistance of advice and training for the conduct of these reforms. But it does little to ensure that there will be enough investment and entrepreneurial drive to push the economies into healthy growth. It has been pertinently observed that the 'IMF model ... assumes away the key issues of what mechanism brings about the resumption of investment';[15] and a range of active policies have been suggested to stimulate growth.[16]

Removal of its trade barriers may be the most significant contribution that the EU can make to the regeneration of the central European economies. Their exports to the EU rose, after 1989, at rates that would double them in only three to four years. For Hungary, this amounted to an addition to GDP of 2-3 per cent a year, offsetting part of the loss from the fall of trade with the countries of the former Soviet bloc and from domestic deflation. But by 1993, this boom was checked by recession in the West and over-valuation of central European currencies, together with remaining restrictions on imports into the EU. If this source of growth is to continue, the EU will have to take very seriously the European Council's decision to accelerate the opening up of its markets.

The EU's open market is one of the keys to private foreign investment in central Europe. But even with complete liberalisation, this is not likely to come soon enough or, for some years ahead, massively enough to provide the dynamism that these economies need. There is also a strong case for a powerful push from public policy on the supply side. One element in this has to be the education and training to inject the managerial and technical skills required in a successful market economy. The PHARE assistance is helpful, but greater effort is needed. There is also useful assistance from PHARE to encourage small and medium enterprises through institutions to provide advice and small amounts of capital. But the economies will not revive until enough state enterprises have been restructured and privatised. For this, institutions of industrial banking, of the type practised in Germany, would seem to be the best instrument. The EBRD is intended to become such an institution, and it can make a significant contribution. But it is not enough. Its capital is 10 billion ecu, whereas it has been estimated that the total funds required for investment in central and eastern Europe, without the former Soviet Union for which the EBRD must also cater, would be not far short of 100 billion ecu a year for several years ahead.[17] Since much of this will be investment in infrastructure, which is suitable for financing from publicly provided capital, and since private investors may lack the confidence to make sufficient investments until a lead has been given by public authorities, there is a strong case for support from the EU and from other western countries to ensure investment on a more massive scale than hitherto contemplated. Private investors are understandably wary of the political and economic risks that they perceive. Yet the success of the central European economies, on which the success of their democracies may depend, is a public good of such significance for Europe as a whole, and the EU in particular, as to justify exceptional measures of public policy.

Private foreign investment on a large scale will be both a cause and a confirmation of success, because it is the most effective means of transferring managerial skills, technology and capital and ensuring access to international markets, and because it will take place only when shrewd judges of the prospects for viability are satisfied that the conditions for success exist. But whatever the scale of aid and the quality of the central Europeans' policies, regeneration of the economies may not come quickly. This leaves central Europe with a dangerously disturbed climate of opinion which could have highly undesirable consequences. The PHARE aid has come to the rescue with food and medical supplies in cases of extreme emergency. But it does little to relieve hardship of the less spectacular kind, which could nevertheless undermine the public support essential for carrying through the reforms. Here again, there is a strong case for western support for welfare payments to the unemployed and other hard cases on a scale that would ensure public support until the economies begin to turn vigorously upwards.

Thus it would seem wise to accompany the policies of stabilisation and marketisation with welfare provision and a push towards investment on a scale that would require assistance from the EU and the West as a whole, far beyond the scope of PHARE as it stands today. This would imply taking the policy concept further than has been done so far, beyond a neo-liberal minimum to that of a social market economy. The effort required of the EU might have to stand comparison with that of the Americans when they devoted over 1 per cent of their GDP to Marshall Aid over a period of four years.[18] To achieve this, the EU would have to enhance its financial power and its capacity to devise and carry out a common foreign policy to a scope that has eluded it up to now. It would also have to develop its paradigm of economic policy far beyond the neo-liberal consensus of the 1980s.

Conditions for Central Europeans: Pluralist Democracy

Member states of the EU have to be constitutional democracies, for quite practical reasons and because that is the political system of the existing member states. These reasons concern both main elements of constitutional democracy: the rule of law and representative government.

Member states must have independent courts that apply the law on the basis of fundamental rights. They must supply judges to the Court of Justice who will, without any shadow of doubt, work along these lines, but most of the cases under EU law are judged in the courts of member states, which refer to the Court of Justice only if they need guidance on the interpretation of the law. The EU could not work without mutual confidence in the integrity of the member states' judiciaries in upholding the rule of law.

There must also be effective representative government. The Council could not accept ministers who did not represent authentically democratic governments, or the laws it enacts would not carry the respect of the EU's citizens. Likewise the European Parliament could not accept members who had not been elected in free and fair elections. Not only do the ministers and members of parliament have to be democratically acceptable, but the Governments of member states must also attain a certain degree of effectiveness, as they are responsible for much of the execution of EU policy. They must, furthermore, appoint properly independent people to the Commission.

Western countries have taken it for granted that their constitutional democracies are supported by civil societies comprising multifarious autonomous institutions in the society, economy and polity. But the Communist regimes in central and eastern Europe sought to destroy the civil society in their countries; and in the economies and the polities, autonomous institutions remained largely suppressed until the changes of regime in 1989-90.[19] Without such institutions there can, of course, be no market economy; the market economy is indeed the economic manifestation of civil society. It is, moreover, a powerful and probably essential support for constitutional democracy; there do not appear to be any examples of such democracies that do not have the support of citizens who exercise the freedoms inherent in economic pluralism. The need for autonomous political institutions is more directly obvious. There are no constitutional democracies without autonomous political parties. Nor is it easy to envisage such a democracy without autonomous interest groups, media, and at least lively and active regional or local governments.

It seems unlikely, too, that constitutional democracies would be viable without a range of autonomous social, cultural and religious organisations. But here the central European civil societies experienced a certain revival from the 1970s, if not before, thus converting what had been totalitarian regimes into what could be called authoritarian ones.[20] While this has certainly made some contribution to the subsequent development of civil society in central Europe, the creation of the economic and political civil society remains an enormous task,[21] whose successful accomplishment is a condition of the consolidation of constitutional democracy. The need for what is sometimes called 'deep', or 'thick', democracy is the subject of some contemporary study.[22] Here we will confine ourselves to the more ordinary term of pluralist democracy, to denote constitutional democracy together with the civil society, including market economy, necessary to sustain it.

Without any active policy beyond the prospect that the new democracies may eventually become members, the EU is of help to the consolidation of their democracy. If the citizens wish to 'join Europe' by being accepted into the EU, they will know that they have to support the democratic system that is a condition of membership.[23] The business class in particular, which can be apprehensive about the results of democracy for the conduct, or even the existence, of their businesses, is both reassured by the EU's juridical framework which protects economic freedoms, and well aware that they will not be able to enter that framework unless their countries maintain a properly functioning democracy. So their support for democracy is assured.[24]

The EU also provides some active support for constitutional democracy and civil society. This can be done through training in the skills required for parliamentary staff, the judiciary and the civil service; and the EU and its member states offer some training of this kind, though it appears to fall short of what is needed. It is also possible, at least where the party systems bear some resemblance to those in western countries, to help the development of effective parties through assistance provided by party internationals and party foundations of the sort that exist in Germany. Such assistance, particularly from the Germans, played a significant part in the Iberian transition to democracy.[25] The EU could do more to stimulate and finance such assistance for the central Europeans and the same could apply to interest groups, particularly trade unions and employers organisations. Training for those who work in the media is equally important.

Whereas a great deal of thought and substantial resources have been put into the programmes of assistance for the transition to market economies, the same cannot be said of the transition to pluralist democracy. The latter is doubtless not amenable to the expenditure of resources on the same scale. But it is worthy of deeper thought and study than has been given to it so far, and of the allocation of more ample resources.

The EU needs, at the same time, to look to its own structure. The reluctance to take risks in accepting the central Europeans as members is a function, not only of their own difficulties in the economic and political transition, but also of the weaknesses in the EU's powers and institutions which give rise to fears that acceptance of the new members would undermine it. The strength of the polity of the Federal Republic of Germany enabled it to take on the daunting task of integrating the five new *Länder* without any prior association. It is legitimate to ask whether the EU could not strengthen itself in ways that would enable it, after a period of association that has enabled the central Europeans to make substantial progress with their transformation, to accept them before they have been able to demonstrate the complete solidity of their market economies and pluralist democracies.

Conditions for the EU: A Federal Reform

The impending enlargement to include EFTA countries may be accompanied by some adjustment of the EU institutions to ensure that they are not weakened by the increase in the number of member states in a system which remains, in many respects, intergovernmental; and such adjustments would shift the balance somewhat from the intergovernmental towards the federal. But these countries are solid pluralist democracies and market economies. They present the EU with nothing like the problems of accommodating the central Europeans.

One such problem is simply quantitative. A score or so of member states would strain the system of intergovernmental negotiation, perhaps to breaking point, so the case for strengthening the federal elements in the institutions would be reinforced.

Qualitatively, the diversity among member states will be intensified, causing difficulties for the working of any form of institutions, but particularly for intergovernmental ones, in which the divergences between national positions are accentuated. Among the features of diversity, the most acute will be the history of over half a century under Fascism and Communism in central Europe and the consequent difficult transition to competitive market economy and stable constitutional democracy based on a strong and responsible civil society. The EU should have the strength to contain countries that are likely still to be undergoing this process of transition, without impairing its capacity to decide and act; and it will need the instruments to help them to complete their transformation and thus take their place as member states without exceptional problems.

The suggestion of this chapter is that the EU will require, if it is to meet this challenge, federal institutions and some powers which it at present lacks.[26]

One such power would be fiscal. The EU's budget has already been transformed by the need to promote 'cohesion' with the less-developed economies of some members, to the extent that the proportion spent on agriculture will be reduced to less than half the total and that the structural funds, which are the main instrument for promoting cohesion, have greatly increased in importance. This can be seen as the beginnings of a 'public finance union', as it has been termed,[27] in which the function of redistribution from richer to poorer is a major element in the fiscal system.

In view of membership for the central Europeans, the EU's capacity for such redistribution would have to be considerably increased.

The EU's cohesion policy is not merely a transfer of money from rich to poor. The funds are used, instead, to promote economic and social development in the poorer regions with the aim of creating a dynamic that will, over time, rid them of their poverty. The PHARE programme can be seen in a similar light; and the more ample aid project considered above would take that concept to a higher level. Thus the EU will, if it wishes to prepare the path of the central Europeans towards membership in a really effective way, anticipate their entry with a larger provision of public funds, already requiring a larger budget. Given the problems of the economic transitions in central Europe, the EU's instruments for the promotion of investment and of structural adjustment would likewise have to be strengthened.

The implications of central Europe for the EU's economic powers and policies may be summarised in the proposition that the EU itself would have to move further towards a concept of social market economy, as defined above with respect to the central Europeans, with more emphasis on remedying the inadequacies of markets by promoting investment and adjustment and by helping the poor and weak - without of course going so far that market failures are outweighed by government failures. Another way of expressing the same idea is that the EU would have to move further from negative integration, which is confined to the elimination of barriers and other distortions affecting economic transactions across the borders between member states, towards positive integration, comprising common policies and laws to promote complementary welfare objectives.

Beyond the field of economics, the EU would, given the environmental disasters in parts of central Europe, have to strengthen its instruments of environmental policy. It should also consider some integration in the field of security and security-related foreign policy, beyond the intergovernmental arrangements of the Maastricht Treaty, in order to make sure that problems of interstate relations in central and eastern Europe do not destabilise the EU as a whole or give rise to international conflicts.

In order to use its powers effectively, the EU would also have to reform its institutions. The requirement of unanimity in the Council or, in plainer words, the scope for the veto, would have to be much reduced. It is hard to envisage the EU responding to the challenges that will surely arise in the future, if it requires the consent to many of its decisions of over a score of member states.

With reform of the system of voting in the Council would go greater scope for the Commission to execute EU laws and policies without detailed control by officials and ministers of all the member states. This is necessary if the executive function is not to grind to a halt. At the same time, democratic control over the Commission would have to be strengthened, which could be done by making it responsible to the European Parliament; and, with the reduction of the power of veto in the Council which has enabled the Ministers of individual member states and hence also their parliaments to exercise an ultimate control over the EU's decisions, the democratic control by the European Parliament over EU legislation would have to be enhanced. The Maastricht Treaty has pointed in these directions, but the principle of cohesion between Parliament and Council would have to be more fully applied.

In short, the argument of this chapter is that the EU will need federal institutions as well as somewhat greater powers. The alternative is at best stagnation, at worst disintegration.

Social Market Economy, Pluralist Democracy and Federal Democracy

After its initial positive response to the onset of reform in central Europe, the EU has performed less well in the task of helping the central Europeans to establish their market economies and pluralist democracies and of paving the way towards their eventual membership. The European Council in Edinburgh in December 1992 decided that in Copenhagen, in June 1993, they would set out, for eastern Europeans, a path towards membership, focusing on the central Europeans who are the subject of this paper. It is therefore urgent that they should grasp what will be required.

The EU should give the central Europeans enough help to ensure their successful transition to competitive market economies, not only through stabilisation programmes and the necessary legislative and institutional framework, but also by giving an impulse to dynamic development through speedier and more thorough trade liberalisation and the provision of more funds for infrastructure investment and structural adjustment, as well as for welfare support to ease the transition. The EU should also pay more attention to the ways in which pluralist democracy can be consolidated through strengthening the political and social, as well as the economic, elements of civil society. The intellectual basis for this is a development of the idea of social market economy and a deeper conception of pluralist democracy.

The EU has also to look to its own capacity to do what is required in ways that are both effective and democratically acceptable. This implies a federal reform of its already pre-federal institutions, in particular through co-decision by the European Parliament with the Council and responsibility of the Commission to the Parliament, together with a development of the EU's fiscal powers and of its ability to conduct a common foreign and security policy.

In sum, the EU needs a strategy for both widening and deepening, through a more thorough effort to help the central Europeans to achieve competitive social market economies and solid pluralist democracies, and a federal reform of its own institutions and powers to give it the capacity to perform effectively as a wider EU with more challenging tasks.

Notes

1. Report by the Commission to the European Council (11/12 December 1992) *Towards A Closer Association With The Countries Of Central And Eastern Europe*, Brussels: European Commission.
2. European Council in Copenhagen (21/22 June 1993) *Conclusions of the Presidency*, Brussels: European Commission.
3. *Der Spiegel*, 42/1991, 024.
4. Communication from the Commission to the Council and Parliament (27 August 1990 *Association Agreements With The Countries Of Central And Eastern Europe: A General Outline*, COM(90) final, Brussels: European Commission.
5 *Congress of Europe*, Resolutions, reprinted by European Movement (1988), Brussels.
6. See Pridham, G. (ed.) (1991) *Encouraging Democracy: International Context of Regime Transition in Southern Europe*, Leicester: Leicester University Press.
7. *Der Spiegel*, loc.cit. (no. 3, above).
8. European Commission, op. cit. (no. 2, above).
9. For EU policy up to 1991, see Pinder, J. (1991) *The European Community and Eastern Europe*, London: Pinter Publishers for Royal Institute of International Affairs.
10. Op. cit. (note 1, above).
11. Op. cit. (note 2, above).
12. For problems and policies regarding Hungary and Poland, see European Commission (1990) 'Economic Transformation in Hungary and Poland', *European Economy*, no. 43, March, Brussels.
13. Economic Commission for Europe (1992) *Bulletin for Europe*, December.
14. Rosati, D. K. (1992) *The Politics of Economic Reform in Central and Eastern Europe*, CEPR Occasional Paper No. 6, London: Centre for Economic Policy Research.
15. Dornbush, R. (1990) *From Stabilisation to Growth*, National Bureau for Economic Research Working Paper no. 3302, New York, cited in Laski, K. (1993) 'Transition from Command to Market Economies in Central and Eastern Europe: First Experiences and Questions', in Richter, S. (ed.) *The Transition from Command to Market Economies in East-Central Europe*, The Vienna Institute for Comparative Economic Studies Year Book IV, Boulder, Colorado: Westview Press, pp. 12-13.
16. See for example Portes, R. (1992) 'The European Community's Response to Eastern Europe', in *The Economic Consequences of the East* London: Centre for Economic Policy Research, pp. 11-12 and Richter (1993), op.cit. (note 11, above).
17. Centre for Economic Policy Research (1990) *Monitoring European Integration: The Impact of Eastern Europe*, London: CEPR, pp. 38-9.
18. See leading article, *Financial Times*, 28 December 1989.
19. See Rau, Z. (1987), 'Some Thoughts on Civil Society in Eastern Europe and the Lockean Contractarian Approach', *Political Studies*, vol. XXXV, December, and 'Introduction', in Rau, Z. (ed.) (1991) *The Reemergence of Civil Society in Eastern Europe and the Soviet Union*, Boulder, Colorado: Westview Press.
20. See Rau, Z. (1987), op. cit., p. 587.
21. See Pridham, G., Sandford, G. and Herring, E. (eds) (forthcoming) *Building Democracy?: The International Dimension of Democratisation in Eastern Europe*, Leicester: Leicester University Press.

22. For example, Held, D. (1992) 'Democracy: From City-states to a Cosmopolitan Order?', in Held, D. (ed.) *Prospects for Democracy,* Special Issue of *Political Studies.*
23. See Pridham, G. (1991), op. cit., particularly the chapter by Whitehead, L. 'Democracy by Convergence and Southern Europe'.
24. Ibid, p. 52.
25. Pridham, G. (1991), op. cit., pp. 239-42. See also Pinto-Duschinsky, M. (1991) 'Foreign Political Aid: the German political foundations and their US counterparts', *International Affairs*, vol. 67, no 1.
26. See Pinder, J. (1992) *The European Community after Maastricht: How Federal* Special Issue of *New European Quarterly Review*, vol. 5, no. 3.
27. Biehl, D. (1985) 'A Federalist Budgetary Strategy for European Union', *Policy Studies*, October.

Part 5

Conclusion

10 Conclusion

Most of the research and debate on the enlargement of the EU has so far focused on the specifics of the countries seeking to accede and, indeed, this book has sought to do precisely that, albeit in a more comprehensive and complete manner than previously published work. However, this procedure has reflected an incremental approach, where the EU was effectively a given variable which was only expected to be marginally affected by enlargement; the forces of change were mainly to be felt by the new member. This is no longer the case. The scale of the forthcoming enlargement, both quantitatively and qualitatively, is such that the EU must change. Moreover, the fact that it is also changing through internal pressures - the Maastricht Treaty - serves to reinforce the trend towards change. In Chapter 9 Pinder begins to address this issue and redress the balance when he not only considers the conditions (or changes) that the central Europeans must effect to be ready to join the EU, but also the conditions that must be met by the EU in order to be ready to receive them. This brief conclusion seeks to continue this train of thought. Specifically, it asks how is the EU likely, or indeed required, to adapt in the face of a potential doubling of its size in the next decade or so?

The question obviously has to be set in the context of the internal agenda and long-run objectives of the EU. This has all been set by the Maastricht Treaty. This, of course, opens up the old 'widening *versus* deepening' debate which now has to be addressed in a potentially acute form because of the unprecedented scale of both deepening and widening envisaged. The dilemma was recognised early in the current context and deepening was protected by not allowing widening, first before the completion of the internal market, second before the Delors II budgetary package (the 1993-99 financial perspective) was agreed and, finally, before the Maastricht Treaty was ratified. The latter requirement was, in fact, relaxed to allow negotiations with Austria, Sweden, Finland and Norway to begin early. However, the principle that deepening had to be secured before enlargement could take place had clearly been recognised.

The risks to deepening that widening may create are clear enough:

- Widening obviously makes decision making and therefore deepening more difficult, because it increases the number of members that have to reach agreement.
- The greater the number of members, the greater the diversity of the EU, the more difficult economic convergence and hence the achievement of economic and monetary union becomes.
- Negotiating the accession of new members ties up the EU and its institutions and reduces the time and energy available to focus on deepening.
- Obviously, there are also concerns about the impact of widening on particular policies. For example, the effect on the EU budget of admitting relatively poor countries from the Mediterranean and eastern and central Europe, and the impact on the EU's embryonic foreign and security policy of accepting neutral EFTAns.
- In an increasingly diverse EU, it becomes more and more difficult to be certain of the commitment of new members to deepening. More specifically, the decision of many EFTA members to seek EU membership represents a very sharp change of mind. This raises questions about whether their efforts to join the EU are based on a commitment to European integration, or an opportunistic assessment of their current options. Some prospective members may press for British/Danish style opt-outs once they have become full EU members.
- There is also a view that certain EU members, particularly Britain, which are characterised as adopting a minimalist stance to integration, support widening as a means of holding back deepening.

However, it is becoming increasingly apparent that the EU has little choice but to pursue widening and deepening simultaneously and to attempt to make them compatible. Not widening is not a costless option. The countries of EFTA have an undeniable geographical, historical and cultural right to be part of any European union and, more pragmatically, they are the EU's major trading partners and cannot be ignored. More fundamentally, the costs of failing to accept the countries of the former Soviet bloc are potentially enormous. There would be an economic cost, in the shape of lost markets. There would be a mass exodus of people from these countries into the members of the EU, leading to unemployment in the EU and a probable rise in nationalist sentiment, and hence political unrest. Finally, the political costs might be even higher in the shape of an unstable and politically explosive region on the EU's immediate borders.

In the light of this, the EU clearly has to adapt to its increased membership on a scale hitherto unimagined. On the economic front, it has to find a means of allowing EMU to proceed with a larger and more diverse membership. In a sense, the admission of the richer and economically well-developed EFTA states may actually facilitate EMU, by enabling the critical mass of half the membership being ready to be reached and EMU to begin early (in 1996, as set out in the Maastricht Treaty). Indeed, this prospect is a specific concern of one current EU member. The Spanish wish the decision as to whether to proceed with EMU early to be based on a majority of the current membership of 12, not of an enlarged EU of up to 16. (Spain fears being left behind in a two-speed Europe.)

However, this difficulty becomes relatively insignificant when considered in the light of the problems for EMU that are likely to be created by subsequent rounds of enlargement in the 1990s. Participation in EMU by the Mediterranean applicants would be difficult, although perhaps not impossible for Cyprus and Malta, but the Visegrad countries and Bulgaria and Romania raise questions of a totally different order, and these countries are unlikely to be ready for some years without economic transfers on an enormous scale.[1] Indeed, some applicant states will need to reform their economies completely before they can participate fully as EU members, and not just the central and eastern Europeans but also the Maltese.[2] The scenario of a multi-speed Europe with only some EU members participating in EMU therefore looks increasingly inevitable, at least in the short run. This is of course envisaged by the Maastricht Treaty and made more likely by the British and Danish opt-outs.

Turning away from the grand design of EMU, there are clearly difficulties raised for specific aspects of the EU's economic operations. Many of these have been aired in the accession negotiations with Austria, Sweden, Finland and Norway. The question of contributions to the EU budget was well to the fore during the closing stages of the negotiations. Of course, the EFTAns will be net contributors (with the exception of Finland)[3] but the opposite will be true of the Mediterranean and central and eastern Europeans, and so their contribution to (and receipts from) the EU budget are likely to be an even more contentious issue. Absorbing the agricultural sectors of new members into the CAP will not be easy, and there are implications (and potential problems) for a whole range of the EU's policies including regional and competition policy and fisheries.

However, in many respects, the most pressing and fundamental issues raised by enlargement relate to the political and institutional spheres.

These were addressed by Pinder in Chapter 9, when he argued for a federal structure to be adopted by the EU to make further enlargement feasible and manageable. In fact, a whole range of critical issues are raised:

- Should there be a shift to a more federal structure with greater powers for the Commission?
- Following on from this, the issue of the democratic deficit in the EU looms even larger. Presumably, a more powerful Commission would require greater democratic control, which could logically be provided by enhancing the powers of the European Parliament.
- The whole question of the balance of power between smaller and larger EU member states and their level of representation within the EU institutions needs to be addressed.
- Moreover, the role and position of small and particularly micro-states in the EU in general has to be considered.

These wider concerns are reflected in a variety of practical dilemmas:

- There is the obvious quantitative aspect. A larger number of members makes all the EU institutions less manageable.
- If the Commission is to become more powerful, then it needs to be streamlined, which could imply only one Commissioner for the larger member states and/or smaller member states sharing a Commissioner.
- The wider use of majority voting within the Council of Ministers seems inevitable if the EU is to press on with the Maastricht agenda.
- The weighting of votes within the Council is important and, in particular, whether the blocking minority required to prevent policies being adopted should be increased after enlargement. This would require a larger minority (in terms of the number of members) required to block policies. This issue was the subject of a major row immediately after the completion of negotiations with Austria, Sweden and Finland. The British, in particular, wished to maintain the old rule whereby two large and one small country could muster enough votes to create a blocking minority. The Spanish also supported this, as it allows them to ally with Italy and Greece and to have the final say on Mediterranean policies which only affect them, without having to rely on fickle Portuguese support which would be necessary if the size of the minority required were increased. It is by no means clear how the uneasy compromise eventually reached - which increases the size of the

blocking minority after enlargement, but still allows legislation to be delayed by the current three country minority - will work in practice.

● The ability and desirability of small states to hold the rotating six-month Council presidency has been questioned, partly on the grounds of the infrequency with which the large countries would hold the office in an enlarged EU. However, the principal concerns relate to the credibility of, and the technical ability of, small countries to run presidencies. This problem has already been partly addressed by a decision to reorder the presidencies, up to the end of 2003, in such a way that the troika (of the previous, current and incoming presidents) always includes a large EU member state.[4]

The other aspect of political union of great importance is the foreign and security policy pillar of the Maastricht Treaty. On the one hand, the accession of neutral EFTAns is seen as problematical, on the other hand, few difficulties are likely to be raised by the prospective Mediterranean members and the central and eastern Europeans are actually enthusiastic about participating in such a policy. The increase in the number of members could clearly make decision-making more difficult but, equally, it would give the EU a more powerful voice.

The EU hopes to evade most of these pressures in the course of the enlargement to include Austria, Sweden, Finland and Norway and delay their consideration until 1996 intergovernmental conference and beyond. This is in spite of promptings from the European Parliament to address them sooner. However, the pressure continues to build as the list of 'prospective Europeans' continues to lengthen. Austria, Sweden and Finland completed their accession negotiations more or less on time and, although those for Norway dragged on into March, agreement was eventually reached. However, all four face difficult referenda to get their populations to support joining the EU and, at the beginning of 1994, none of them was able to muster even 40 per cent of the popular vote in favour of membership.[5] Indeed, the fact that the Norwegians were ultimately left haggling over fish does not bode well, because the referenda results will be largely determined by the terms of accession which have clearly not been all that the prospective members would have wished. The European Parliament also has to approve their accessions and may create difficulties if some progress is not made on institutional reform.

Equally, however, the agreed terms of accession have not been entirely to the satisfaction of the EU. Whilst there must always be compromise in negotiations, the British press was somewhat cynical about some of the concessions made.[6] Even when the four new members are paying their full contribution to the EU budget, it will amount to only about half what was originally expected, and Finland will break even. In the short run, full contributions will not actually be paid, as the new members will be allowed rebates to cushion the effects on their farmers of having to align their prices with those of the EU (which are lower).[7] Farmers will also be assisted in the longer run as well: the Alpine farmers of Austria are poor enough to qualify for existing EU aid and special arrangements are being made for the Arctic farmers of Scandinavia. Finally, Austria is to be allowed to keep its restrictions on the transit of EU lorries for an extended period. Whilst these concessions may be necessary to ensure (or at least increase the likelihood of) 'Yes' votes in the forthcoming referenda, it is quite possible that the EU is storing up problems for the future. Over-generosity at this stage not only increases future expectations, but sets in stone agreements which the EU may well come to regret.

Turning to the other 'live' applications for EU membership, from the Mediterranean, these have only been delayed. The Greek Cypriots are doing their best to give the impression that the review of their position in January 1995 will amount to a decision to go ahead in the absence of Turkish Cypriot involvement. Whilst it is far from clear that this is the EU's intention, expectations are being raised. Meanwhile the Maltese continue to press their suit (with some justification). On a visit to Brussels in early 1994, the Maltese Prime Minister was very positive. He argued that the economic reforms in Malta set out in the Commission's Opinion were well under way and that, despite the institutional issues raised by Malta's application, he felt that accession negotiations could be completed quickly, and in 1996.[8] Last, but certainly not least, there is the question of Turkey which the EU will have to address sooner or later. The Turks will not go away and are as ardent in their pursuit of EU membership as ever.

Finally, the pace is increasing in central and eastern Europe. The Hungarians expressed an intention to apply for membership in April 1994 with a view to negotiations beginning in 1997,[9] and did indeed apply, quickly followed by the Poles. However, the Poles are less further forward, recognising that the costs of their participation in the CAP and in the EU's regional policy preclude membership in the near future. However, they have advocated a partial membership in the short term, through involvement in the EU's foreign and security policy and the justice and home affairs pillar of the Maastricht Treaty.[10] The Czechs recognise that they need more time,[11] which makes participation in an accession round along with Hungary and Poland difficult, but remain anxious to join, as do the Slovaks, Bulgarians and Romanians. It is clear that the EU could spend the next decade or so involved in a steady stream of accession negotiations.

This means that the broad issues raised by enlargement, as indicated above, will have to be addressed. Whilst all the debates of principle, listed earlier, are important, the essential question comes down to a choice between two basic scenarios: adapt in such a way as to allow the deepening envisaged by the Maastricht Treaty to proceed (widening with deepening) or, adapt in a way that creates a much looser or possibly a multi-tier EU (widening without, or instead of, deepening). Indeed, and even more fundamentally, it comes down to the old decision between a supranational (federal) or intergovernmental (looser) EU, although with the nuance that it may be possible to have both simultaneously. An inner core could pursue federal-style deepening, whilst an outer group might be granted a looser form of membership.[12] A core of current EU members undoubtedly prefers widening and deepening, but there are doubts about some other member states either in terms of their motivation or their ability to pursue the Maastricht agenda. The same categories of attitudes to deepening (want to, don't want to, can't) are also apparent amongst the dozen or so aspiring EU members and it may well be that their membership bids tip the scales in favour of a multi-tier EU. Ultimately, if widening is inevitable, the EU has to decide to adapt in a way that makes deepening possible for all, for some or for none. Some very hard and fundamental decisions have to be taken in the 1990s. They can no longer be delayed.

Notes

1. Pinder argues for an effort of a similar order to the Americans' provision of Marshall Aid after WW2. See p. 182 above.
2. This is made explicit in the Commission's Opinion on the Maltese application for membership. See p. 143 above.
3. Details of the Commission's assessments are given in detail in *Agence Europe* (1994) no. 6174, 19 February, p. 6 and summarised in the *Economist* (1994) 5 March, p. 43.
4. See *Agence Europe* (1993) no. 6127, 12 December, Report on the conclusions of the European summit, Brussels, 11-12 December, p. 3.
5. See the *Economist*, 5 March 1994, p. 43.
6. The *Financial Times* announced the agreement of terms with Austria, Sweden and Finland with the headline 'Cash carries the day in enlargement talks', 2 March 1994, p. 2 and talked sarcastically of a deal for Finland which 'looked as though it had declared the entire country an Arctic region eligible for special agricultural support'. Meanwhile, the *Economist* (1994) 5 March, p. 38, talked of 'bribes'.
7. In fact, these are not really needed in Sweden which has already aligned its farm prices with those of the EU and so they are to receive a genuine budget rebate.
8. *Agence Europe* (1994) no. 6163, 4 February, p. 8.
9. *Financial Times* 8 March 1994, p. 2 and *Agence Europe* (1994) no. 6182, 3 March, p. 7.
10. Ibid and *Financial Times* 9 March 1994, p. 3.
11. Ibid.

12. Of course, questions might be raised about the practicability of this. Certainly, Europe *à la carte* does not seem viable. This is the ill-advised road of the Maastricht opt-outs, where individual countries are allowed to opt out of different bundles of policies. With one or two countries this might be feasible, but with more it is a recipe for chaos. It is simply not practical to have different countries coming together in different combinations for different policies and is almost certainly not acceptable for the core of current EU members which wish to pursue the Maastricht agenda fully. A multi-tier Europe with various levels of membership involving involvement in groups of policies is practical, although the drawing of the line which separates those countries with full participation in decision making from those with only partial voting rights will be critical.

Index

202   *Prospective Europeans*